COMMODITIES

Commodities was produced by Commodities Project
Limited for Channel Four Television.

COMMODITIES

How the world was taken to market

Nick Rowling

With illustrations by Phil Evans

'an association in which the free development of each
is the condition of the free development of all'

Free Association Books / London / 1987

First published in Great Britain 1987 by
Free Association Books
26 Freegrove Road
London N7 9RQ

© Nick Rowling, Phil Evans, Firefret Ltd,
Channel 4 TV Co Ltd 1987

British Library Cataloguing in Publication Data

Rowling, Nick
    Commodities: how the world was taken to market
    1. Commodity exchanges—History
    I. Title
    332.64′4′09   HG6046

ISBN 0-946960-67-4

Typeset by Sunrise Setting, Torquay, Devon
Printed and bound in Great Britain by
Commercial Colour Press, Forest Gate, London E7

COMMODITIES: The TV Series

Commodities, six films for television commissioned by Channel Four's 'Eleventh Hour', was first broadcast in July and August 1986. The series was directed and produced by Sue Clayton and Jonathan Curling in conjunction with independent film makers in Brazil, Colombia, Hong Kong, China, Zimbabwe and other countries.

This book draws on the experience and information gained while researching and producing the series, sometimes quoting from interviews originally done on film, but much of the time extending into areas not covered by the films themselves.

The book is intended to provide a broad framework within which the films can be used for education, for developing analysis and arguments that no television film could embark upon.

The films are available on videocassette from:
The Other Cinema,
79 Wardour St,
London W1.

For international sales please contact:
Jane Balfour Films,
110 Gloucester Avenue,
London NW1.

For educational distribution and classroom materials please contact:
Pergamon Educational Publishing,
5 Dean Street,
London W1.

Contents

Introduction

A commodity appears, at first sight, a very trivial thing, and easily understood. Its analysis shows that it is, in reality, a very queer thing, abounding in metaphysical subtleties and theological niceties.
Karl Marx, *Capital*, vol. 1, ch. 1, section 4

The word 'commodity' in medieval English meant anything which had a use value. Cows, fields, rivers and ports were all referred to as commodities. Gradually, the notion of use value was replaced by that of exchange value, and 'commodity' came to mean anything which could be bought and sold. However, as Marx observed, a commodity is a queer thing; it is not necessarily a 'thing' in the normal sense of the word. A human being, for example, would be a commodity if he or she were a slave. And since it is possible for people to sell their labour power, labour too can be called a commodity. 'Commodity' can also mean something even more abstract than labour power. Knowledge, for example, as a pure abstraction is, in certain circumstances, a commodity which can be bought and sold. Although money is a concrete thing when it takes the form of gold, silver, coins and banknotes, it is also an abstraction in the sense that it is a notion of value or equivalence; insofar as it is bought and sold, it, too, is a commodity.

Given these metaphysical subtleties, it is best to start with the more familiar examples of 'commodity'. Since time immemorial, people have produced innumerable vegetable products – like wheat, potatoes, maize and rice – which have become commodities. The same has happened to many animals and animal products, like beef, wool, pork and leather. Some commodities are botanical products like timber, rubber and quinine. Minerals like iron, coal and tin have a use value in manufacture; others, particularly silver and gold, have also been employed in a more complex matrix of human exchanges, namely as money.

Other commodities are more complex than they seem at first sight, even though they are part of our everyday lives. Sugar, for example, is not drained out of trees like rubber but is the product of complex chemical transformations. So, too, are rum and other distilled liquors; and coffee beans and tea leaves are both products of sophisticated taste-extraction processes, as we shall see.

Everything which we now think of as being a commodity – whether it is a foodstuff or a mineral, wood or an animal skin – was at earlier stages of human history neither used nor traded. It was production for sale on the market place that made these things commodities, and most commodities then became produced and exchanged in increasingly complex ways. Nothing is intrinsically a commodity; if something is not recognized as saleable, then it is not a commodity. A gardener looking at a dead sunflower is not looking at a commodity; a farmer looking at 50 acres of dead sunflowers, however, almost certainly is. Almost anything can become a commodity under certain conditions; for example, dog shit on the street is today not a commodity, it is merely a filthy, anti-social inconvenience. In nineteenth-century London, however, it was a commodity when it was collected and sold for curing leather. Likewise, rats are not normally thought of as commodities, but under certain conditions, such as sieges, and in certain places, such as China, they too have been caught, prepared and sold as food.

We have selected sugar, coffee and tea because they exhibit central aspects of the history of capitalism. Attempts to control their production and marketing have provoked countless wars. Whole cultures, tribes and civilizations have been destroyed so that other civilizations could consume these commodities, parts of the earth have been devastated by their cultivation, millions of people have lived miserable lives and died in producing them; people and societies elsewhere have been enriched by them, sometimes in unexpected ways.

COMMODITIES AND HISTORY

Any commodity has a history, linked to the histories of those societies which first recognized its utility, enhanced its value by cultivation or processing, and began to trade it. Even the humble cucumber has a history which started

'Sewer rat' collecting saleable items (from *Mayhew's London*, 1849)

If everything is potentially a commodity, how is it possible to write a history of commodities? Obviously, we have to be selective. We cannot include in a single book even short histories of commodities as various as water melons (which were first cultivated in West Africa), coconuts and breadfruit (which came from the Celebes), cucumbers, bananas and rice (which originate in south east Asia), and so on.

We have, therefore, concentrated on four commodities which are of particular interest. Two are drugs: tea and coffee. One is a foodstuff which is also a poison: sugar. Then we look at money, the most complex commodity of all. Finally, we look briefly at petroleum, high technology and financial futures, which in many ways are the core commodities of contemporary capitalism.

in south east Asia, where it was first cultivated three thousand years ago. It arrived in Europe as an expensive delicacy. It was cultivated in monastic gardens and served on medieval tables, before being mass-cultivated for pickling factories all over the world. The processes of that transformation constitute the history of the cucumber; not an earth-shattering history perhaps, but a history nonetheless. The perspective of this kind of history is necessarily global because it stresses the links between economic, political, social and cultural developments in different parts of the world; unlike most histories, it focusses, nct on great individuals, but on the lives of the billions of people who have produced, desired and consumed the commodities which constitute our history.

Very early on in human history there was a stage when people began to see nature in a different way, when certain kinds of grass, for example, were recognized as being edible if treated in certain ways. Gathering would have been followed by a stage when these grasses were cultivated and later traded. This seems to have happened first in Anatolia (now northern Turkey) around 8000 BC. Trade, at first, was by barter when one valued commodity was exchanged for another. After 600 BC, money in the form of coinage (a Lydian–Greek invention) increasingly became the medium of exchange along the trading networks of Asia, Europe and Africa.

For a long period of human history, many different species of plant and animal were known and used only in their areas of origin. For example, turkeys, avocado pears, potatoes, cocoa, tomatoes, pineapples and chillies were unknown and uncultivated outside the Americas until the sixteenth century. In China, from at least the first century AD, the leaves of the tea bush had been cured in various ways, but the drink was hardly known outside east Asia until the seventeenth century. The berries of the coffee bush were being eaten by Ethiopian nomads for centuries before anyone thought of extracting the beans from the berries and roasting, grinding and brewing them into a liquor; coffee as a drink only became known outside Arabia in the sixteenth century.

In this book, we use the metaphor of a chain to trace the processes of production and exchange of commodities, and what we shall find as we examine the chains are the various factors which link them together. We will see how one chain becomes entangled with other chains, and how, as links break, they are re-welded. At the same

'Treasury of ivory, South Africa'

COMMODITIES

time, we shall try to explain why the chains evolved in particular ways, what forces acted upon the commodities, and how they were transformed as they shifted along the chains.

THE MODE OF PRODUCTION

In charting the story of commodity capitalism, the term 'mode of production' is often used. The mode of production refers to the way that labour is regulated and its product distributed. Peasants who cultivate crops and tend animals for their own consumption with tools they have made on land not claimed by anyone else, employ a very basic mode of production. In many parts of Europe and Asia, small scale production was replaced by larger productive units fairly early in history. Large scale production of foodstuffs on plantations using slaves and free labourers was already established around the Mediterranean two thousand years ago when grain, olive

oil and wine all figured as important trading commodities.

In order for extensive trading to develop, the Romans, Greeks and Arabs needed some recognized medium of exchange. Coinage, guaranteed by a powerful government, provided that. With the collapse of the Roman Empire in the fifth century AD, that ancient stage of mass commodity production disappeared, and trade withered away in most of Europe.

Was the subsequent phase of feudalism a precondition for capitalism? Feudalism certainly played a significant role in Europe. Feudal power was essentially the creation of hegemonic states, ruled in theory by monarchs; their authority was established on the ground by feudal lords who controlled, and in many instances owned, the labour power in their territories. They also profited from the sale of the commodities produced by their serfs. From local merchants they bought essentials such as salt

Mountain of 20,000 billiard balls, produced by the slaughter of 2,000 elephants

and various luxury items. However, the merchants were not themselves subject to feudal controls. In Florence, the richest merchants actually became feudal landlords through a system called the *contado* which guaranteed them cheap foodstuffs and many of the raw materials they needed for their manufacturing operations. Elsewhere, in general, landlords lacked capital but owned land, whereas merchants had money but lacked land. Gradually a symbiosis occurred whereby merchants acquired control over land and production, while landlords intermarried with the daughters of the mercantile elite. But this development was delayed by the extravagance and violence of the feudal lords, who expended a significant amount of the small surplus available on wars against each other and in crusades against other Christians and the Turks. Such elites also delayed the development of a centralizing power which was necessary if coherent mercantile and colonial policies were to develop.

Both the withering away of serfdom and the establishment of a wage labour system were complete in England by about 1400, though serfdom persisted in other parts of the British Isles and in Europe until well into the eighteenth century. By about 1500, in Europe at least, most merchants had aligned themselves behind strong monarchs; together they dismantled feudal power. In return for a share of the profits of their operations, merchants were guaranteed protection by the monarch and his state apparatus. Thus there was, in the more enlightened nation states, a stimulus to trade and to the expansion of production.

The shift to a mercantile system was important because it integrated land ownership, labour power and trade networks into a coherent system. Such alliances between merchants and the crown often created acute misery. In sixteenth-century England, peasants were evicted from the land so that sheep could be grazed for their wool. Many starved, but some were employed in the early factories, like that of Jack of Newbury, which employed hundreds of labourers. English wool and cloth was then sold through Antwerp and later Amsterdam. Flemish and Dutch money flowed into England and speeded up the production of other commodities; coal and lead mines were opened up, while shipbuilding developed to carry the coal and the wool, and in general, the economy expanded.

By 1600, the elements of plantation agriculture, the factory system, arms manufacture, trading networks, the use of currencies and credit systems, insurance, banking, taxation and aggressive governmental policies, had all emerged in various parts of Europe. Under the impact of European conquest, the entire world was increasingly compelled to mass-produce commodities in a system which aimed only to maximize profits by exploiting labour.

TRANSPORT AND TRADE

Whosoever commands the sea commands the trade; whosoever commands the trade of the world commands the riches of the world, and consequently, the world itself.
Sir Walter Ralegh, 'A Discourse of the Invention of Ships', *Works*, vol. VIII, p. 325

Trade, which links the producers with the consumers, is dependent on other commodities for transport. These have included camels (from central Asia), asses (from north Africa), horses (from the Russian Steppes), boats of various description, railways after the mid-nineteenth century, and trucks and aeroplanes in the twentieth. Always, at the end of the chain, there is a market of some description. Most towns and cities, of course, developed as markets.

Haymaking, early 17th century

COMMODITIES

Given the distances which commodities travel and the costs of transporting them, it is obvious why early long-distance traders concentrated on commodities such as spices and precious metals which are small in bulk and which sell for high prices in distant markets. Given the value of such commodities, it is not surprising that this early stage was extremely dangerous, for traders risked losing everything to bandits and pirates.

The ancient world had many kinds of craft. The earliest large cargo carriers, which could carry loads of up to 500 tons, were capable of making long-distance voyages, though rarely out of sight of land. They were trading in the Mediterranean and Arabian Seas in the first century BC. Such ships needed unprecedented amounts of timber and other materials, as well as the technical skills to build, rig, sail and navigate them. After 1500, seaborn trade was increasingly dominated by European capitalists who developed and built ships for specific uses. The 25-ton Portuguese *barca* which crept down the

coast of Africa in the fifteenth century evolved into the *caravel* which came back with the riches of the East in the sixteenth. At the same time, Bristol fishing boats were risking the icebergs of the north Atlantic to catch cod off Newfoundland. The trade of the Arab *dhows*, which dominated the Indian Ocean before the arrival of the Europeans, was eventually overwhelmed by the massive bulk carriers invented by the Dutch in the sixteenth century; and these were later adapted to carry the ever-increasing trade of Europe with Asia and the Americas. Such innovations, which led to the modern container ships, helped to determine the patterns and scale of world trade.

The making of ships required other commodities, not least timber, which was already becoming scarce in many parts of Europe from the 1550s onwards. The Dutch adapted their grain carriers to bring back timber from the Baltic as well as hemp and pitch. By the seventeenth century, forests were being destroyed over much of the Caribbean and the Americas to provide the Dutch, British, French and Portuguese with ships. As in all other commodity chains, those who built and manned the ships saw little of the profits. Those who captained the ships saw more, because captains were usually traders themselves; but it was the owners and the capitalists who benefitted the most.

As some merchants prospered, they preferred to lend

(top right) Drake's astrolabe
(below left) Building a cog, 15th-century Germany

their money to other traders rather than take the risks of trade themselves. Admittedly, they risked losing their money, though they often held the borrower's goods as collateral. They also lent money to the landowners who controlled cultivation. Increasingly, merchant-capitalists came to control every aspect of production through their moneylending operations. They financed cultivation, processing, transport and marketing; initially only taking interest on the loans, they eventually came to own the land, capital and transport systems themselves.

THE FRUITS OF LABOUR

Throughout history, labour – the source of profit – has always received a minute proportion of the profits of production and marketing. This is not simply due to the greed and cruelty of the landowners and capitalists who controlled production, though that plays a part, but to the institutionalized power that employers have over labour.

Through capitalism, labour increasingly became a commodity which could be bought and sold, or tied to the land or capital in various ways. Capitalists and land-lords either made the laws or bribed and influenced those who did; therefore they could hang, whip, mutilate or burn any slaves or indentured servants who might try to escape or who demanded fair remuneration for their labour. Even if they lacked this authority, where, for instance, wage labourers worked for wages rather than as slaves, employers could restrict the workers' right to cultivate the land themselves by claiming ownership of the land and by evicting labourers who refused to work on the employers' terms. So the choice for most 'free' (waged) labourers was poverty as a worker for a landlord or capitalist, or starvation as a landless vagrant.

To extend cultivation, landlords and planters needed credit to buy slaves or to hire labour, to buy title to the land (from whoever claimed title to the land), or weaponry to enable them successfully to seize and protect it against interlopers. They also needed to buy tools for their labour force to clear and work the land; they also needed to buy food, clothing and supplies for themselves and their workers. Further, as competition

'The Fruits of Labour', George Grosz, 1923

COMMODITIES

increased, they needed to buy machinery to process their commodities and to retain their share of the market.

Thus, the middle of the chain came to be dominated by capitalists who advanced credit to landowners and who profited from the interest on the loan. The capitalist might well have been another planter who had prospered, a merchant who not only advanced credit but who sold the product when it reached the market, or another trader; he might even have been a retired pirate. Within this capitalist mode of production, labour received only a small percentage of the goods, or the money equivalent of the goods, which it produced. The rest was taken by the owners of the land and capital which labour made productive. This surplus was the landowner's or capitalist's profit. Increasingly, clear divisions emerged. There were some, the capitalists, who accumulated the profits, whether in the form of goods which they could sell, or as money which was a store of wealth, and others, the workers, who produced commodities for subsistence wages, or in the case of slaves, were merely given enough of what they produced to stay alive.

This process occurred both in the colonies and at home. Native peoples, naturally, resisted European encroachment, but lacking guns they were almost all, eventually, wiped out or taken into various forms of slavery. Often imperial conquest was followed by the vast transfer of populations. Twelve million Africans were shipped across the Atlantic before the ending of slavery, and more than five million Asians were moved around Asia or taken to Africa and the Caribbean after that period.

The same military and legislative machinery was also used to oppress the domestic population. Peasants were deprived of their land and forced to work for landlords on large estates or in the factories which produced the commodities upon which imperial expansion depended.

In the nineteenth century, slavery was abolished within the European empires, and labour movements began to set limits on exploitation. Yet capitalists retained control of both the factory system and plantation agriculture. Through wage labour discipline, they were able to compel their workers to produce a greater value of goods than the value of wages paid – the difference being the profit (or surplus value). Thus they continued to extract the profits produced by their workers. In effect, this process means that labour produces commodities for capital. The wages earned by labour are then used to purchase the commodities which it has produced. Labour consumes and capital accumulates. Thus, the extraction of surplus value from labour is the precondition upon which the whole edifice rests.

Historically, the capitalist mode of production was geared to the production of commodities for sale. The poor had little money and few goods to exchange for the products of capitalist enterprise; if they could not afford the market price of food, they starved. Production was therefore orientated to potential consumers with money. The expansion of a money economy in Europe greatly increased the size of the market, but it remained restricted to the middle class until working class wages rose above subsistence level.

In the twentieth century, mass consumerism has changed the products of commodity capitalism quite remarkably. Few countries remain outside the trading networks established initially by Europeans. Beyond simple survival, the desire to own consumer products remains a compelling reason why people continue to work for, and thus sustain, the system which exploits them. Meanwhile profits appear to arise from some special powers of capital or from the skills of the capitalists; their origin in human labour remains hidden.

TAXATION

Commodity capitalism is embedded in political structures because governments have always needed taxes to protect their own class interests. Taxes which derived from land were limited by the amount of profit which could be extracted from agricultural labour – if too much was taken, labour starved and the revenue ceased. But taxes which derived from trade increased with trade. Therefore, as trade developed in medieval Europe, monarchs and governments tried to obtain as large a proportion of the profits of trade as they could. Sometimes they seized traders' goods, under various pretexts –

a short-sighted solution, since their theft of the profits from trade resulted in the collapse of trade itself.

It was precisely to avoid this contingency that many of the great European trading cities evolved outside the jurisdiction of higher authorities: Amsterdam, Venice, Genoa, Florence, London and the German cities were all essentially self-governing for long periods of their histories.

Other cities, however, could only evolve with the consent of their traditional overlords. In these cases, the government became responsible for law and protection of the realm and taxed the merchants in order to pay for the costs of administration and defence. Most governments soon came to realize that it was better to encourage the expansion of trade rather than to limit it, since increases in trade bought increasing customs revenues. It is this which explains the historical alliance in Europe of government and mercantile interests. By the seventeenth century, exclusive trading rights or monopolies were often in the hands of favoured traders who had purchased them from the government. This obviously did not please other middlemen, traders and merchants, and exclusive trading rights were usually replaced by a tax on traded goods, which provided a regular revenue for the ruler or government.

Often, though, taxes were very high; one tenth of the British government's revenues in the eighteenth century, for example, was raised by a tax on tea. When a commodity was heavily taxed, consumers bought less of it; merchants sold less, profits for refiners and traders became smaller, and eventually the tax burden fell on them as well. In order to pay they demanded that tariffs and taxes be lowered or abolished under the slogan of 'free trade'.

Free trade was never free, of course. All it meant, and means today, was an extension of the right to trade to those who can successfully compete with the privileged monopolists who established the system in the first place. And successful competitors, once established, become as vigilant in the defence of their privileges as any monopolist. Governments like those of seventeenth-century Holland and England, which actively promoted trade,

Tax collector, 16th-century France

became richer than all their competitors. And because they spent much of the revenue derived from trade on arms, warships and soldiers, they were able to grab vast tracts of the earth and coerce native populations into producing the commodities upon which their prosperity depended. Furthermore, once conquered, those populations were taxed to finance the administrations and war machines of the imperial powers.

SMUGGLING

Conventional historians rarely pay much attention to smuggling, since it is poorly documented and difficult to estimate. However, smuggling always follows taxation, and is therefore crucial to an understanding of commodity capitalism. Smuggling was, and remains, an essential component of the system. The potential profits from successful smuggling are, of course, immense, which explains why it is attractive to so many people. Producers are happy to sell to smugglers and consumers are happy to buy from them.

In certain historical periods, so great was the amount of smuggled trade that it is not possible to calculate how

Smuggler pursued by customs officer, 18th-century England

grounds of health. At various times the sale of tea, coffee, alcohol and tobacco was prohibited, but these prohibitions were so widely evaded and opposed by traders, growers and consumers that the governments usually rescinded the ban and returned to their customs revenues.

It often happened that while one government promoted a trade another prohibited it. For instance, the British government in the eighteenth and early nineteenth century encouraged the production of opium in Bengal and its sale in China. When the Chinese Emperor objected to the poisoning of his subjects, he was gunboated into submission.

Many countries and communities depended on smuggling in order to survive. The Dutch were adept smugglers in the seventeenth century and much of their trade was carried on in defiance of both foreign and Dutch regulations, under flags of convenience. The Dutch government turned a blind eye, realizing that smuggling was essential to the Dutch economy. For the same reason, no Andean government today will suppress a cocaine trade which brings dollars into a starving country. Nor will any Jamaican government seriously attempt to limit the production of marijuana for the US market, when marijuana sales total more than all Jamaica's legal exports put together.

RISK

We can usefully characterize capitalism as a global gambling game in which there are few players, since almost everybody lacks the risk capital with which to gamble. The tokens are people's lives and the commodities they need to have in order to survive. The high potential profits from successful gambling were (and are) linked to high risks. Throughout history, the players have attempted to minimize these risks in various ways.

The thirteenth-century European merchants, who abandoned the risks of trade for the different risks of moneylending, developed insurance mechanisms to help minimize their risks. At the same time, a number of players of the game realized that it was in their interest not to compete to the point of economic extinction, but

much actual trade was carried on at all. For instance, it has been calculated that in certain years in the eighteenth century, four times more tea was smuggled into England than was legally imported. Sometimes, smuggling has developed because governments have attempted to forbid certain types of trade altogether, usually on

rather, to form alliances of various kinds. Merchants joined other merchants as associates, and these associations were later transformed into joint-stock companies; thus, they shared the risks of any operation. By the eighteenth century, outsiders with spare capital were permitted to buy shares in these companies, thus spreading the risks further.

High risks were linked to the possibility of high profits. One of the most refined aspects of capitalism was the activity we now call 'speculation'. There are many variations on this game, but essentially it is played by those who have money to spare (risk capital); rather than buy another yacht or another painting, the players attempt to make money from the initial sum. This is possible because the operations of commodity capitalism are continually changing; it is a dynamic system constructed with chains, whose links might break at any moment. There might be a revolution in Peru or an earthquake in Mexico; ships might be attacked by pirates, or governments might increase the tax on a commodity; there are numerous factors which can destabilize an operation and bring the price of a commodity up or down.

By the seventeenth century in Holland and London, there were people who were prepared to gamble on various possibilities. In part, this development occurred because the distances involved in commodity trading and the time required for communication between different parts of the world were so immense that there was considerable uncertainty about the state of the market. If a fleet of sugar carriers was sunk, if the harvest in a distant part of the world was destroyed by floods, or if the subject population producing the commodity rebelled, the price of that commodity would rise very rapidly, owing to its scarcity. Equally, if a large number of ships arrived in port at the same time carrying the same commodity, then the price would fall rapidly. The speculators were merely people with risk capital who, in effect, betted on the various possibilities.

Paradoxically, the activities of speculators have often helped stabilize the market. Their activities have meant that merchants could buy at a guaranteed price and that plantation owners could sell at a guaranteed price (under ideal conditions, though conditions are rarely ideal). Insofar as they helped to stabilize the market, they stimulated production. Speculators, however, were not simply interested in predicting accurately the state of the market; they often attempted to manipulate the market to their own advantage. They might, for example, spread rumours that cargoes had been lost so as to profit from the sudden rise in prices which the scare would produce; they might hoard a commodity to ensure that its price rose through shortage; or they might attempt to corner the market, that is, to buy up enough of the commodity in advance to ensure that they could dictate the price at some future date.

NATIONALISM

That's your glorious British navy, that bosses the earth. The fellows that never will be slaves, with the only hereditary chamber on the face of God's earth, and their land in the hands of a dozen gamehogs and cotton-ball barons. That's the great empire they boast about — of drudges and whipped serfs — on which the sun never rises.
James Joyce, *Ulysses*

The historical alliance between European capitalists and the state was linked to evolving concepts of 'nation' and to the ideology of 'nationalism'. Nowhere, however, was this process straightforward since neither concept is easily defined. Perhaps the clearest example of a 'nation' in the pre-modern world was China, which, in 1500, had recognized frontiers, an emperor, a state religion and language, a national legal and fiscal system, and a centralized administrative bureaucracy which maintained order and collected taxes. The Chinese also had a strong sense of common identity and, like the ancient Greeks, called all outsiders 'barbarians'.

No European country at that time could so easily be defined as a nation. Italy was a collection of antagonistic independent states which shared only a common language. The emerging powers on the periphery of Europe, Portugal, Spain and England all had national languages and legal systems with their populations living within recognized frontiers. But even this is an over-simplification: for example Spaniards in 1500 included Basques, Catalans, Gypsies, *Moriscos* of Arab descent and Africans; England by 1700 included Cornish and Welsh speakers as well as refugees from most of the countries of Europe.

Nationalism – which gave the inhabitants of certain places certain rights, while denying 'outsiders' those rights – had emerged early on in Europe. The Jews, for example, were expelled from England in 1290; 200 years later, they were expelled from Portugal. In both cases, the legal reason given for expulsion was heresy; the actual reason, financial rivalry. A parallel symptom of emerging nationalism was the English Navigation Acts, passed in the 1380s, which excluded foreign vessels from English ports; although these were never efficiently enforced until the seventeenth century, they were symptomatic of a growing nationalist ideology among 'home' merchants.

In Europe, the evolution of nations into powerful states was largely linked to their imperial ambitions. Those countries with strong governments and a tax-gathering bureaucracy could assemble the armies and navies which made conquest possible. Once they had established footholds abroad, the plunder financed further expansion and territorial control, and so on, until eventually they turned on each other. During the most innovative and dynamic phases of capitalist development in Europe, when various European countries were emerging as world powers, those capitalists who focussed their operations abroad were remarkably unfettered; they (and their agents) were permitted by their governments to operate on the principle that 'might is right'.

Not all imperial powers were monarchies. Holland, for example – or more strictly the United Provinces – was a loose confederation of states, which for various reasons, had fought for independence from the Catholic Habsburg empire. The new state was ruled by a committee of rich merchants with the support of a handful of landowners, and was dedicated to the pursuit of profit unrestrained by dynastic ties or religious loyalties to

fellow Europeans. Yet, by 1700, Holland had a more extensive empire than any other European power.

In Holland, as elsewhere, political power was restricted to the owners of land and property. The Dutch were quickly superseded as a world power by the British, and to a lesser extent by the French and the Germans. In each case, a new kind of state had evolved which declared its subjects equal citizens before the law. The law was made by men of property: 'English law is the best that money can buy' was Voltaire's astute comment on the power of the rich. Property determined privilege – but the right to die for one's country was the prerogative of everyone, particularly the poor. The poor were usually pressed or conscripted into defending 'their' country, while the rich rallied them around national flags and legitimated plunder in the names of their God and their kings. Patriotic duty meant that now the mass of the population were obliged to make sacrifices, and if necessary to die, to protect the nation that guaranteed them equality before the law.

European colonialism was advanced by arms; 'nation' came to mean 'empire' as armies of native soldiers were recruited to advance the imperial flag. Imperialism operated successfully as an ideology, not least because of the high ideals it proclaimed: Christianity was 'the true religion', imperial conquest brought 'progress' to subject territories, European trade, technology and science helped 'modernize' the non-European world. While nominally, perhaps, retaining a monarch, this new kind of state had become the property of a national bourgeoisie. With flags and rhetoric, they portrayed their interests as 'the national interest' and used nationalist sentiment which appealed to all sections of society to disguise their own particular interest.

Merchants and bankers, however, showed little loyalty to the nation which advanced their interest. Whenever they saw advantage in shifting their operations abroad, they switched allegiance to other states. The Genoese went to Portugal and Spain, the Dutch to England, the English to the US, just as now bankers with American Express cards are citizens of the world. The condition of those who lacked title to the land belied the

JOHN BULL Happy.   JOHN BULL going to the WARS.

JOHN BULL'S Property in danger. J.G! in. et. fecit. JOHN BULL'S glorious Return.

lofty ideals which capitalists upheld. While their masters could steal thousands of acres of land with impunity and could ransack the world for gold, the poor could be hanged for stealing a chicken. To satisfy the capitalist lust for profit, millions of English, Scottish, Welsh and Irish peasants lost their land, and many thousands were transported to distant parts of the earth to work on their master's plantations.

This enormous crime did not go ahead unopposed. During the English Civil War, the Diggers occupied common land from which peasants had been evicted according to the Enclosure Acts. Gerard Winstanley articulated their opposition in *A Declaration from the Poor Oppressed People of England* (1649). The recognition of shared misery is evident in the subscript, 'signed for and on behalf of all the poor oppressed people of the whole world'. Meanwhile, in the colonies conquered populations were defined according to a hierarchy of race, ranging from white, yellow, red, brown to black. Positive attributes were ascribed to whites, negative attributes to others. Thus, in the organization of labour the allocation of people to particular roles was made to seem a result of natural differences among 'races'. Racism complemented nationalism by denying subject populations political power, legal rights and the right to share the wealth which their labour created.

Naturally, European imperialism was bitterly resisted from the very beginning. Many of the early forts and settlements established by the invaders were wiped out by native resistance, but once the European powers had

19

COMMODITIES

Belfast graffiti, 1977, on the 25th anniversary of Queen Elizabeth's accession

established a military presence they were less easily dislodged.

Even so, the US rebelled against Britain in the 1780s; Latin America rebelled against Portugal and Spain in the 1820s; the colonies of Holland, Portugal, France and Britain in Asia and Africa have all won some form of independence in the twentieth century. None, however, has been able to escape their imperial inheritance. Their languages, economies and political systems have been moulded by the experience of European conquest.

HISTORY AND PROGRESS

Men make their own history, but not of their own free will; not under circumstances they themselves have chosen but under the given and inherited circumstances with which they were directly confronted. The tradition of the dead generations weighs like a nightmare on the minds of the living.
Karl Marx, 'The Eighteenth Brumaire'

History is a nightmare from which I am trying to awake.
James Joyce, *Ulysses*

Our sense of ourselves and our world is unavoidably determined by the past. At home, at school and in society we inherit language, concepts, 'facts' and intellectual

tools, and all of them mould our view of the world. Many of these fundamental concepts are never queried. Yet, if we are to unravel the difference between what happened in the past, and what the victors claim happened, then we need to re-examine some of them. The first, and possibly most important, is the notion of 'progress'. Progress, almost invariably, is measured in material terms. 'Advanced' societies are defined as those which have the greatest concentration of material goods, cars, hospitals, food, weaponry, and so on. 'Backward' or 'underdeveloped' societies are those which have least. 'Progress' occurs when advanced societies give or sell their knowledge, skills, products and tools to backward societies, allowing them to catch up in the march of progress.

Such a notion is, of course, deeply flawed. As an ideal, it is very attractive, but in reality it has never happened. 'Progress' for a particular country or class has usually meant a corresponding loss for other countries or classes. These losses, however, are ignored, as if the overall benefits outweigh individual disadvantage. For example, the notion that 'Europe brought progress to Africa', which underlies most European literature on Africa, must be replaced by analysis of the processes whereby Europe underdeveloped Africa. The same is true of most of the other territories we shall look at in Latin America and Asia. European expansion and conquest provided many of the material benefits which define Europe's progress, but that progress was achieved by reducing other societies to servility and misery.

Often this notion of progress is associated with other less material 'gifts', like 'democracy', 'law', 'freedom', 'a true understanding of God', 'nationhood' and so on. However, these bequests turn out to be essentially destructive. Wherever we look, whether at the culture of Pacific islanders, African tribes or American Indians, we find laws, democratic institutions and means of determining territorial and domestic disputes long before the arrival of Europeans. Equally, it has yet to be proved that the imposition of European laws and political systems, which wiped out earlier systems, provided any significant benefits at all for most societies. Often the legacy of European conquest has created a degree of misery quite unknown before the Europeans arrived.

After European conquest, the Central African nomadic peoples, who are now starving in their millions, lost their traditional grazing rights; the timber and forests on which they depended were cut down. Because the climate has changed, water holes and rivers have dried up and the topsoil has blown away. When people attempt to travel to find water and food they are blocked by the 'national' frontiers drawn up at the Congress of Berlin in 1884. Those 'nations', created by European statesmen (who had no knowledge of Africa whatsoever) comprised tribes and kingdoms which had always been independent of each other; by virtue of their being now defined as 'nations', they are locked in civil and tribal conflict long after the Europeans have seized what they wanted and departed.

ALIENATION

Throughout this book we will emphasize the impact of capitalism on the people who ultimately created its profits. This anecdote, by a Jesuit priest working in Sri Lanka today, alerts us to many of the issues involved:

'I was with a superintendent on a tea plantation, and he asked me to be present when he allowed workers to come to him with their problems. The workers came in one by one. Then a young man stood opposite. I did not notice any defiance. The superintendent (a good Christian gentleman, who does not miss his Sunday mass) said, "Put your bloody hands down, that is not the way to talk to me". The man, meek as a lamb, put his hands behind his back and said, "Master, I have only come to see you about the pension of my father who is dying". At that moment I remembered the words of Isaiah, "I am a worm and no man, an outcast of my people". The boy was made to feel he had no human dignity at all. Marx has spoken of the four types of alienation in industrial society: he says man is alienated from what he produces, from his productive activity, from his fellow men, and from his species

being. Now I never understood before what Marx meant by "alienation from his species being", but I understood it that day. That lad was a textbook illustration of Marx's four forms of alienation.' (Paul Caspersz, speech at the International Conference on the Problems of Plantation Workers of Sri Lanka, April 1983, quoted in Selbourne)

The boy, like all plantation workers, is alienated from the commodity he cultivates. It is not his; he does not own it, value it or love it in any way – he is merely part of the process which produces it. And since he works for others, he does not work according to his needs and capacities, producing things which he values and which give his labour meaning. His labour power is therefore alienated or taken away from him. He is alienated from his fellow workers because he has been reduced to a condition of degrading servitude. In sum, he is no longer a person but a beast of burden.

That condition of alienation is ever-present in the history of the commodities we present in this book. Whether in the sugar slavery of the West Indies or in the high tech factories of south east Asia, inherent in the production of all commodities today is this dehumanizing and unjust pattern of alienation.

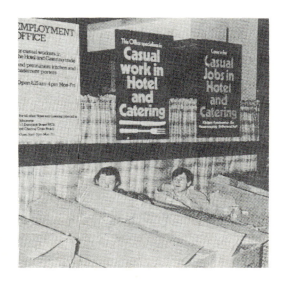

Casual hotel workers sleeping outside employment office, London, 1981

In this chapter we look at the role of three trading centres in the sixteenth century, in the context of an evolving world economy: Portugal, Spain, and Holland. Each enjoyed a commanding position as mercantile centres for a brief period; as one declined, another rose. The rise of the various centres was rapid and was based on the commodities which promised vast profits (like pepper, sugar and spices), and on the various mechanisms for financing their exploitation (banking and commercial institutions). Ships were available to transport commodities, and territorial control could be enforced by new armaments with the support of expansionist governments. Foodstuffs were needed to feed the population during a period of expansion; labour was needed (whether slave, unskilled, or skilled); markets, distribution centres and fairs (like those of Antwerp and Amsterdam) were needed; and manufactured goods were needed to supply their colonists and traders (providing a crucial stimulus to manufacture in economies like those of England, Hungary and Sweden).

THE WORLD IN 1500

In the sixteenth century the world's population was much smaller than it is now and it was increasing, if at all, slowly. Everywhere in the world people were smaller than they are today and they lived shorter lives; many women died in childbirth, and infant mortality was very high. Although most peoples, by 1500, had become relatively immune to their particular parasites, increasing commercial links meant that whole populations were frequently decimated by diseases and epidemics to which they had acquired no resistance, like bubonic plague which rats carried along the Euro-Asian-African trade routes, or like smallpox which decimated the native Americans. Almost everywhere in the world there were occasional famines because few governments or communities had the resources to transport and store grain and other bulk staple commodities. These famines were usually due to sudden changes in climate and were unlike our modern 'man-made' famines when millions die even though resources exist to avert disasters, because people have been evicted from the land and deprived of the means of producing food.

In 1500, there were still hunters and gatherers to be found in every continent as well as settled communities and civilizations. Where there were cities, few were self-governing; most owed allegiance to an overlord of some description. Both cities and monarchs often owed allegiance to an emperor. The empire in which they lived was in general the boundary of their knowledge and experience. The twelve million inhabitants of the Aztec empire, for example, probably had no knowledge at all of the ten million subjects of the Inca empire which stretched almost 2,000 miles down the Andes. And neither empire, of course, was known to Europeans at that date. Only a handful of traders and sailors had crossed either imperial borders or continental boundaries, and few people anywhere had much knowledge of the world beyond the community into which they were

COMMODITIES

born. Moreover, since very few people anywhere could read and write, the things which they had seen or heard about were mostly misremembered or misunderstood.

Towns and cities were fewer and much smaller than their giant modern counterparts. In 1500, there were only five cities in Europe (Milan, Paris, Venice, Florence and Naples) which had more than 100,000 people. Outside Europe there were bigger cities. Istanbul had a population of perhaps 300,000 and Nanking and Peking in China may have had populations of half a million. But growth, in every case, was limited by the logistical problems of providing daily supplies of water and foodstuffs to the inhabitants.

Diets differed all over the world: the staple of the Aztec empire was maize; the Incas had potatoes; the people of China had rice and millet. Yams and bananas had spread from Asia to Africa by 1000 BC. Rice had spread across Asia from southern China and was being cultivated in Africa and Europe by the first century AD. Wheat and barley were grown in many parts of Asia, Africa and Europe. Sugar, too, although a rarity outside Asia, had been cultivated in the Nile valley since the ninth century, and on various Mediterranean islands since the tenth. But these foodstuffs apart, most diets were largely restricted to produce of the locality, and to salt as a preservative and additive. Many fruits and vegetables were very localized

in their use, and most of the things we see on fruit and vegetable stalls and supermarket shelves today were unknown in most parts of the world in 1500.

The soils of the world in 1500 were more fertile and more abundant in forests than those of the modern world. Because there were more forests, the soil held more water. Soil erosion was therefore rarer and deserts were smaller in area than they are now. Because there were fewer people and more forests, there were more animals, and many more species of animal. Since 1500, those species which people breed and domesticate have increased in numbers (cattle, sheep, pigs, chickens, turkeys), while those which people kill for their meat, skins and other things are close to extinction (for instance, whales, bison, elephants, tigers, parrots, birds of paradise). Other animals were exterminated because people took over and destroyed their habitats, or they were destroyed gratuitously, like the dodo. Many peoples, too, have been exterminated since 1500. The last Aboriginal Tasmanian died in 1876. After the Spanish conquest of Mexico and Peru, the native population dropped from about 20 million to less than two million. The Carib and Arawak peoples of the Caribbean, who numbered perhaps a quarter of a million in 1500, had, by 1700, mostly been exterminated by Europeans.

In 1500, Europe was less advanced in many ways than

Venice, 1480

other parts of the world. The Inca civilization had high-ways linking its cities which were capable of with-standing earthquakes; there was a highly-trained, numerate bureaucracy; the state owned the land; there were food warehouses to control production and to prevent famine; and all Inca subjects were entitled to sick-ness and old age benefits. The closest parallel to such a society in 1500 was China, which was secure, richer and more varied than the Inca empire. China had been unified by the Ming emperors, and despite subsequent changes of dynasty, its essential order remained unaltered. Its great canal system, providing transport and irrigation, had been started in the eleventh century. Although it was essentially a peasant society, most of the population was well fed, and towns and trades flourished. Paper was a Chinese invention, and paper money had been circu-

lating there since the eleventh century. By that date, the Chinese had invented gunpowder, compasses, spinning wheels and water-driven clocks. The printing press was also a Chinese invention. From the ninth century, prin-ters were engraving wooden blocks, and from the four-teenth they were using moveable metal characters. By 1500, the Chinese had a vast printed literature : technical treatises, encyclopaedias, histories and so on. There was also a daily newspaper in Peking. Chinese craftsmen, too, were unsurpassed in almost every technical skill.

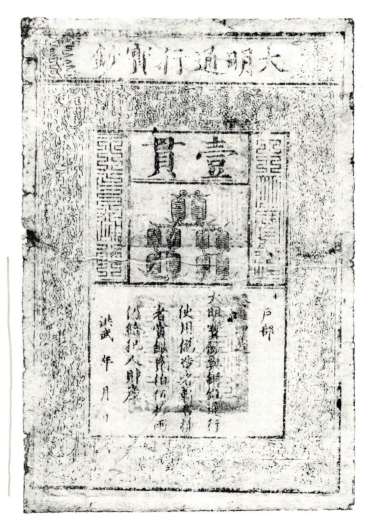

(*top left*) Incas harvesting potatoes, 16th century
(*below right*) Chinese paper money, 1380

COMMODITIES

Bronze casting, pottery, textile making, silk weaving, painting and printing were all prized and considered as art by the rich, while cheaper designs were being mass-produced for the richer peasants and townspeople. In 1421, the imperial capital was moved from Nanking to Peking, and by 1500, Peking was the largest, best designed, most exquisitely built and orderly city the world had ever known. It is significant that when Marco Polo returned from his voyages in 1295 and described the wonders of the Sung civilization at Hang-chow, no one in Europe seriously believed his account. His encyclopaedia of Asia, the greatest work of European learning of its age, was read as fable, on a par with the *Arabian Nights*.

The most extended trading empire in the world in 1500 was that of the Arabs. It covered the southern coastline of the Mediterranean to southern Spain, circled the Sahara, and extended east through Persia and northern India to Indonesia. Although most of the sultans and caliphs who ruled the separate states were independent, it still meant that Arab traders could safely travel over vast distances. For example, the Arabs were selling Chinese porcelain in Africa by 1300, long before it arrived in Europe. The scientific and cultural achievements of the Arabs were also remarkable. They had invented algebra, the concept of zero, and many accounting techniques. Their knowledge of optics, astronomy, medicine and chemical processes was far ahead of Europe's, and their castles, domed mosques and palaces were the result of building techniques which far surpassed those of Europe.

The African civilization of the Nile Valley was, of course, one of the oldest and greatest civilizations in the world. Cairo, the focus of trade routes spanning three continents, was in 1500, probably bigger than any European city. Benin, in the Equatorial jungle of West Africa, was described in glowing terms when it was first reached by Dutch traders; it was the only place outside Italy and China where the complex processes of bronze casting were fully understood. Arab traders also contributed significantly to the development of sub-Saharan civilization. The vast kingdoms of Mali and Songhay were both extremely prosperous, according to Arabic accounts. When the ruler of Timbuktu, Mansa Musa, went to Mecca in 1324, his gifts of gold were said to have lowered the value of gold in Cairo by 12 per cent. Of other great kingdoms, like the Kongo, which had an extensive trade in ivory with other parts of Africa, we know little because the population (of probably more than a million) was decimated in the sixteenth century by European slavers. On the east coast of Africa, the civilization of Zimbabwe erected impressive stone buildings and exported gold and copper through Sofala to Arabia and India.

The richest and most populous continent by far was Asia, with the Chinese Empire in the East, the largely Hindu civilization of south India, various Moslem empires in the middle, and the Ottoman Empire in the West. All were linked by local and long-distance trade networks from an early date, though China was largely self-sufficient. In the Red Sea, Persian Gulf and the Arabian Sea, Moslem traders in their *dhows* had already

Timbuktu (René Caillié's *Travels*, 1830)

established commodity chains all the way along the coast from Zanzibar to Indonesia. Here, they traded in pearls from the Persian Gulf and the Coromandel Coast, tin from Malaya, ambergris from whales tossed up on the Arabian Gulf, spices from the Malaccas, and textiles made by the celebrated craftsmen of southern India. Africa, too, had been opened up by Arab traders, who shipped copper, slaves, gold and ivory out of East Africa, and who had established the trans-Saharan trade routes which bought gold, 'Moroccan leather' and slaves from the Gold Coast to Morocco, where they were exchanged for tools and other commodities. So when the Portuguese, and later the Dutch and the English, seized control of this trade, they were appropriating, and ultimately destroying, one of the greatest trading empires in history.

South India, one of the safest trading coasts in the world, had some very wealthy cities, like Bombay, Calicut, Cochin and Madras, where Tamil, Parsee, Armenian, Hindu and Banyan merchants had complex trade and banking networks. Not the least of the reasons for India's prosperity and its great artistic achievements in architecture, sculpture, painting, literature, music and crafts, was that it had long been the duty of the state to construct and maintain an extensive irrigation system, with vast reservoirs, and canals which took the flood waters of the largest rivers to distant areas. This was paid for by a land tax, which amounted to a third of the peasants' produce. When the British arrived, they seized the tax revenues and neglected the irrigation system, which largely contributed to the Bengal famine of 1770 when ten million Indians died.

Before 1500, almost all the long-distance trade in the world was in valuable commodities, like gold, silver, ivory and spices. Bulk trade of grain was almost invariably by water since the cost of land transport was much higher. This explains the importance of water transport over much of the world, along rivers like the Rhine, the Ganges, the Nile and the Yangtze.

The Moslem Ottoman Empire, by 1520, controlled most of the eastern Mediterranean, stretching from the Red Sea to the Black Sea and from the Balkans to Iraq. It was through the Levant trade (as trade with the Ottoman Empire was known) that Europe had learned about the riches of the East and long-distance trade. Long-distance trade developed much later in Europe. One problem which faced European traders until well into the seventeenth century was that there were few commodities they could offer in exchange which the Chinese, Arabs or Indians did not already have: those they did offer, in the early days, were often treated with contempt.

In the tenth century, Europe had essentially been marginal to the great trading empires of Africa and Asia. But slowly, fairs evolved in Europe to market the goods from what little long-distance trade there was. Most goods came in from the Levant through Venice, across the Alps, and up the Rhine Valley. Soon European commodities, particularly Italian and Flemish textiles, began to be sold in these occasional fairs. Local markets serving local needs expanded, and by 1500 most parts of Europe were linked in an expanding network of trade. Towns around the North Sea had formed the Hanseatic League, Italian cities were trading extensively among themselves, with the Levant, around the Mediterranean, and across the Alps.

In most places in the world, societies were divided into rulers, their soldiers, agents and officials, and those they ruled. Merchants, because of their wealth, were often the closest advisers and associates of kings. The mass of the population, however, was at the periphery of all commodity chains. They worked in the mines, whether in Peru, Mexico, Hungary, Malaya or Northumberland, in workshops, or on the land. Most crafts were manufactured at home. Mass production techniques were rare and confined to particular industries and places, like the Arsenal in Venice which employed ten thousand workers in its shipyards, the textile factories of India, China, Italy, Flanders and England, which employed several hundreds of people under a single roof, the pottery industries of China and Persia, or the printing works in China, Geneva, Augsburg and Antwerp.

All these societies were hierarchically ordered: the material basis of that order was control of the land. Only in western Europe had a fundamental legal distinction

(*top*) Cotton weaving, c. 1800, China
(*right*) England, c. 1340: ploughing and sowing, above; threshing corn, below

evolved between the rights of property and the rights of authority; even there, the various monarchies and states could effectively block the 'free' use of land and trading opportunities. However, merchants increasingly gained control of the means of production from aristocratic grandees and monarchs because they could always supply the commodities and credit on which the rich were beginning to depend. So, by 1500, European merchants and traders, although they were regulated, taxed and controlled by the princes within whose territories they traded, enjoyed more rights and privileges than the mass of the population. Increasingly after 1500, because of the luxuries and rarities that the merchants provided for the princes, and because of the money, arms, supply and credit they could advance them, the merchants themselves became powerful and able to influence the actions of their masters as well as the policies of their governments.

If merchants were 'free', the mass of the population emphatically was not. Wage labourers were free to starve or to work at prices determined by their masters. Serfdom, where peasants were legally tied to the land and compelled to work a certain number of days for their landlords, was still widespread in much of Europe though it had disappeared in England by 1400. Slaves were widely employed both in southern European cities like Genoa (where one tenth of the 80,000 population were slaves), and in agriculture on many Mediterranean islands, in Spain and Portugal, and in Arab countries bordering the Mediterranean. Some of those slaves were brought from Russia and the Ottoman Empire, but most were transported across the Sahara and forced to work on the land or in Moslem households where there was a market for castrated Africans. By 1500, perhaps five million Africans had been transported by Arab slavers through Zanzibar and Egypt to Moslem countries.

We have used the term 'territories', but what do we mean? Before 1500, the world's boundaries were essentially inchoate and temporary. Most of the world was unmapped, with the important exception of the Mediterranean and Black Seas which had been accurately charted by Catalan sailors before 1300. By 1500, the Atlantic coast was being charted as well. Other coastlines, like that of West Africa, were only partly known and inaccurately charted. Sailors almost everywhere were forced to depend on local pilots when sailing in unfamiliar waters. By 1500, the compass, the astrolabe and the lead (for depth sounding), were in general use among European sailors. But, even in Europe, until the eighteenth century navigational skills were so rudimentary that few captains could sail far out of sight of land.

Apart from the sailors, people's knowledge of the world beyond their horizons was mostly based on fable. Many believed in various deities, angels, witches and spirits; and even educated Europeans believed tales, like those of Sir John Mandeville, of cannibals, basilisks, gryphons, giants, leviathans, and men whose heads grew beneath their shoulders.

DISCOVERY

The motive behind the early European voyages of discovery, was not, as is commonly supposed, the desire for knowledge about new worlds. When Bristol fishermen reached Newfoundland in the 1490s, three hundred years after the Vikings, they kept quiet about their discovery for fear of competition. The Portuguese crept down the African coast in their tiny boats in order to bring back pepper, gold and slaves. Columbus's diary rarely refers to the 'noble' motive of discovery at all, but at least sixty times to the possibility of finding gold.

The greatest voyages of discovery before those of Columbus, had been undertaken by the Chinese, when the Ming Emperor had sent the court eunuch Cheng Ho to discover what the territories beyond his own supplied. The voyages, between 1405 and 1433, were peaceful and successful. A vast flotilla of 50 junks and 27,000 men was assembled at the imperial shipyards, which sailed on longer voyages into the unknown than had ever been sailed before. The voyages mapped out the contours of

Portuguese ships with sea monsters, early 16th century

the Asian coast, visited Sumatra, Java, Sri Lanka, India, the Arabian Sea, the Persian Gulf and its greatest city, Ormuz, and as far south as Mogadishu, the great trading port on the Somali Coast. In 1433, when the fleet returned from its seventh voyage, the Emperor pronounced himself satisfied. He and his mandarins had sampled and discussed the merits of the commodities and facts which Ho's mission had brought back and there was nothing that the Emperor required. This lack of official interest in expansion overseas blocked any development of Chinese commercial imperialism and later left China vulnerable to predatory empires, like those of the Portuguese, the Dutch and the British.

Portuguese route to India, Italian map of Africa, 1508

It is against this background that we need to measure the achievements of the Portuguese 'explorers', (though the name slightly dignifies them). Each of Cheng Ho's junks had been 500 tons; the Portuguese sailed in the 25-ton *barca*, crewed by seven men. A Portuguese expedition had seized Ceuta in Morocco in 1415, which became the bridgehead for further exploration down the African coast. The Portuguese rediscovered the Azores in 1439, followed by the Madeiras and the Cape Verde Islands, where they established sugar cane plantations by the 1470s. In 1448, they established their first African trading base at Arguin in Senegal, where they obtained the slaves to work on their plantations. By 1500, three thousand slaves a year were being taken from 'the Slave Coast' (Senegal, Gambia and Guinea) back to Portugal.

Before 1450, these expeditions had largely been sponsored and financed by the Portuguese Crown. But once pepper was discovered, Genoese merchants arrived, followed by others from all over Europe; this was because pepper was then worth almost as much as gold (the dowry of Isabella of Portugal, when she married Charles V in 1526 was paid in pepper). Foreign sailors gravitated to the Portuguese boats, attracted by the rumours of rich rewards. The shipyards built bigger boats, and by 1460, the *barca* had been replaced by the sleek *caravel*, which could sail to windward and carry cargo and cannon. In 1469, the Portuguese Crown leased the rights to the Guinea trade to a wealthy merchant, Fernando Gomes, for five years, in return for an obliga-

tion to explore 100 leagues of coast each year. In that short time, Portuguese ships reached the Ivory Coast and the Gold Coast (Ghana), as well as the islands of Fernando Po and São Tome, where they also established sugar plantations. In 1482, Diego Cam 'discovered' the Congo. By 1488, the Portuguese had rounded the Cape of Good Hope and reached the Great Fish River on the Indian Ocean. Then, in 1499, Vasco da Gama reached Calicut in India, though he lost two out of his four ships on the voyage. By 1500, the Portuguese had a string of forts and 'factories' (trading warehouses) along the West African coast, where they traded with African kingdoms for pepper, gold, ivory, and slaves. The slaves were used as household servants by the rich and as workers on the sugar plantations.

Sugar, after gold, silver, and pepper, was the most valuable commodity in Europe. It was a luxury enjoyed only in small quantities by the aristocracy. So, once the Portuguese had territories they could plant and control, finance to invest in sugar production, and ships to transport it to markets, they systematically began to exploit the production of sugar. To grow and refine sugar, they needed labour (black slaves), capital (provided by the Genoese merchants) and a market. Venice and Genoa controlled the Arab-European sugar trade, so Portuguese merchants sent the sugar to Antwerp for refining and marketing.

Columbus, like other Genoese sailors was attracted to Portugal in the 1480s by the stories of gold. In Lisbon, he attempted to interest the merchants and the government in the idea of a sea route to India which would bypass the Arab and Venetian middlemen. No European knew where Africa ended; in Europe, Africa was thought to end in mountains of ice. Columbus suggested another route to the Indies, which he had read about in the fables of Marco Polo and Mandeville, and which he had discussed with the foremost geographers in Italy. Like most sailors, he knew that the earth was not flat yet he underestimated the circumference of the world by several thousand miles; he suggested a route past the Azores and the Canaries, and then west with the trade winds along the equator to India. Neither the Portuguese government nor the merchants were attracted to this risky investment. Although they disbelieved the stories about the ice, fire and hell south of the equator, they preferred to invest in the possibility of a route around Africa. When a Portuguese expedition led by Diaz returned in 1489 with news of a route to the Indian Ocean, Columbus was forced to take his wild scheme elsewhere.

The Portuguese, however, had not yet demonstrated

that their route was profitable. Columbus went to Castille and was financed by Queen Isabella and a consortium of Genoese bankers. He returned in 1493 and announced that he had discovered the route to the Indies. In fact he had 'discovered' the Bahamas, the north coast of Cuba, and Hispaniola. The 'Indians' (as he mistakenly called them) that he encountered there were friendly. During his next voyage (1493–4), he explored the coast of Cuba (which he believed to be China). During his third voyage, Columbus 'discovered' Trinidad and

(*top*) Warehousing grain and spices, 16th century
(*below*) Calicut, south west India, c. 1500

COMMODITIES

German woodcut, c. 1500, with inscription stating that the native Americans 'eat each other . . . become 150 years of age, and have no government'

Venezuela, behind which he believed lay terrestrial Paradise. And during his fourth voyage, he explored the coast of the Isthmus of Panama, Nicaragua and Honduras, which he took for Indochina. The most immediate consequence of that contact was that by the year 1500, syphilis was an epidemic in Europe and smallpox and measles had begun to decimate the Indian population of the Caribbean.

TRADE AND INDUSTRY IN EUROPE

Before 1500, the bulk of European trade had been in a few commodities. The Baltic was essential as a source of timber, pitch, tar and hemp for shipbuilding. Swedish iron was also essential for shipbuilding, and for the rapidly expanding armaments industry. The other major commodities were English wool, French wine, and Flemish and Italian textiles. The mercantile oligarchy of Venice controlled the European end of the valuable Levantine trade, and the Genoese oligarchy controlled trade with the Black Sea. Florentine merchants dominated trans-Alpine trade between Italy and northern Europe.

During the sixteenth century, there were clear signs of capitalist development in which ownership of the means of production had become separated from the labour power which produced commodities. The wool and textile industries were major employers in England,

Flanders and northern Italy. Silk production was extensively capitalized and concentrated in centres like Genoa, Florence, Venice and Tours. There were extensive copper, silver and iron mines in Hungary, controlled by the Fugger banking dynasty. Many industries already depended on a large proletariat which was employed in building, mills, furnaces, forges and mines. Yet despite industrial development in these countries, for a brief period, the commercial initiative passed to Portugal and Spain. Why?

PORTUGAL'S TRADING EMPIRE

Even before the development of its fifteenth-century trading empire, Portugal had long-established links with northern Europe and the Mediterranean. The Portuguese aristocracy was declining, but in their decline they had successfully held down the peasantry; thus food was relatively cheap, and so too was wage labour. Portuguese agriculture had long been specialized; olives, wine, and cork had been traded with northern Europe and the Mediterranean since Roman times. Since 1300, merchants in particular had prospered as they handled this lucrative trade. By the 1450s, Lisbon was the focus for many foreign bankers, particularly the Genoese, who had a long experience of sugar production in the Mediterranean, from Sicily, to southern Spain, and who rapidly invested in and prospered from the development of the Portuguese–African trade in ivory, pepper, gold dust, and slaves.

In 1494, the Treaty of Tordesillas granted discoveries west of 60° longitude to Spain; those east of that line went to Portugal. Thus Portugal had a monopoly of trade with the Indies. Calicut, where Vasco da Gama first landed in India, was by chance one of the great trading centres of India, receiving pepper, ginger and cinnamon from Sri Lanka, cloves from Malacca, and tin from Malaya. When da Gama returned in 1501, his cargo was worth 60 times the cost of the expedition, though he had lost two ships. Such a quantity of spices could not be handled by Lisbon, so they were shipped to Antwerp and unloaded there. In 1503, the Portuguese had established a warehouse in Antwerp (the Casa de India), and for the next 60 years the fortunes of these two places were closely linked. Through Antwerp came Hungarian silver and copper (controlled by the Fugger banking dynasty, whose trading empire was based in Antwerp). This copper and silver passed down the chain and paid for the extension of Portuguese trade and conquest. Through Antwerp, Portugal also obtained grain from the Baltic to feed its expanding dependencies, as well as other essential commodities.

In 1501, the King of Portugal, Manuel I, optimistically entitled himself 'Lord of the Conquest, Navigation and Commerce of Ethiopia, Arabia, Persia and India', which reveals that the motive behind Portugal's extraordinarily swift expansion was not simply territorial aggrandizement but the extension of trade. The next 150 years saw Portuguese sailors and traders making effective that grandiose claim. By 1509, Portugal was powerful enough to defeat the combined Indian and Egyptian fleets, which gave it a series of key trading bases along the coast from Sofala on the Zambezi to Nagasaki in Japan. In 1557, Portugal seized and fortified Macao, an island off Canton, which gave them access to the China trade.

Despite the fact that taxes on traded goods were levied by the Crown at between 30 and 60 per cent on the value of the goods, the profits from trade were so enormous that taxation did not restrict expansion. It is significant that when the Portuguese sailor Cabral 'discovered' Brazil by mistake, in 1500, on a voyage to the Indies round the Cape of Good Hope, no further voyages were undertaken to that coast for 20 years because it offered no immediate trading advantage. It was not until 1549 that Bahia was founded in Brazil, and sugar plantations were established using African slaves; in less than 30 years, it became the richest sugar-producing area in the Western world.

By 1580, Portugal had a global trading empire which extended from Brazil to the Gold Coast and Angola, and from Sofala, through India to Malacca, Canton and Japan. Never before in the history of the world had such an extensive transcontinental trading network been established. But in that year, Portugal was annexed by Spain and it remained under Spain until 1640. However,

(*top*) Lisbon, 16th century

(*below*) Dutch conquest of Ceylon (now Sri Lanka)

by then its trading empire had been undermined by Dutch and English interlopers; Portugal was rapidly declining.

SPAIN AND SILVER

When Columbus returned from his first voyage in 1492, his main difficulty was in raising capital to finance further exploration. Queen Isabella sponsored his voyage, but most of the money was put up by wealthy Spanish merchants. Queen Isabella appointed an official to organize Columbus's second voyage and she created a Council of the Indies to control the exploitation of the Americas. Seville was authorized as the sole port for the Americas, with responsibility for revenue collecting, licensing of territories, and so on. The Crown claimed all gold, silver and jewels for itself, and it taxed one fifth of the value of all other commodities.

Columbus's second voyage took colonists to the West Indies, but they were rapidly wiped out by the Caribs. His last two voyages also were not particularly profitable. It was Spanish *conquistadores* led by Cortes in the 1520s, and Pizarro in the 1530s, who reaped the benefits of his 'discoveries'. Destroying the Aztec and Inca Empires, they seized control of a vast territory stretching over 4,000 miles from Mexico to Chile, and this territory supplied the most valuable of all commodities, gold and silver. There was already in Europe a serious shortage of gold and silver; what had not been turned into costly ornaments for popes and princes had been exported to the East to pay for Arab spices and luxuries. It was Spanish conquest which restored the supply. This gold and silver (like Portuguese pepper and spices) was increasingly taken to Antwerp and exchanged for all those commodities (armaments, ships, salted foods, grain and tools) which Spain, like Portugal, needed to sustain its expansion overseas.

The Spanish colonial system was essentially feudal, with a class of grandees ruling over native populations, raising taxes which were remitted to the Spanish government. Apart from silver mining (to pay the taxes, which financed the process of conquest and control), Spanish colonies were not encouraged to become self-sufficient or to develop industries and manufactures of their own. It was not until their independence from Spain in the 1820s that they became important as producers of other commodities like sugar and coffee.

In general, mercantile wealth provided the capital for Spanish expansion. It was the Augsburg banking dynasty, the Fuggers, which advanced loans to the Spanish monarch, Charles V, so that he could bribe his way to the throne of the Holy Roman Empire; when he came to the throne in 1519, he combined Spain and the Habsburg empire under a single monarch. But he needed more gold to consolidate his claims, so Spanish silver and gold flowed increasingly to northern Europe, via Antwerp into the hands of northern merchants, bankers and mercenaries. Charles, however, was unable to consolidate his territories because the expense was too great. In 1556 he abdicated, and his empire was divided.

At the same time, the importing of gold rapidly led to price rises and unemployment, first around Seville and soon all over Europe, because it became cheaper to buy goods and manufactures in regions where costs had not yet begun to rise. It was the poor, of course, who suffered most, since prices rose faster than wages; but inflation was convenient for entrepreneurs, since the difference between wages and prices allowed them to accumulate capital which they invested in trade, industry and agriculture.

BANKING AND COMMERCE

Discoveries, trade and the extension of agriculture, however, are not alone sufficient to explain developments at this time. The problem which faced both Portugal and Spain was the lack of banking and mercantile expertise; to fill the gap, in the early days of expansion, they relied on local merchants and the skills of Sephardic Jewish merchants. Later, the Genoese moved in and took control of the operation; the Jews were expelled from Portugal in 1487 and from Spain in 1492. Many Jews went first to Antwerp, and later, in order to escape the Catholic Inquisition, on to Amsterdam and the Caribbean; others were invited by the enlightened Sultan Beyazid II to settle in Istanbul. By 1500, Jewish and

Italian bankers had developed many of the fundamental operations of modern banking. As early as the thirteenth century, bankers from Pisa adopted Arabic rather than Roman numerals, and double-entry bookkeeping was being used in Italian financial centres from the fourteenth century. Paper transactions were being widely used in Flanders by the fifteenth, which speeded up business, provided credit, guaranteed rates of interest (at a time when usury was condemned by the Church), and dispensed with the necessity of coin and bullion. The first public bank was established in Genoa in the early fifteenth century, and bills of exchange for settling distant debts were common among Florentine bankers and their distant branches in Flanders from the 1440s. Marine insurance was being used in Palermo as early as 1350, and by 1500, it had spread to Flanders. Equally important was the Florentine *societas* or association, in which several members of a family or associates put up money for fixed periods to finance trade. Such companies also accepted deposits, which paid interest of six to ten per cent, and

made loans at between seven and 33 per cent. Elsewhere, in places like Genoa and Venice, bankers would put up money for risky ventures and take 25 per cent or more of the profit.

MERCHANTS AND THEIR CITIES

Historians often fail to emphasize that one of the fundamental determinants of history has been mercantile activity. Even though a great city might have been created by imperial decree, it was the merchants who created the chains which built and sustained Peking, Cairo, Timbuktu, Istanbul, Rome and Seville. In Europe, in particular, merchants not only sustained cities but they created their own, and through their civic power determined the successes and failures of governments.

In Europe, by the middle of the fourteenth century, no government could attempt to extend its territorial control or contain rebellion within its border without the credit and supplies of merchants. But merchants in general had prospered outside those borders; in their free towns, outside the jurisdiction of the Church, which prohibited usury, they found ways of increasing trade. All the inventions which we have mentioned (double-entry bookkeeping, credit, insurance and banking), they liked to keep far from the predatory eyes of princes; their cities were self-regulating havens of trade. By 1500, the Portuguese had extended mercantile chains beyond the boundaries of Europe to the whole world, but they lacked a market. Antwerp became that market.

It was in the cities which merchants themselves controlled (like Antwerp, Venice, Genoa, Florence, Bruges, Amsterdam and London) that first mercantile and then industrial capitalism evolved. Venice, in many ways, had been the prototypic mercantile city. It owned dominion to no overlord. It was an imperial power with a monopoly over the Levant trade. It had colonies which supplied it with essential and valuable commodities and a banking system. Mass production was characteristic of its Arsenal, which was the largest shipbuilding and armaments complex in the world. Its mint forged coins which were accepted at a premium all over the world. However, the arrival of Portuguese spices in Antwerp

'Commerce', 15th-century tapestry

marked the beginning of Venice's decline. Access to the Mediterranean was now worth less than access to the oceans of the world.

ANTWERP

Antwerp rapidly rose to prominence in the sixteenth century because it was there that the Portuguese and German commodity chains met. The Portuguese brought in spices, which they bartered initially for German textiles, copper, silver and tools. Then the German merchant bankers began to finance Portuguese voyages to the Indies. The Baltic trade, controlled by Flemish sailors, supplied ships and grain. These chains also intersected with the English wool trade, which exported cloth for finishing in Antwerp before distribution to other markets in northern Europe. French and Rhenish wines were shipped into Bristol and exchanged for dry cod, which was taken to Portugal. Such a volume of raw commodities encouraged technical innovation, and Antwerp had both the credit and the incentive to rapidly industrialize in order to supply its new markets. Metals and vegetables were refined and processed there. Metalwork, the armaments industry, glass making, paper making, instrument making and publishing all flourished. Part of the success of Antwerp was due to the fact that little money needed to circulate on its markets. Antwerp merchants preferred to give and take credit, and the richest merchants were secure enough in their credit to make loans and to take deposits. Much of this credit capital was invested in industry and so secure was its system that the Antwerp Bourse became the financial centre of Europe; merchant bankers like the Fuggers averaged 50 per cent profits in the period between 1511 and 1525.

The Antwerp money market was secured on commodities, but the most profitable (and risky) loans were made to various princes. At first, the symbiosis of private bankers and governments led to a massive expansion of credit operations. Then, in 1549, the Portuguese Crown defaulted and the Fugger banking empire collapsed. In the 1550s, the Portuguese withdrew their spice monopoly, the textile market collapsed and

Dunkirk pirates attacked Antwerp shipping. The Spanish-American trade also slumped in the 1550s, when the gold ran out. The Spanish Crown declared itself bankrupt in 1557, and the Antwerp merchants lost the money owing to them, which was two shiploads of silver. In 1560, the Portuguese Crown followed suit, and the Antwerp banking system finally collapsed. There were harvest failures; foreign merchants diverted their trade to other cities, particularly to Amsterdam. In 1572, Antwerp and the northern Flemish provinces rebelled against Spanish rule (the Revolt of the Netherlands). Antwerp was recaptured in 1576 and sacked by Spanish troops. In 1585, the Dutch blockaded the Scheldt, which cut Antwerp off from the Rhine and German trade. Antwerp's golden age was over.

THE UNITED PROVINCES

The United Provinces, as Holland was called in its early history, was a federation of seven provinces, all quite different, united only in their opposition to Spain. They had aligned together during the Revolt of the Netherlands, inheriting little more than a swampy stretch of islands on the delta of the Rhine. While fighting an intermittent, 80-year war against Spain between 1568 and 1648, they had revolutionized the economy and productivity of their country to an extraordinary degree.

By 1600, Amsterdam's economy was the most dynamic and powerful in Europe, the hub of European trade and finance, controlling two thirds of Europe's shipping with an ever-increasing volume of trade in primary commodities and manufactured goods. By 1700 (which dates, in retrospect, the beginning of Holland's obvious decline), the Dutch fleet was still as large as the combined fleets of the rest of Europe. Dutch merchants controlled a trading empire which stretched from Japan to the Caribbean. Amsterdam bankers were the richest in Europe. Holland's crafts and industries were almost unparalleled. But already it was being overtaken by London as the core power in world trade. What factors then explain the rapid rise and decline of Holland?

It is useful to divide Holland's development into four phases: the period when the Provinces were still under

Flemish control (to 1589), a transitional period which was dominated by the war with Spain (1589–1609), the period of the Regents (1609–1660), and then the period of the Republic (1660–1789). Holland's phenomenal rise greatly puzzled contemporaries when they attempted to explain it; how could a cluster of muddy islands create a world empire? What principle lay behind its policies? When contemporaries looked for material causes, they failed to find them. Holland was merely a loose alliance of states, covering a total area less than the size of Devon, much of it below sea level and thus liable to flooding, with no minerals, forests or decent farmland.

The first phase in Holland's rise, was a period in which the Dutch came to control the fishing industry of Europe. Dutch herring boats, fishing off the Dogger Bank, gutted, salted and barrelled up the herring, which were then taken by smaller craft all over Europe, before being loaded onto larger ships. By 1540, Dutch salted herring was one of the staples of long sea voyages. Inshore fishing for wet fish, cod fishing off Iceland, and

whaling off Spitzbergen together equalled in value that of the herring fleets. The profits from this lucrative trade (effectively a monopoly since no other fleet could sell fish as cheaply as the Dutch), provided much of the early capital for economic developments. It is important to note that fish and grain, the two key commodities in Holland's economic development, were bulk commodity trades, unlike the spice and precious metal trades of the Iberian peninsula. Both, therefore, depended on the massive expansion of shipping, which was fundamental to Holland's development of an interlinked world empire.

It was also in the early period that Amsterdam sailors first seized control of the Baltic trade. Initially, they were permitted to trade fish and salt for grain; by the middle of the sixteenth century Dutch ships controlled the corn trade between the Baltic and the Iberian peninsula as well. Amsterdam was mocked as 'the corn bin of Europe', but control of the trade was yet another crucial contributor to its prosperity. From the Baltic came

37

timber, pitch, tar and hemp, all essential for the Dutch shipbuilding industry. Finally, Swedish iron ore, an industry which had largely been developed by Dutch capital, provided the raw material not simply for Dutch shipping, but also for armaments, tools, machines and technical instrument manufacture as well.

The Dutch shipbuilding industry was in itself extraordinary, and rapidly surpassed that of Venice. Holland's ability to monopolize the Baltic trade meant that it enjoyed a guaranteed supply of all essentials; ships were mass produced and mechanical saws and hoists were employed. It took eight weeks to build a ship, and the yards at Saardam just outside Amsterdam were capable of turning out 50 ships a year. The great ship invented at these yards was the *fluyt*, a bulk carrier which could be crewed by seven men, and which had a carrying capacity much greater than other ships of the same length. Dutch *fluyts* could therefore always undercut rivals, since transport costs for low value commodities like grain, fish and salt largely determined the price which those commodities could command in distant markets. The shipyards were also expert at salvaging and repairing ships; Amsterdam rapidly became the secondhand ship

Dutch fluyts, 1647

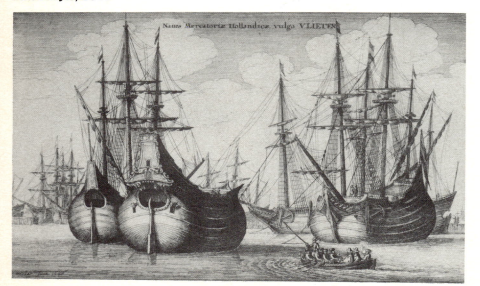

market of Europe, for credit was cheap and easily obtained, and there was never a shortage of cargoes.

By 1600, Holland was the most densely-populated country in Europe; over half the people already lived in towns. The feeding of such a vast population was made possible by an agrarian revolution which began after 1500, when rivers were banked, canals cut, and windmills constructed to pump the land. Urban waste was used to manure the reclaimed mud, wheat was planted, crops were rotated, and turnips were grown to feed the cattle, which were selectively bred so they yielded unprecedented quantities of milk. Each cow produced on average three pails of milk a day, which were made into butter and cheese and then exported all over Europe. The cattle, of course, also manured the land. New experimental crops were planted like maize and potatoes from the Americas, flax, hops, tobacco, rape, and dyes like madder and woad (used in the textile finishing trade, itself rapidly expanding in Leyden, Haarlem and Amsterdam). Even wheat yields per ton planted matched those of England, which at the time were the highest in Europe. By 1700, Holland was growing half the wheat it needed. Market gardening flourished too, as the towns expanded and as more roads and canals were built to link villages and urban markets.

A crucial factor in Holland's evolution was its policy of religious toleration. This amazed contemporaries, who could not believe that a state could cohere without an official religion. Although the majority of the population was Protestant there was no state church; Lutherans, Jews, Calvinists, Presbyterians and Catholics all worshipped openly. This policy was forged in the war against Spain; the stepping up of religious persecution by the Catholic Inquisition had forced a third of the Antwerp merchants to settle in the United Provinces. Most focussed their activities on Amsterdam. Many were Sephardic Jews and their expertise, particularly in exchange and credit operations (both crucial in an economy which had little coin or bullion, and which was beginning to trade with the world), as well as their links with Iberian and Levantine trade, greatly extended Amsterdam's horizons.

By 1600, Leyden was established as one of the great

textile centres of Europe. Haarlem silks were already cheaper than those from Lyons and Tuscany. The exquisite mass-produced pottery of Delft was shipped as ballast to England, the Iberian peninsula and the Americas. Amsterdam contained the largest printing industry in Europe. Dutch printed maps and telescopes (another Dutch invention) were used by sailors everywhere. Optics, clock making, diamond cutting, navigational instruments, armaments – almost everything which sailors required and traders could trade – were manufactured in Holland. Even mud was made into bricks in the largest brickworks in Europe, taken to England as ballast, and traded for unfinished cloth.

Probably the majority of the skilled craftsmen were religious refugees. Holland also attracted many poor immigrants from Germany who worked in the docks and warehouses, collected refuse, and worked on the land. If there was any single shortage in Holland, it was a shortage of labour. For this reason, Holland was not even a nation in a linguistic or an ethnic sense: Walloons, Portuguese, French, German, Swedes, Danes, Jews – all were Dutchmen. But although immigrants prospered in varying degrees (and although even peasants prospered), power in Holland was in the hands of the mercantile oligarchy.

Nominally, between 1609 and 1660, power lay in the hands of the Regents, but the Regents were connected by family and business links with the merchants. Thus they were effectively the merchants' puppets; they raised taxes in the merchants' interest and the poor carried most of the fiscal burden. The Regents enforced the law; they controlled wages in the towns and suppressed any discontents. According to John Evelyn, who visited Holland at that time, vagrants were put to work and orphan girls were made into good housewives and taken by 'men of good worth' (Evelyn, p. 26).

By 1620, Holland was remarkably secure against invasion. Prince Maurice of Nassau had completed a string of earthworks and forts which held the eastern frontier. The border was turned into a military academy, where German and English mercenaries flocked to learn the basics of their trade, using the most advanced weaponry

Soldiers armed with the arquebus, the main firearm of the 16th century

and skills of the time. Foreign policy was in the hands of the States General, which contained representatives of the various provinces. But since foreign policy was funded by the merchants, they ensured that it served their interest. In general, after 1609, Holland pursued a policy of peace, since trade inevitably suffered during periods of conflict. Holland even intervened in a Baltic war in 1654, because it was damaging (Dutch) trade.

DUTCH CAPITALISM

In Holland, money and commerce were free. Nothing restrained their operation; neither usury nor wealth was condemned, they were both seen as increasing the advantage of the state and its subjects.

Holland financed its early development by commodifying its seas and its land, and from the sale of herring and corn it had funded its other trades. The Dutch always enjoyed a healthy trading surplus so foreign gold, silver and copper coins flooded in. Some of this was reminted in Amsterdam, and recirculated as Dutch dollars. So colossal was the volume of Dutch trade, however, that something apart from coins were needed to sustain it; the substitute discovered was credit. Essentially, this meant that anyone with whom the Dutch traded could obtain Dutch goods on credit, in return for a share of future profits, whether through processing or trading. The importance of credit can be seen in a crucial sector of the

39

COMMODITIES

Dutch economy, the docks. Amsterdam, being an entrepot, needed to turn ships around as quickly as possible; five days was the general rule. Such a trade needed quick and easy settlements. The ships were unloaded, goods were stored in warehouses and then another cargo was assembled and loaded, and all this was done on credit.

The provision of cheap and easily obtained credit largely explains the rapid development of Dutch trading links abroad, as well as the rapid economic development of Holland itself. All manner of manufactures and industries were built up on credit. The Bank of Amsterdam, which was founded in 1609, greatly facilitated this development, because after credits and debits had been entered in its books, most of the transactions cancelled each other out. The system also incorporated bills of exchange which could circulate as paper money. The commission trade was also crucial. This enabled a merchant-capitalist to advance anything between a quarter and three quarters of the expected profit from a sale to another merchant, who would undertake to get the goods to market.

Death of Herr Credit: 'When you've got the money, I've got the bread' (German satire, 17th century)

Foreign merchants and princes soon came to rely on the Amsterdam Bourse, leaving as collateral land, jewellery, tax entitlements, even on one occasion the Crown Jewels of Russia. However, when the French Govern-

ment suspended payments in 1788, this seriously undermined both Dutch credit and general confidence in its operation.

THE DUTCH EMPIRE OF TRADE

Until 1600, Dutch mercantile activity focussed on the North Sea, the Baltic and the Channel ports, which, as we have seen, were effectively Dutch lakes. It is significant that it was English shipping, unable to compete with the Dutch in these waters, which first opened up direct northern European trading links with the Mediterranean and access to the Levant trade through Istanbul.

The Spanish and the Portuguese had acquired their empires through a mixture of accident and aggression, and between them, and with the connivance of the Pope who issued the Treaty of Tordesillas, they had divided the trading empires of the Americas and Indies. The English and Dutch, being Protestants, did not recognize the Treaty, but initially they lacked the seapower to break the Iberian monopoly. By the 1570s, however, English privateers had discovered the ease and advantage of attacking Portuguese and Spanish shipping. Pirates, like Drake and Hawkins, plundered carracks, traded slaves to the Caribbean, and amassed large fortunes. Piracy was easy compared to the much more complex and costly operations of trade. The Dutch, too, indulged in occasional acts of piracy. By 1600, however, the Portuguese were well prepared and well armed and they sailed in convoy. Besides, the general policy of Holland (when it suited Holland) was peace.

In 1596, a group of Rotterdam merchants sent a captain to Portugal to enlist in disguise on a Portuguese East Indiaman. He was discovered and thrown into jail in Goa. The Rotterdam merchants bailed him out, and, on the basis of his report, they prepared an expedition to the Indies, which returned in 1601 bringing a cargo worth 400 per cent of the cost of the voyage. A group of wealthy Amsterdam merchants, hearing of the voyage, then approached the States General and argued that what was clearly needed was a government operation as well funded as that of the Portuguese. In 1602, the Dutch East

India Company (the V.O.C.) was floated; predictably, most of the subscription was taken up by the great trading oligarchs. The Company was granted a monopoly of trade with Asia, which obviously angered the traders who already had opened up links with the East, though they were temporarily silenced. The capital raised by the flotation was enormous: 6.5 million florins or the equivalent of 64 tons of gold, a sum ten times greater than that raised by the English East India Company two years earlier. Such funding allowed the Company to assemble vast convoys of specially constructed East Indiamen; by the 1690s, the Company was estimated to have between 100 and 160 ships, all armed with 30 to 60 cannon apiece, employing perhaps 8,000 sailors. Its payroll also included Dutch and native soldiers and an army of perhaps 10,000 agents based in Asia. In short, the V.O.C. was a formidable fighting force and commercial operation combined.

By 1600, Portugal had enjoyed a century of relatively peaceful trade across the Indian Ocean to China and Japan, as well as half a century of trade with its colony in Brazil. A revealing report of one of the early Dutch voyages to the Indies tells how the Dutch found themselves sailing beside a Portuguese carrack; cheese and wine were exchanged, and they fired a single shot salute (economical but polite) as they parted for their separate spice islands.

From the first, the Company combined aggression with trade. Its captains were prepared to trade peacefully, but happy to use force. In 1604, they attacked Malacca. In 1605, they captured the Portuguese fort of Amboyna. Three times, by 1610, they had tried to trade in Canton, thereby challenging a Portuguese monopoly. In 1616, they were trading in Japan. In 1619, they seized Batavia (now Djakarta in Indonesia) on what were then called the Spice Islands. By 1620, the Company had established a string of factories and forts along the Indian coast. In 1641, it took Malacca and (with the exceptions of Macao, Bombay and Goa) extinguished the Portuguese empire in the East.

The basic principle behind the V.O.C.'s policy was the extension of its mercantile empire and the imposition of

Dutch merchant points to V.O.C. ships in Batavia (now Jakarta), 17th century

monopoly control in every way possible. For example, in order to create a monopoly in cloves, the Dutch uprooted trees in Malacca and restricted production to Amboyna. They restricted mace and nutmeg to Banda. They uprooted cinnamon bushes all over the Indies so they could profit from Sinhalese cinnamon (having seized Sri Lanka in 1661). When native labour was rebellious or unavailable, the Dutch shipped slaves to Java and South Africa; there the slaves were compelled to grow sugar, coffee, spices and wheat. The Company also controlled the gold mines of Sumatra and the tin trade in Malaya.

Commodities were bartered for other commodities or exchanged for metals and jewels, which, however, could only be obtained in certain places. Company ships were therefore sent to China for gold and silk and to Japan for silver and copper; they traded Indian cottons and Chinese vases to Europe and took elephants to Bengal. They bought Spanish silver in Manila, until they stupidly sacked the treasure fleet and killed the golden goose.

The directors of the Company profited not only as shareholders but also as traders. They operated 'a ring' which ensured that they could purchase the commodities bought in by Company fleets at very low prices, thus cheating the ordinary shareholders, who received surprisingly low dividends given the visible success of the operation. Quickly, the factors and agents followed the directors' example and soon the Company was notorious for the luxury and corruption of its employees; they squandered company money, spent it to buy slaves and luxuries, advanced credit to smugglers, and even peculated (on credit).

The corruption and coercive policies of the V.O.C. soon rebounded. Other merchants, angered by the high prices that the Company's monopoly encouraged, set up rival East India Companies flying Danish, Swedish and Norwegian flags. Increased competition from such interlopers and from the English caused a rapid rise in the prices paid for commodities in Asia and a fall in selling prices in Europe. To maintain confidence, the V.O.C. continued to send out vast fleets, but these increasingly returned half-empty.

The activity of the other government-sponsored monopoly, the Dutch West India Company, is equally revealing. In the 1450s, the Portuguese had established sugar plantations using African slaves around Bahia and Olinda in north east Brazil; they shipped the sugar to Amsterdam where it was refined and then marketed. This was an extremely profitable operation both for Amsterdam and Portugal. In 1621, however, the States General licensed a company to plunder Brazil, the Dutch West India Company. In 1624, its fleet looted São Salvador, the capital. The city was retaken next year, but in 1629 it seized the sugar growing town of Olinda, its port Recife, and loot worth a million gold dollars, which gives some indication of the profits the Portuguese had made from sugar. Four years later, the Dutch occupied Paraiba and a long coastal strip, but their carracks were unable to reach the sugar growing areas; the Amsterdam refineries were bankrupt and the price of sugar soared. In the meantime, the Dutch had been selling arms to the Portuguese, so the Portuguese successfully expelled them in 1654. Once again, a Dutch company had killed the golden goose.

By 1700, the Dutch had a trading empire which stretched around the world. They had colonized Sri Lanka, Java, South Africa, Curaçao and Surinam. Their banking system was the most advanced in Europe, likewise their industry and agriculture. They had the largest fleet in the world. Why then was Holland so rapidly overtaken by London?

The first reason was that in order to secure its conquests and extend its trade, Holland had to fight its competitors. After the Dutch had defeated the Portuguese, they were increasingly challenged by the English. The English Navigation Acts, tightened up and more rigorously enforced, were directly aimed at eliminating Dutch competition; the only ships allowed to berth in England were English ships or ships carrying their own country's commodities, which struck at the heart of the Dutch control of England's trade. The three Anglo-Dutch wars (1652–54, 1665–67, 1673–74) were provoked by the Navigation Acts and commercial rivalry, and they were more costly for Holland than for England, because England captured many Dutch ships. At the same time, Holland was increasingly at war with France, though the French, unable to sail the ships they captured, sold them back to the Dutch or to the English, even though this was costly.

Many Dutch merchants and bankers moved to England after 1650, attracted by Cromwell's aggressive mercantile policy and the rich trading opportunities offered by England and its new colonies. Others moved wherever their money took them, settling all over the world, from Russia and France to the Americas. For a country with such a small population, the loss of skills and capital was serious. After 1660 and the establishing of the Republic, life for the rich in Holland became increasingly luxurious. However, since trade was becoming increasingly competitive and profits were falling in Holland, more and more money was simply gambled away on speculative bubbles. Holland, manipulated by England, also paid heavily for the protracted war with France, the War of Spanish Succession (1702–13).

Holland was also ultimately undermined by the principle of self-interest, which meant that the Dutch would trade with anyone who wanted to trade. The Dutch traded with their official enemies even when this undermined state policy. Typical was an episode which occurred when the French were at war with Holland in 1697. There was a grain famine in France, the army was dying, and the French were about to capitulate. The price of grain was going through the roof. The shortage, predictably, was ended by supplies from Dutch ships flying Danish flags, and, according to an astonished French witness, by ships boldly flying Dutch flags as well. There was nothing the States General could do to stop the trade; self-interest was a principle of state. But it also meant that Dutch money moved out of Amsterdam, and inevitably, of course, it helped capitalize resistance to Dutch monopolies.

Finally, Holland was over-extended. When the links holding their commodity chains broke, the Dutch had few means of repairing them and regaining the advantage. They held on to their colonies but by the 1720s, the Dutch world empire of trade was effectively finished. Control had now passed to London.

LONDON

Between 1660 and 1700, English merchants and seamen seized the advantage from Holland. The Anglo-Dutch wars provided the English with many Dutch *fluyts* and warships. Many Dutch traders and craftsmen came to England and helped develop the English economy; for instance, it was a Dutchman, Vermuyden, who engineered the draining of the Fens in England in the 1630s. Dutch craftsmen came to England after the Great Fire in 1666 and helped to rebuild London. Dutch financiers were attracted to London because interest rates were much higher than those in Holland. This shift of Dutch expertise and capital abroad diminished the advantages which the Dutch enjoyed over their competitors. Also, it was difficult for so small a country as Holland, with a population of less than three million, to increase its share of the world market above a certain level; it was not difficult for interlopers to take over Dutch operations when Dutch supply lines were so extended.

Even so, England's challenge to Holland was very quick and decisive. In 1641, when Civil War broke out in England, nobody would have predicted that England might play a major role in Europe. England's economy was in tatters after twenty years of royal mismanagement. England had no coherent foreign or economic policy; its only colony was Wales, which had been sucked dry by the Normans. Ireland was theoretically a colony (the Irish, of course, disagreed about this), but, in reality, it was a swampy island in which generations of English soldiers had lost their lives and reputations, and which certainly was not, in any sense, a profitable operation. Scotland was neither a colony nor a source of profit to English capitalists; it only became important in the eighteenth century. New England was a colony, but hardly a thriving or profitable one at this time. Apart from tin in Cornwall and a flourishing coal mining industry in Northumberland, England had little mineral wealth. Dutch ships regularly evaded the Navigation Acts. Yet 20 years later, England was established as a European power. By the end of the seventeenth century, England was the greatest hegemonic mercantile and capitalist power in the world. The two key commodities which explain this development were sugar and slaves, which we will now look at.

Bristol port, c. 1730

King Sugar

This kingdom's pleasure, glory and grandeur are more advanced by sugar than by any other commodity we deal in or produce.
Sir Dalby Thomas, *An Historical Account of the Rise and Growth of the West India Colonies*, p. 349

Sugar is the most influential and protean of substances. It is present in most of the things we eat and drink; yet 900 years ago it was unknown outside China, India and the Arabic Empire. No other foodstuff has had such an impact on world history as sugar. To produce it, millions of Africans were enslaved and transported to the Caribbean; bases for future colonies were established in Africa; African nations, languages and cultures were destroyed; the native population of the Caribbean was exterminated; European colonialism was established in the Caribbean and Brazil; and Chinese and Indian peasants were shipped halfway round the world. The profits of sugar funded innumerable industrial, economic and cultural developments in the countries which financed its production, and attempts to control its production provoked innumerable wars.

The history of sugar is also crucial to an understanding of at least five colonial empires, those of Portugal, Holland, England, Spain and France, who fought for control of its profits and who subsequently abandoned their colonies. Yet even today, white European capitalism still retains control of the world sugar industry. About 60 per cent of the sugar sold on world markets today derives from cane. Sugar cane employs about six million people, and all of it is grown on tropical plantations. The rest is supplied from sugar beet, grown in temperate climates. The beet production process is heavily capitalized and mechanized so it requires a much smaller labour force, probably less than a million people. Refining, which is even more mechanized, employs only a few hundred thousand people. However, millions of people are employed in sugar-related industries like food processing, soft drinks manufacture, brewing and so on. Overall, sugar is both a major employer and a major provider of calories in most parts of the world.

Seven hundred years ago, when sugar first arrived in Europe, it was the most expensive of all foodstuffs. It was often called 'white gold' and was as expensive as silver, pound for pound. Over the next seven centuries, however, its price gradually dropped. By the 1840s, the clever money was beginning to shift from sugar into banking, industry, mining and railways. In 1985, the price of sugar hit an all-time low, selling at three US cents a pound on the world market ($80 a tonne), a price far lower than its actual cost of production.

The patterns of sugar's consumption have been equally varied. Sugar was almost unknown in Europe in 1500; by 1800, it had become an essential component of the middle-class English diet and was used (as rum) to invigorate and intoxicate the Royal Navy. During the nineteenth century, it was fed to the English working class, in tea, to increase capitalist production. By 1900, it was supplying one fifth of the calories in the British diet. Today, the British figure is even higher, and the rest of the world (regrettably for its health) has begun to catch up.

To understand the history of sugar we need also to understand ourselves, because the story of sugar is not simply a story of human consumption but also of addic-

**Sugar harvest,
Philippines, 1980s**

But when the crops are ripen'd quite,
'Tis then begin our saddest pains;
For then we toil both day and night,
Though fever burns within our veins.

tion. People have not simply learned to eat sugar, but also to crave it. In some ways, therefore, it mimics a drug – though it is not exactly a drug. Furthermore, although it is a foodstuff, it is not essential to the human diet. In fact the body, quite evidently, is much healthier without it. How then could it have had such an influence?

To simplify a complicated topic, chemists make a distinction between basic sugars and combined sugars: the basic types are glucose (which occurs naturally in honey), galactose (which is present in mammalian milk), and fructose (which is the sugar found in fruit). Sucrose (what we normally mean by the word 'sugar') is created artificially by a complicated refining process which starts with fructose. Fructose, which occurs in all plants, is a carbohydrate; carbohydrates, along with proteins, fats, vitamins and trace elements, are essential to a healthy diet. So a natural diet would include sugar (as fructose) and starch, which pass into the bloodstream to be converted into energy.

We are primates descended from arboreal ancestors who were fruit-eating apes. Our taste for sweetness probably evolved as a survival mechanism enabling our ancestors to distinguish food from everything else, because the ripest (and sweetest) fruits contain greater concentrations of fructose. Since other mammals also seem to like sweet tastes, it has also been argued that such a taste is innate, that mammals are genetically attracted to the sweetness of mammalian milk, just as the pacifying effect of glucose on young babies appears to be universal. The digestive system is itself triggered by various chemicals, of which by far the most important is sugar. When that has been extracted by the intestine and absorbed into the bloodstream, the process stops.

Sugar is sweet, but so are many other substances. Ripe fruits, mammalian milk, dried fruits, berries, wine, fruit syrups and honey are all sweet and have been cultivated and consumed for thousands of years. But sucrose, derived from sugar cane (and later beet) is a late addition to the human diet. During its early history it spread slowly; it was not until about 1650 in Europe that it began to reveal its extraordinary potential, overtaking all other forms of sweetener in food and drink. By the nineteenth century, clear differences in patterns of sugar consumption in each society had emerged. Sugar was used in different foods and drinks, was consumed at different times of the day and at different points in the meal. It was fetishized differently, used in certain rituals in one place and for different rituals in others. Britain, for example, had a per capita consumption of sugar ten times higher than that of France. Cheap sugar, after the 1850s, meant that in Britain it also became a staple of the working class diet. Women traditionally consumed sugar in different ways to men, adding it to different foods and drinks, consuming less alcohol than men and more sweet foods. Since the 1950s, sugar consumption worldwide has followed the American pattern, with increasing consumption everywhere of fizzy drinks, prepared foodstuffs and quick energy candy.

Sugar consumption is also associated with disease. The reason for this is simple: the industrial processes which convert fructose into sucrose are in effect replicating the

46

human digestive processes. If pure sucrose is eaten, it is rapidly absorbed by the bloodstream and the digestive system is switched off. Although sucrose is the most concentrated source of energy known to us, excessive consumption is inevitably detrimental to the digestive process, since in switching it off, the gut no longer exercises its musculature, or absorbs essential foods. Habituation to sugar means that enzymes which convert fructose and starch are inhibited. This inevitably leads to constipation (because the gut is now paralyzed), and malnutrition (because essential vitamins and minerals cannot be absorbed by the colon). In the long term, too, excessive sugar consumption is associated with maturity-

onset diabetes (unknown among peoples who do not add sucrose to their diet), alcoholism, high blood pressure, heart disease, strokes, duodenal ulcers, cancers of the colon, stomach and pancreas, obesity and dental decay.

Consumption of sugar also becomes increasingly addictive, because the addict's blood sugar level rises and falls very rapidly. This exhausts the pancreas and the body experiences a feast-famine syndrome in which the addict necessarily becomes a compulsive sugar eater. Children in particular are seduced into sugar addiction through government policies which make sugar-based foodstuffs cheaper (calorie for calorie) than sugar-free alternatives and through ignorant parents, and shops and supermarkets which tempt them with their poisonous wares. Children who become compulsive sugar eaters are also much more likely to become addicted to alcohol when adults, because sugar alcohol also gives a lift to the blood sugars: 'Candy's dandy but liquor's quicker!', as Dorothy Parker noted. Sugar, in short, after hard drugs, tobacco and alcohol, is the most poisonous addictive substance we consume.

SUGAR CANE
Until the nineteenth century, all pure sugar was obtained from sugar cane. There are at least six species of cane. The most valuable as a source of sugar is 'puri', or 'creole' sugar as it came to be called. One of the crucial characteristics of sugar cane (and the same is true of sugar beet) is that no other crop produces larger quantities of utilizable calories per land unit. Per acre, sugar cane grown under optimal conditions yields about four tons (or eight million calories) of sugar, and about eight tons of 'trash' which is used as fuel (the equivalent of one ton of oil), as well as half a ton of molasses, which can be used as human or animal feed or even as fertilizer. To produce this quantity of calories from potatoes would require four acres of land, from wheat about ten acres, and from beef about 135 acres. These statistics alone explain sugar's phenomenal emergence as a foodstuff to feed an increasingly urbanized and densely populated world. Whatever its nutritional value, sugar's calorific qualities are unparalleled.

(*left*) UK government nutrition propaganda, 1940s

Cane grows quickly and is ripe for sugar extraction after a period which varies between a year and 18 months. It only produces fructose if grown on fertile soil in tropical climates, because low temperatures kill the canes. The cane is propagated from cuttings which have at least one bud. The cuttings need constant irrigation and weeding, and a constant temperature if they are to flourish. When the cane is mature, the outer leaves (trash) are burned off, or stripped off with machetes. The newly cut cane has to be milled within 24 hours. In the mill it is chopped, crushed and pulped. The muddy liquid obtained from the process is boiled and cooled. Cooling produces a crystallized substance and sludge, called bagasse, which is used for fuel and animal feed. The crystallized fructose is then boiled again several times producing muscovado, which is still technically unrefined sugar. The processes of Arabic refining, which were used elsewhere until well into the nineteenth century, produced, apart from muscovado, a fully refined white sugar, an unrefined yellow sugar, and a liquid, molasses. Molasses could not be refined further, but when distilled, (though this was not discovered until later), it could be used to produce rum.

A constant factor in the history of sugar is that the greatest profits have always been made by the final refiners. Milling has to be carried out on the plantation because cane only yields its sucrose if it is milled and refined immediately after cutting. The second stage could also be carried out locally if there were an adequate fuel supply and the necessary machinery, but merchants have always resisted such a development, since their profit has traditionally derived from being the middlemen between planters and consumers. So, from the sixteenth century onwards, most 'advanced' markets like Antwerp, Amsterdam, London and Bordeaux controlled the final refining process. If prices dropped because of a temporary fall in demand, they refined less, knowing that the planters could not flood the market: when prices rose again, the refiners could take a disproportionate part of the profit. Refiners also effectively operated as wholesalers, so they could always guarantee themselves a large margin between the price they paid for semi-refined sugar and the price they could command from the retailers. Because of this, the greatest sugar fortunes have always been made by the refiners. When planters at various times attempted to export white sugar they were heavily taxed at the instigation of the home refiners: this happened to the Barbadian planters in 1685 and to the Cuban planters in the nineteenth century. So, necessarily, planters were forced to either export the lower value products, (muscovado, molasses and rum), or else engage in smuggling.

The cane itself, native to Polynesia, was diffused by water currents and tides around south east Asia, and may well have reached India by 6000 BC. From there, it was probably taken to China where it was being cultivated by 1000 BC. At this time, sugar cane was only used as a source of sweet syrup, but by 350 BC it was being used in India to flavour rice and to ferment alcohol. By 400 AD it was being used as a medicine.

At this time there was only one other concentrated form of sweetness, honey, which was used all over the pre-modern world. However, its collection was dif-

Domestic sugar mill, early 19th-century Brazil

ficult, and the cultivation of bees for honey was both unsophisticated and uncommon. Even so, it was honey which provided the main source of sucrose in northern climates. It was used as a sweetener for fruits and meats, as well as being the basis of mead, an alcohol made from fermented honey. In warmer climates, particularly around the Mediterranean, wine was also drunk as a substitute for sugar (wine, interestingly, does not inhibit digestion). But after Mohammed, the founder of Islam, banned the use of alcohol by his followers in the seventh century AD, sugar cane growing and sugar refining were introduced into Persia. From there, the cane was taken by the Arabs wherever they conquered. Sugar, like Arab citrus fruits, rice, cotton, hard wheat, plantains, mangoes, aubergines, chess and algebra, followed the Koran.

European historians tend to belie the achievements of Arabic science and technology, but in the case of sugar technology the Arabs were both pioneers and masters. They developed new forms of irrigation, adapted the Persian bucket wheel and water screw, and discovered many of the fundamental processes of refining and distillation: processes which have given us words like 'sherbet', 'syrup' and 'julep'.

No plant can be commodified unless its qualities are recognized as valuable. This might seem self-evident in the case of most commodities, but in the case of sugar it certainly is not. It required the genius of Arab pharmacology to discover and identify sugar's particular qualities. Sugar helps preserve other foodstuffs (a major factor in its increasing use by the modern food industry); it lessens the effect of certain poisons; it is a solvent (i.e. it can be used to liquify certain other substances); it can be combined with many other foods to give them consistency, bulk or body (which is why it is used in bread and confectionery); it stabilizes other chemicals in foodstuffs; it masks bitter and unpleasant tastes (which is why it is used in medicines and for coating pills); it can combine with other tastes to produce syrups; it is a demulcent (i.e. it can soothe internal and external wounds); and, finally, it can be used in perfumes. All of these uses were either known or discovered by the Arabs. To this list we can add several more uses: it has a pacifying effect on young babies; no other foodstuff provides such a quick and intense supply of energy to the human bloodstream; its waste products are important (cane after milling and the extraction of sugar can be used as a fuel and also to make paper and similar materials); and sugar itself, though the Arabs did not exploit this discovery, can be used to make alcohol, both to drink and as a fuel.

The Arabs employed slaves on their sugar plantations; they were not the first to use slaves to grow crops commercially. The Roman *latifundia* system employed, by the first century AD, over one million slaves, and the revolt of Spartacus (73–70 BC) is an indicator of the miseries they endured. But it was the Arabs who pioneered sugar slavery. The first sugar plantation revolt recorded in history was among East African slaves working on Arab plantations in ninth-century Iraq.

By the tenth century AD, the Arabs had taken sugar cane to Syria, Palestine, Egypt, Morea in Greece, Cyprus, Malta, Rhodes, Crete, Sicily, North Africa and southern Spain. It first reached England around 1100, and sold for its same weight in silver. Consequently, it was used almost entirely by the very rich. Apart from luxury consumption, its most important early use was an additive to the nauseous (and generally worthless) medicines which early pharmacists concocted for their wealthy clients.

It was through Crusading contact that sugar first entered Europe – indeed, the seizure of sugar from the infidel was one of the Christians' motives as is clear from the Pope's 1306 appeal:

> In the land of the Sultan, sugar grows in great quantities and from it the Sultans draw large incomes and taxes. If Christians could seize these lands, great injury would be inflicted on the Sultan and at the same time Christendom would be wholly supplied from Cyprus . . . Morea, Malta and Sicily. (Dufty, p. 31)

The history of the Mediterranean islands on which sugar was first cultivated by the Arabs prefigures the subsequent European wars for control of the Caribbean sugar islands. Sicily fell to the Normans, then it was

18th-century map of Jamaica

taken by the Genoese; Cyprus was seized by the Venetians and then taken by the Turks; Malta was seized by the Knights of St John, Majorca by Spain, and so on. By the thirteenth century, the Venetians had established sugar plantations on Crete and Cyprus. The Genoese had also tried (and failed) to grow cane commercially in Sicily. In many ways, the fate of these unfortunate islands also foretold the fate of the Caribbean – once sugar cultivation had destroyed the forests and the soil, the planters moved on, leaving the population to scrape a subsistence living from the ruined (and by now parched) earth.

Between 1100 and 1500, the main locus of Arab/Christian contact was Spain. It was through Spain that many of

the greatest achievements of Arab culture first became known in Europe. The Arabs were finally driven out of Spain in 1492, but before that the Portuguese had adopted Arab technology and planted sugar on the Azores, the Madeiras and São Tome (off the coast of West Africa). The Spanish also planted it (using German capital) on the Canary Islands.

Both the Portuguese and the Spanish, after a brief experiment with convict labour, followed the Arabs and began to use slaves on their plantations. After the 1450s, almost all these slaves were kidnapped or purchased in West Africa. The Spanish were the first to take sugar to the West Indies. Columbus planted 'puri' sugar cane on

KING SUGAR

San Domingo, and later it spread into all the Spanish Caribbean. But Spanish colonial policy did not encourage plantation agriculture, so it was never particularly successful or important until the eighteenth century, when the richest Cuban landowners evicted the small farmers and tobacco growers and established mills and plantations to cash in on the European sugar boom.

Much more significant was the pioneer role of the Portuguese who took cane to north east Brazil in the 1520s, where they attempted to coerce the Indians to work on their plantations. This policy failed when the Indians fled into the jungle, so the planters brought slaves over from Africa. By the 1550s, the area around Bahia and Olinda was established as the main supplier of American sugar to European markets. This achievement was not easy because sugar production requires an immense amount of capital and a much more profitable crop at the time appeared to be tobacco. However, by 1700, sugar had easily eclipsed tobacco as a valuable trade commodity. Tobacco could be grown and cured by small farmers who needed little capital, so prices fell rapidly in Europe as more tobacco flooded onto the market in response to the early profits. But, because the costs of sugar production were so high, there was no risk, once supplies were secured, that the market would be swamped by new producers. So sugar attracted capitalists who sought to establish monopoly control over scarce commodities, and there was a tendency everywhere for that control to pass into fewer and fewer hands.

Spanish and Portuguese sugar was mostly consumed in the Iberian peninsula until about 1550, when it began to reach a much more lucrative market via the refineries of Antwerp, Amsterdam and London. However, there was not a sudden glut on the market. Sugar was still an enormously expensive luxury in northern Europe, and the costs and difficulties of establishing plantation agriculture meant that it was not until 1650 that New World sugar provided more than half the sugar consumed in Europe; the rest came from the Atlantic islands or was imported through Venice from the Levant.

After the decline of Antwerp in the 1560s, Amsterdam became the main refiner and market for Portuguese sugar. But after the Dutch West India Company had broken the links between Brazil and Amsterdam in its incompetent attempt to conquer Brazil, the Dutch were forced to look elsewhere. They took sugar to Barbados, and from there it spread to Jamaica, and finally to all the other Caribbean islands. By 1800, the Caribbean was supplying 80 per cent of Europe's sugar and receiving 80 per cent of the slave trade from Africa. By this date, half the shipping of western Europe was employed in trade or the protection of trade between Europe and the Caribbean. Thus, sugar was not simply one commodity among others but the most valuable and politically significant commodity of them all.

SUGAR PRODUCTION

One of the fundamental characteristics of sugar production from sugar cane is that it rapidly exhausts the soil and the available timber supply. So, throughout its history, sugar has continually moved from place to place, and a sugar boom has been invariably followed by ecological, economic and social collapse. A further characteristic of sugar cane agriculture is that until the 1830s it was almost invariably produced by slave labour. The links between the two were vehemently defended in an anonymous English pamphlet printed in 1749:

> The most approved judges of the commercial interests of these kingdoms have ever been of the opinion that our West India and Africa trades are the most nationally beneficial of any we carry on. It is also allowed on all hands that the trade to Africa is the branch which renders our American colonies and plantations so advantageous to Great Britain: that traffic only affording our planters a constant supply of negro servants for the culture of their lands . . . The negro trade therefore, and the natural consequences deriving from it, may be justly esteemed an inexhaustable fund of wealth and naval power to this nation. (Calder, p. 451)

But negroes were not 'servants' as the pamphlet suggests. In English law, their status had been defined by

51

Slave auction, southern USA, c. 1840

two court decisions of 1677: 'Negroes being usually bought and sold among merchants . . . (are) merchandise' (Calder, p. 263); and, 'Negroes ought to be esteemed goods and commodities within the Acts of Trade and Navigation' (Calder, ibid). Other crops like tobacco and cotton were produced by slaves, but the ratio in the early days for these crops was rarely more than two slaves per planter. Sugar ratios were always five slaves per planter and sometimes as high as 200 slaves. The reason given for this by the defenders of sugar slavery was that it was impossible for whites to do the work, because it was astonishingly arduous. Before the introduction of steam technology in the 1850s, all the work was done in the humid heat of the tropics; all the physical labour from cutting trees, clearing the land and cropping the cane, to working in 130-degree temperatures in the mills, 16 hours a day, six or seven days a week, surely constitutes the most exhausting agricultural work ever undertaken in human history. No one would ever have worked under such appalling conditions unless they were compelled to. Capitalists and consumers, however, were greedy for their sugar and thus ignored

the injustices and misery of hard labour upon which their sugar depended (and upon which it still depends, as we shall show). Slaves were treated as commodities which could be bought and sold; they were seen merely as part of the planter's capital. However, slaves were never cheap; they had to be bought from slaving oligarchs in Africa, who demanded high prices for them, and were then shipped at considerable expense to the plantations. To the planter, the cost of slaves was about four times that of the cost of his land and machinery. Thus, the slaves constituted the bulk of his investment. Capital had to be borrowed at high rates of interest from merchant bankers in the Caribbean or in centres like Lisbon, Amsterdam and London. This burden of debt partly explains the ruthless exploitation of African labour.

Of the slaves captured (possibly 15 million Africans in all), perhaps a quarter never reached the Caribbean. Of the 12 million who survived the crossing, the next stage of their lives was even more terrible. It was in the slave traders' interest to deliver live slaves, but the planters' profits derived from working the slaves until they dropped. The slaves had to cut back the jungle, clear the land, plant cane, set up the buildings, install the machinery, harvest the cane, and spend four months milling, crushing, boiling, and refining it. Only at the end of this period was the plantation established. Only a year after that could the planter expect to have begun to pay interest on his loan. That the system was brutal in the extreme was inevitable once it had commodified human labour. If slaves could be bought and sold like animals then they could be treated like animals, and worked to death like animals.

Another characteristic of early sugar production was that it was generally concentrated on islands. Planters needed to grow the crop as fast as possible, in order to repay the interest on the loans they had raised, even before they could begin to think of repaying the loan. Because sugar was by far the most valuable crop they could grow, they rarely planted other crops with which to feed themselves and their slaves. Thus, they were dependent on the import of foodstuffs, slaves and essential machinery. For these reasons the early plantations were strung along the coasts and in the immediate hinterland. Production was also concentrated on specific islands, because planters needed markets where they could sell their sugar and buy their slaves and supplies. After the timber had been cut and when the soil was exhausted sugar producers moved to other islands. Thus, the characteristic pattern of plant, boom, slump, bankruptcy, hit every sugar island in turn.

Finally, it needs to be stressed that sugar production was essentially an industry. It was controlled by entrepreneurs, required enormous amounts of capital as well as a large, controlled labour force (an 80 acre plantation, producing an average 80 tons of sugar a year, needed 100 slaves or labourers, as well as mills, boiling houses, curing houses, a distillery and a warehouse). Industrial capitalism was first seen on this scale, not in the dark satanic mills of Lancashire, but on the plantations of the West Indies.

SUGAR AND MERCANTILISM

After the 1580s, a theory of mercantilism had evolved in Holland which stressed the advantages of trade as a source of national prosperity against the feudal notion that land was the only source of wealth. Sugar capitalism was, however, a synthesis of these two ideas; a system 'which combined the vices of feudalism and capitalism with the virtues of neither', as Eric Williams noted (Williams, p. 13). It was both feudal and mercantile, because merchants soon realized that the profits of sugar were greatest when they also had control of production, which meant that they needed land (by conquest) and labour (through coercion). Trade provided bullion, capital and credit facilities; therefore, the theory argued, it was the obligation of the state to encourage, advance and defend mercantile ambitions. Taxes from trade would provide the revenue for building and maintaining a navy. Labour should be forced off the land to work in factories to make textiles, guns and machinery, or taken to plantations where it would produce foodstuffs at much lower costs. Everyone, it was argued, would become infinitely richer. For these reasons, conquest and colonization were at the centre of mercantile strategy. The core powers like

England and Holland needed colonies as suppliers of cheap commodities and as markets for their own manufactures. To the question, 'What was in it for the colonies?', the answer was, 'Very little'. From the beginning, they were created to play a subordinate role; therein, of course, lay a crucial contradiction, but one which would only become significant when the operation was in decline.

Mercantilism was eagerly adopted and advanced by the mercantile interest in early seventeenth-century England, and it was one of the crucial issues which led to the Civil War of the 1640s when most merchants sided with Parliament against the Crown. After Cromwell had crushed the Levellers in 1649, the City of London enthusiastically funded and supported his foreign policy, which was astonishing in its global ambitions. It saw the tightening up and enforcement of the Navigation Acts in 1652, war against Holland to open up the East Indies to English shipping, followed by a treaty in 1654 which guaranteed England's leadership of the Protestant alliance (as well as attracting much needed capital into England). A commercial treaty with Sweden in 1656 to keep open the Baltic for English ships followed, as well as a commercial treaty with France in 1655. Dunkirk was taken in 1657, which gave England a trading base in northern Europe. War against Spain began in 1654 and ended in 1657; the aim was to open up the Caribbean to English ships, but an ill-equipped expedition failed to take Hispaniola and took Jamaica instead, though the blockade of Cadiz resulted in booty worth over £1 million. Blake's expedition against the Barbary and Corsair pirates, which allowed the English to trade in the Mediterranean, also forced Portugal to agree trading terms to English advantage, such that Portugal thereafter was in essence an English protectorate. It was the London merchants, too, who enthusiastically organized and supplied the naval expedition which sailed to Bermuda, Barbados, Virginia and Maryland between 1651 and 1652, restoring Parliamentary control over the colonies.

During the Civil War, the English colonies had enjoyed a period of free trade. It was particularly in this period that Dutch influence made itself felt, for it was the

COMMODITIES

Dutch who advanced cheap credit and slaves to planters who could supply them with sugar. Cromwell's policies, however, undermined the power of the Dutch. Besides evicting them from English ports, he supplied an army of convicts and Irish Catholics to work on the English plantations. From then on, it was inevitable that England would attempt to control the slave trade, because mercantilism enthusiastically adopted the principle of slavery, arguing that it was in the nation's interest to support the trade and to protect the shipping which sugar capitalism required.

Carib carvings on a rock, Grenada

THE CARIBBEAN

The colonization of the Caribbean was never easy, for no other race has so vigorously resisted the encroachments of capitalism as the Caribs. The Caribs, who came from the Amazon basin, had reached most of the islands by canoe before the arrival of the Spaniards, in the process decimating the peaceful, vegetarian Arawak Indians who had settled there before them. For two hundred years, the Caribbean was one of the most contested territories in the world. The Caribs were heroic and fierce; until the 1750s they posed the most constant threat to European expansion in the area. Barbados was settled by the English precisely because it was out of reach of Carib canoes, but early settlements on islands like St Lucia, Grenada and

Trinidad were often destroyed by Carib raids. Despite heroic resistance, most Caribs were eventually killed by European guns or by diseases. The last Carib survivors, along with several Arawaks, were rounded up by the British in 1796 and dumped on the so-called Mosquito Coast (Nicaragua and Honduras).

It was the Dutch, in search of salt deposits for their herring industry, who first made settlement by the French and the English possible in the Caribbean. The Dutch often aligned with the French and the English to oust the Spaniards, and were willing, as always, to advance goods, slaves and machinery on credit. But such alliances between Europeans were always temporary; indeed, there was no guarantee that the English would even support each other, since they were all competitors. Whenever war was declared between the European powers, local planters would seize the opportunity to invade neighbouring islands, where they would destroy their competitors' crops and mills and steal their sugar and slaves. When concerted action was proposed against the marauding Caribs, the English planters on Nevis refused to join the English planters of Antigua and Montserrat, preferring to see their competitors eliminated. When the Nevis planters were invaded by the French, however, they quickly surrendered and pleaded to be allowed to keep their canes. King Sugar was indeed the god and the religion of the Caribbean.

BARBADOS AND JAMAICA

The English played no part in early sugar production history – characteristically, they seized it from the Spanish as booty, which is how it first reached the English market in large quantities. In 1600, England had no colonies at all in the Caribbean; yet by 1700, it had more than either the Dutch or the French. Its first island was Barbados which was claimed in 1625 and settled two years later by colonists financed by a London merchant; within five years the 2,000 settlers were close to starvation because they had killed all the wild pigs and failed to plant adequate crops. By 1640, however, the island had recovered, and the surviving planters had established their own Assembly, which from then on resisted all attempts by London to control its affairs. At this time Barbados had a serious labour shortage, and it was Cromwell who shipped over large numbers of Irish soldiers and vagrants, after the invasion and conquest of Ireland in 1652, to provide an initial source of cheap and easily coerced labour. This trade was stopped in 1657 when it became clear that thousands of poor, bewildered, Irish peasants were being kidnapped by English and Dutch merchants to be sold in the Caribbean, irrespective of whether they were alleged to have committed crimes.

In 1652, the Barbadian governor invited the Dutch to trade slaves and supplies. The Dutch, exhausted by their attempt to colonize Brazil and control sugar production there, provided sugar cane, capital and machinery to Barbadian planters. The price of sugar in Amsterdam was very high because of the shortage of Portuguese sugar from Brazil, and the first harvest from Barbados proved so lucrative that in two years, more slaves were being imported. Barbadian planters also went to Holland to arrange cheap credit, and returned with skilled 'sugar masters' who knew how to refine sugar.

From Barbados, sugar spread to the other Leeward Islands. Initially, the plantations were small; after the English Civil War, however, many royalists went to Barbados with what capital they could salvage from their lost cause. Soon, they had bought out the small farmers who were forced to work on the bigger plantations. One cavalier reckoned that £14,000 was needed to start a sugar plantation, which was an enormous sum (the equivalent of the price of a large country house). Added to this, there was a yellow fever epidemic brought in by African slaves, in which a third of the population died. Again, it was the richest planters who weathered the crisis and bought up the plantations and slaves of the smaller farmers.

By 1655, over 7,000 tons of sugar were being produced annually in Barbados, an island no bigger than the Isle of Wight. By 1660, it had a population of 40,000, and had been transformed from a net exporter of foodstuffs into an island which needed to import three quarters of all its food. By 1670, Barbados had overtaken Brazil as the major sugar-growing region in the Americas. By 1680, all the trees on the island had been cut down, and the mills were dependent on timber from other islands. There were 3,000 property owners on Barbados, but the richest 125 owned half of the land and an average of 60 slaves each. It was these rich planters who formed the first planters' oligarchy and who from then on controlled the politics and law of the English islands. Before the ending of slavery in the 1830s, over a quarter of a million Africans had been sold to die on its soil.

Sugar planting, Barbados, 17th century

From the 1650s, despite being heavily taxed, the English colonies enjoyed, through the Navigation Acts, an effective monopoly as sugar suppliers to England. Sugar had rapidly become by far the most valuable of colonial imports, and it seemed that demand for sugar in England would always keep pace with supply. But within 60 years, Barbados was already beginning its serious decline. Yields were already higher on newly-settled islands among the Windward and Leeward groups, and Barbados had begun to be overtaken by Jamaica.

From the beginning, the Caribbean settlers rejected metropolitan control. The Barbados planters sent their first Crown-appointed governor back to London in chains, and in 1674 when a Barbadian planter butchered his mulatto brother and 80 Caribs on Dominica, despite being condemned to death by the Crown, his fellow planters acquitted him and elected him speaker of their island parliament. In 1710, the Antiguan planters killed their governor; the next, who was more compliant with planters' demands, finished up in an English gaol. Typical was the comment of one customs official who wrote, 'I dare not go to St Kitts for I shall certainly be assassinated if I attempt it'. Planters made their own law and supported each other against outsiders. The creditors of the biggest planters were obliged to accept chattels in settlement of debts, at values determined by other planters. However, the poorer farmers had no such defence against the plantocracy. The rich foreclosed on their poorer neighbours when times were hard; since they were the creditors and assessors of the debtors' property, they took exactly what they wanted. By these means the rich increasingly ousted the smaller farmers from the best land.

Jamaica, 25 times the size of Barbados, had been settled by the Spaniards in 1500 but subsequently neglected. In 1655, it was easily seized by the remnants of the English expedition dispatched by Cromwell to seize Hispaniola. After the English had enslaved the 1,500 Spaniards on the island, the black slaves, brought in by the Spaniards, escaped into the hills and formed a guerilla army. For the next 80 years the maroons, as they were called, were a constant threat to the white planters of Jamaica.

Until 1671, Jamaica was in a kind of limbo. The Spanish claimed sovereignty over the island but lacked the means to recover it, while the English government left the invaders to consolidate their territory as best they could. The first English governor of Jamaica invited the scattered buccaneers of the Caribbean to use Jamaica as a base from which to attack the Spanish treasure fleets. All the riffraff of the Caribbean flooded in: French, English, Welsh, and Flemish pirates, criminals, desperados and whores. From their base in Port Royal, the pirates attacked Spanish shipping and raided Cuba and the Isthmus of Panama. These expeditions were led by Henry Morgan (later knighted by a grateful monarch who received a fifteenth of the profits). Port Royal became one of the largest, wildest and (temporarily) richest towns in the Americas, until it was destroyed in an earthquake in 1692. In 1680, peace was made between England and Spain and Morgan was appointed Lieutenant Governor. He attempted to encourage settlers and to control the piracy, though pirates still threatened the stability of Caribbean trade for the next 60 years.

After 1680, sugar planters began to arrive with their slaves, followed shortly by Sephardic Jews who came to play a crucial merchant banking and trading role in the Caribbean. Within 40 years, Jamaica had overtaken Barbados as a sugar producer. Kingston, the new capital of Jamaica, also became the unofficial colonial capital of the English West Indies, providing an entrepot for the other islands as well as having the largest slave market (over 600,000 slaves were sold there in just 100 years). Jamaica was also the focus of most of the inter-island trade. But even by the 1780s, there were only four whites per square mile and only 20,000 whites in the whole island, whereas there were 200,000 slaves, and the average plantation employed 500 slaves. Jamaica's notorious history of violence and rebellion can in part be ascribed to this low ratio of white masters to black slaves.

THE REBELLIONS

From the beginning, both white servants and black slaves rebelled against the system. Dozens of poor whites were executed for plotting against their masters in Barbados in 1634 and 1649. Fed a starvation diet of porridge, beans and potatoes, and living in shacks without furniture or bedding, their conditions were appalling, as Richard Ligon reported in 1673:

> If it chance to rain and wet them through, they have no shift but must lie so all night. If they put off their clothes, the cold of the night will strike into them: if they complain they are beaten by the overseer; if they resist, their time is doubled. I have seen an overseer beat a servant with a cane about the head till the blood has followed . . . Truly, I have seen such cruelty there done to servants, as I did not

think one Christian could have done to another. (Ligon, p. 45)

Although these servants had been promised land when their time was finished, they were cheated out of it and often compelled to sign new indentures when their contracts were completed.

One planter, Christopher Jeaffreson, went to London in the 1680s to buy labour from London gaols, and having bribed the gaolers, the Recorder, and the Secretary of Trade, he shipped out what was, in his own words,

'a parcel of as notorious villains as any that have been transported this long time . . . As they went down to the waterside, notwithstanding a guard of about 30 men, they committed several thefts, snatching away hats, wigs, etc. from several persons whose curiosity led them into the crowd.' (Calder, p. 261)

But Jeaffreson lost money on the operation; when he got them to the Leewards, he found that the planters did not want to buy them, even at knockdown prices.

Both on Bermuda and Barbados, white servants were discovered plotting with African slaves, a clear indication of the common misery they shared. Add to these slaves the thousands of convicts who were shipped out in the 1650s, and we can understand this comment about Barbados in 1655:

'This island is a dunghill whereon England doth cast forth its rubbish: rogues and whores and suchlike people are those which are generally brought here. A rogue in England will hardly make a cheater here; a bawd brought over puts on a demure comportment; a whore, if handsome, makes a wife for some rich planter.' (Calder, p. 259)

Slaves were intentionally split from their own families and countrymen, which compounded their misery and loneliness even further. The reason for this policy was that 'the disproportion of blacks and whites being great, the whites have no greater security than the diversity of the negroes' language', as a planter put it in his evidence to the Lords of Trade in 1680. Working conditions were acknowledged to be terrible, even by the planters. One planter calculated that a third of the slaves would die even before they began work:

When they are seasoned, and used to the country, they stand much better. But to how many mischances are they still subject? If a stiller slip into a rum cistern, it is sudden death, for it stifles in a moment. If a mill feeder be catched by the finger, his whole body is drawn in, and he is squeezed to pieces. If a boiler get any part into the scalding sugar, it sticks like glue or birdlime, and 'tis hard to save either limb or life. They will quarrel and kill one another, upon small occasions; by many accidents they are disabled, and become a burden. They will run away, and perhaps be never seen more: or they will hang themselves, no creature knows why. (Lyttelton, p. 19)

On St Kitts, scores of men and women escaped into the woods, but as the smaller islands were cleared, this became more difficult. Escapes and rebellions were commonplace, particularly on Jamaica, where escaped slaves could join the 'maroon' guerillas, but punishment was vicious, even for those suspected of plotting. In 1675, six slaves were burned alive in Barbados, and 31 were beheaded. A black slave was burned alive for cursing his master in 1685. Yet a slave rebellion controlled the Dutch island of St John for over six months in 1733, and in the 1720s, life in Jamaica was constantly threatened by the maroon army under its greatest general, a Coromantee named Cudjoe. The last slave rebellion in Jamaica occurred in 1760. It resulted in the deaths of 400 maroons and 60 whites, as well as the execution of hundreds of sympathetic slaves.

The news shocked English opinion and did much to arouse a better informed debate about slavery. Dr Johnson, who had an implacable hatred of planters and was one of the earliest English champions of black rights, proposed a toast in Oxford 'to the next insurrection of negroes in the West Indies'. 'How is it', he also asked,

COMMODITIES

'The Black Man's Lament', a picture series for children, 1826

'that we hear the loudest yelps for liberty among the drivers of negroes?' (Boswell, vol. III, pp. 200, 201)

None of the planters seemed to have realized that they had become trapped by the system which they apparently controlled, and most lived in a state of constant fear. A Jamaican planter in 1734 spoke of:

> 'The insecurity of our country, occasioned by our slaves in rebellion against us, whose insolence is grown so great that we cannot say we are sure of another day, and robbings and murders so common in our capital roads, that it is with the utmost hazard we travel them.' (Calder, p. 464)

THE END OF SLAVERY

We, the British House of Commons, have been sitting this fortnight on the African Company. We, that temple of liberty and bulwark of Protestant Christianity, have this fortnight been pondering methods to make more effectual that horrid traffic of selling negroes. It has appeared to us that six and forty thousand of these wretches are sold every year to our plantations alone – it chills one's blood. I would not
have to say I voted for it for the Continent of America. (Horace Walpole, 'debate on the Royal Africa Company monopoly 1750', in *Letters* vol. II, pp. 432–3)

One sometimes reads that the earliest critics and opponents of slavery were the Quakers. This, of course, is nonsense. The earliest critics and opponents of slavery were the slaves themselves. Once gathered on the plantations, they organized and rebelled. The planters adopted the most extreme tortures and terrors imaginable in order to pre-empt rebellion. They chained slaves together with locks on their necks and ankles; female slaves had iron muzzles locked over their heads; intransigent male slaves were whipped to death or castrated or burned alive starting with the soles of their feet. The Antigua Assembly in 1724 explicitly acknowledged the everyday treatment of slaves when it published an Act to 'prevent the inhumane murdering, maiming and castrating of slaves by cruel and barbarous persons (as has been too much practised)'. (Calder, p. 460) Since planters could also claim compensation if slaves were executed for theft or rebellion, old and disabled slaves were often tried on trumped-up charges and hanged. The women were constantly raped by their masters, (virgins especially, because they were thought to cure syphilis). Pregnant women were worked till they aborted, and if they gave birth they were forced to neglect their children. Their infants rarely survived because, being unable to work for the first seven years of their lives, they were 'uneconomic'; the planters forced the mothers back to work in the fields within days of giving birth. Blacks could expect to survive no more than ten years under such conditions, and they had no recourse but rebellion. They had no rights in law – the planters made the laws and executed them and slaves were not even permitted to bring charges or give evidence against their masters.

Historians also emphasize the importance of the British anti-slavery movement, but this obscures the fact that slavery withered away when slaves ceased to be profitable investments. It was recognized, from the very beginning, that the slave trade itself was repugnant;

Captain Thomas Phillips a Welsh slave trading captain, repenting in his old age, wrote that blacks,

'excepting their want of Christianity and true religion, are as much the work of God's hands and no doubt as dear to him as ourselves . . . I can't think there is any intrinsic value in one colour more than another, nor that white is better than black, only we think it so because we are so.' (quoted in Calder, p. 354)

Also, the slave trade was not particularly profitable. The slaves, by starving themselves to death or by jumping into the sea to drown, bit into the traders' profits:

'The negroes are so wilful and loathe to leave their own country that they have often leaped out of the canoes, boats and ship into the sea, and kept under water till they were drowned . . . they having a more dreadful apprehension of Barbados than we can have of Hell . . . I have been informed that some commanders have cut off the legs and arms of the most wilful, to terrify the rest . . . I was advised by some of my officers to do the same but I could not be persuaded to entertain the least thoughts of it.' (ibid)

Another slave trader, John Barbot, commented that when the slaves tried to starve themselves to death, 'I had been necessitated sometimes to cause the teeth of these wretches to be broken . . . and thus have forced some sustenance into their throats' (ibid). Olaudah Equiano, who was captured by traders at the age of ten, believed that the whites were cannibals and that they were being taken to the West Indies to be eaten; this terrifying belief was quite common.

The barbarity of the trade killed many slaves en route. That, too, was unprofitable. The Dutch had supplied most of the slaves to the English planters up to 1660, but after the Restoration, Charles II eagerly promoted the trade as a royal monopoly. The second Anglo-Dutch war was sparked off by English attacks on Dutch forts along the Slave Coast, though the Dutch quickly regained the forts and continued to trade slaves. In 1672, the Crown granted a slaving monopoly to the Royal African Company; the Duke of York, later James II, was both its governor and the largest shareholder. But the monopoly was ill-organized and failed to supply enough slaves to the planters; it also tried to force up the price of slaves to cover its losses. The planters therefore bought their slaves off Dutch and English interlopers. In 1686, the Royal Africa Company conceded defeat and taxed other English slavers ten per cent for the right to trade, though it omitted (predictably) to spend its monopoly profits on its forts, which were wiped out by the French in the 1690s. Ironically, the most lucrative part of the company's operation was selling English manufactures to the African traders, and at one time it even wanted to stop trading slaves, but found that it had to continue 'to keep up the credit of the trade' with the African merchants.

The Royal Africa Company's monopoly finally lapsed in 1712, but by then Bristol merchants, initially assisted by the Dutch, controlled the operation. By 1730, they in turn had been undercut by 300-ton Liverpool slave ships, trading Lancashire cottons and Black Country knives and guns. Almost everyone in Liverpool was involved in the trade in some way. The raw frontier town of 1700 expanded over the mudflats, growing bigger and bigger and richer and richer. In a typical year, 1771, 104 Liverpool vessels alone shipped as many slaves as all the French slavers together, taking 30,000 slaves to the Caribbean and selling them for an average of perhaps £60 a head before returning with muscovado sugar for the Liverpool refineries. In fact, the Liverpool traders were so ruthless and successful that they flooded the Caribbean with slaves. The planters became increasingly worried by the fear of black rebellion and tried to restrict the trade. But the planters' Acts attempting to limit the trade were revoked by the government in London on the grounds that 'we cannot allow the colonies to check or discourage in any degree a traffic so beneficial to the nation'. By 1800, Liverpool was one of the most impressive cities of Europe, every building financed and bonded with the sugar and blood of slavery.

One important reason for the declining profitability of slavery was that the African rulers and oligarchs who

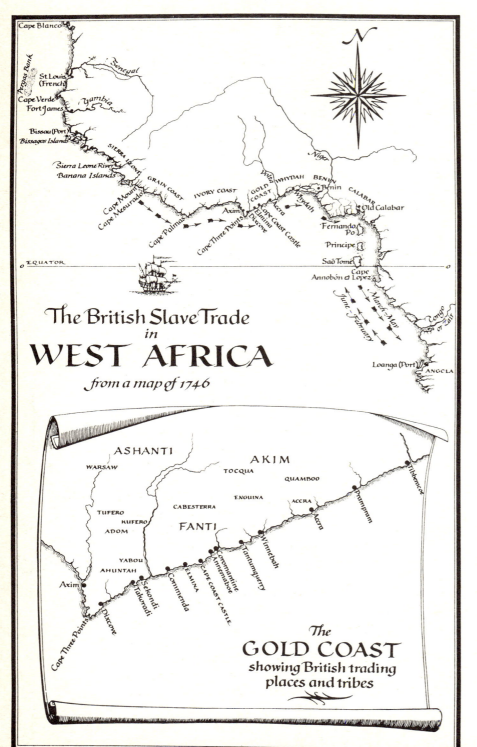

The British Slave Trade
in
WEST AFRICA
from a map of 1746

The
GOLD COAST
showing British trading places and tribes

controlled the Slave Coast end of the operation were just as ruthless in their bargaining and devious in their tricks as any of their European counterparts. The operations of some oligarchs paralleled those of the whites with whom they traded. One John Kabes traded ivory and slaves and controlled the salt industry and maize plantations which supplied the European forts. He also owned a flotilla of canoes which he hired out to the white traders. Like their white counterparts, such men also lived on credit. The European forts, John Barbot said in 1732, 'have but little authority over the blacks, and serve only to secure the trade, the blacks here being of a temper not to suffer anything to be imposed on them by Europeans' (Calder, p. 348). To trade successfully, Europeans needed more than a hundred different commodities. One trader listed guns, gunpowder, tallow, knives, woollens, blankets, carpets, pewter, basins, lead, iron bars, Indian textiles, and many other commodities as well.

But if the trade was no longer profitable except to the cheapest and cruellest slavers, slavery as an economic investment in agriculture still appeared to be. It was less economic in the Caribbean because the sugar planters worked their slaves to death so quickly. But elsewhere, particularly in North America, slavery was increasingly paternalistic and legitimated on the grounds that blacks were like children, so it was kind to enslave them and to look after them, and to encourage them to breed and have more slaves. The Quakers in the early eighteenth century had increasingly adopted this view; thus it came as a shock to many when, in 1758, the London Yearly Meeting of Quakers condemned the 'iniquitous practice' of slaving; three years later it threatened to exclude Quakers from meetings unless they severed their links with the trade. The Methodists followed in the 1770s. But, even here, Christian charity and good economic sense went together, because the freed slaves in the American colonies were then employed as cobblers, sail-makers, clerks and seamen, or else they borrowed money to set themselves up in trade, and traded particularly with the Quakers, because of the Quakers' well-deserved reputation for honesty. Thus, Quakers did not suffer through their moral opposition to slavery.

At the same time, defence of the slave trade was expensive for the English government, which had to maintain the forts and factories on the African coast. The government also had to protect its merchant shipping in war time, and war was endemic in the 'golden age' of capitalism. Also, in times of war, merchant seamen were drafted into the Royal Navy and merchant ships were diverted to other cargoes; at such times, the slave trade ceased.

Then, during the long interruption of trade during the Napoleonic Wars between 1803 and 1815, planters began to realize that their slaves were increasing in value because of the shortage, so they had some incentive to treat them better. Also, because slaves were more valuable due to the shortage, the bankers had better collateral. Ships, scarce because of the war, could be used to transport more profitable commodities. So it was for these reasons, as well as the more obvious philanthropic ones, that the slave trade was declared illegal by Britain in 1807. That didn't mean that the trade ceased. Liverpool slavers and others continued shipping Africans to Cuba and Brazil until the 1870s; it was competition from these slave plantations which did most to undercut the British sugar islands in the nineteenth century.

SUGAR MONEY

The history of sugar is also the history of those who profited from its cultivation. One of the distinctive features of sugar capitalism is that its producers have rarely seen much of the profit (the labour force, of course, saw none). From early on, even when it was being financed by the Genoese in Sicily, the growing of sugar was revealed as a very risky way of making a fortune. But the fact is that fortunes were made; financiers lent money to planters and merchants at very high rates of interest, and the refiners profited from the sale of the sugar when it reached the metropolitan markets.

The early financing of sugar production was merchant capitalist, but increasingly in the Caribbean, this role passed to successful planters, those who had managed to repay the crippling loans (and interest) which all sugar planters started with. So it was these planters who financed smaller operations; when those went bankrupt, they collected the land, machinery and slaves, which was their collateral. This explains the increasing size and wealth of a few plantations, particularly in Jamaica, and the frequent bankruptcies of the rest. Those planters who did prosper returned to England, where they built vast country houses, invested their money in stocks and shares and purchased political power; in the early eighteenth century, at least 60 MPs were retired sugar oligarchs.

Peter Beckford was one such successful planter. He arrived as a small trader in Jamaica in 1662. When he died in 1710, he was said to be worth £1.5 million in bank stock, as well as owning 20 estates, and 1,200 slaves. (His fortune was squandered by his son William, who spent most of it building a mock-gothic mansion, Fonthill, which was higher than Salisbury Cathedral, and which blew down in a storm in 1807).

By 1750, the balance of trade between the Caribbean and the metropolis was overwhelmingly in the planters' favour. The English islands were producing half the sugar consumed in Europe and all the sugar consumed in North America, but overall they lost out on the deal. Jamaica alone in the 1750s was providing profits of over £1 million a year to English investors and traders, money which could either be reinvested in the trade, or invested in English agriculture and industry. The interest on loans went to the bankers, and the profits on the market went to the refiners and the capitalists. Merchants, men like the Norrises, owners of Speke Hall, members of parliament and lord mayors of Liverpool, began to organize and

(left) Slavery abolition badge, 1790

invest in the slave trade. The following instructions, given to the Captain of the Blessing in 1700, give a good picture of the 'triangular trade'. First, he was to go to Kinsale in Southern Ireland to pick up provisions because they were cheaper there; then he was to proceed to Africa: 'I hope you will slave your ship easy and what shall remain over and above slaving your ship lay out in teeth [ivory] which are there reasonable'. Then the captain had to go to the West Indies and load

> 'sugar, cotton, ginger if to be had . . . We leave the whole management of the concern to you and hope the Lord will direct you for the best . . . Endeavour to keep all your men sober, for intemperance in the hot country may destroy your men and so ruin your voyage . . . We commit you to the care and protection of the Almighty.' (quoted in Calder, p. 357)

Such mercenary hypocrisy was commonplace. At the London end, investment in sugar was risky; rebellions, earthquakes and hurricanes could easily wipe out the collateral. However, the bigger investor, who spread his risks over various islands, could generally make very comfortable profits. Many Americans, by advancing credit to Caribbean smugglers and planters, finished up with sizeable estates in the West Indies; two American presidents, George Washington and Thomas Jefferson, owned land in Barbados. Often those who advanced credit to younger sons to set up plantations in the West Indies found themselves in possession of land, slaves and equipment after the planter/debtor had gone under. But since most of the debt was accumulated interest, the creditor/investor often found, despite the bankruptcy of the planter, that the collateral was worth much more than the initial loan and could therefore be sold at a profit. Many of the biggest plantations therefore finished up in the hands of families with large estates scattered over England and Ireland as well.

Other industries, apart from refining, also developed to support the sugar and slave trades. The development of manufacturing industry around Liverpool, Birmingham and Bristol, turning out knives, guns, nails, woollen cloth, clothes and tools for the slave traders and the West Indian planters, was a crucial stimulus to the early industrial revolution in England.

For these reasons, sugar money underwrote English commercial and cultural developments, from the expanding towns and cities to the grandest country houses and new buildings in the universities. The library at All Souls College in Oxford, for example, was built with a bequest of £10,000 from Christopher Codrington, the inheritor of the largest planter fortune in the West Indies. Jane Austen also reminds us of these links when she tells us that the Bertram fortune, upon which Mansfield Park was built, derived from a rebellious plantation in the Caribbean.

An attempt has even been made to quantify the debt. It has been calculated that every half ton of sugar sold in London before 1660 cost one African life; after that, a ton was the equivalent; by the time of the abolition of slavery, perhaps two tons. Even if these figures are slightly high, the resulting benefit of slavery to England can hardly be disputed.

SUGAR AFTER SLAVERY

By 1790, the British, French, Dutch and Spanish all had a stake in the Caribbean, essentially supplying their own markets. The first successful challenge to European hegemony was the revolt of Haiti against the French, followed by the unification of Haiti with the Spanish part of the island (San Domingo) under the black revolutionary leader, Toussaint l'Ouverture, between 1791 and 1801. This loss to France of its most lucrative sugar colony stimulated the search for alternative supplies. A German scientist long before had discovered that sugar could be extracted from many vegetables, particularly sea beat (or sugar beet as it came to be known). After 1801, directly as a consequence of the loss of Haiti and the British blockade of the West Indies during the Napoleonic Wars, the French government encouraged experimentation with beet. By 1810, the growing and refining of beet was already established as a commercial alternative to cane. This discovery sealed the fate of the Caribbean; from then on production of beet in temperate climates would increasingly undercut tropical sugar.

Between 1800 and 1900, the annual sugar harvest of Jamaica dropped from 100,000 tons to 5,000 tons, which gives some indication of the scale of the decline.

After the emancipation of their surviving slaves in 1837, the British planters in the Caribbean were paid £20 million compensation for the loss of their slaves (the slaves, predictably, got nothing at all for the loss of their families, homes and freedom). Almost all this money went to pay off the London bankers who were owed money by the planters. The period between 1830 and 1850 was one of crisis for the British planters. Over 1,000 went bankrupt and there were more than a hundred sugar trading bankruptcies. Tariffs which hitherto had protected the planters against foreign competition were gradually reduced, until the tariffs were abolished altogether in 1851. The planters attempted to stem the tide, and persuaded the British government to pass legislation compelling ex-slaves to work as 'apprentices', but most of them refused to work on terms which were little different to slavery, preferring to squat and raise their own vegetables. The planters also passed legislation prohibiting blacks from voting or owning land, so the blacks were either forced to work for the planters for subsistence wages or to escape into the ports and from there to North America. A few of the biggest estates shipped Asian indentured labourers halfway round the world to provide a substitute labour force, but this was only a temporary solution. Of 140,000 Chinese coolies shipped to the West Indies, only a quarter survived the journey. Most left the fields to establish themselves in trade when their indentures were completed. The surviving planters finally gave up when they could no longer compete with cheaper sugar from Cuba. Some turned to other crops, others sold out to the transnationals who began to move in by buying up cheap land. Some, like Tate & Lyle and Booker McConnell still grew sugar, but others concentrated on less labour-intensive agriculture like bananas.

After the 1830s, smart money (both English and American), moved into Cuba, where slavery still operated. The first railway in Latin America was completed there in 1845; new steam machinery was introduced; the mahogany forests which once covered the island were torn down, and cheap sugar flooded the European market. This cheap sugar was then used to fuel another cheap source of labour power, the English working class, which itself produced manufactures, textiles and machinery at subsistence wages for export all round the world, forging yet another link in the complex chains of sugar capitalism.

The nineteenth century was a transitional period in sugar history. The collapse of Haiti as a cane producer encouraged capitalists to plant sugar on other islands apart from Cuba, like Hawaii and the Philippines. But as cane cultivation was extended, the price began to fall, encouraging producers to grow even more cane in order to maintain their overall profits. They also, increasingly, had to compete against northern beet sugar, which, in France from 1810 and in Germany after 1880, was protected by tariffs, further restricting the cane producers' markets. By 1885, beet had overtaken cane as a traded commodity, though cane enjoyed a brief boom during and after the First World War when the European beet industry was paralyzed. But never again would sugar monoculture dominate the Caribbean.

SUGAR CONSUMPTION

It is extremely difficult to grasp the scale of sugar consumption. Between 1650 and 1970, it appeared that demand for sugar would always keep pace with supply. The consumption of sugar by individuals or nations doubled and then doubled again in shorter and shorter periods, until the world consumption of sugar reached absolutely colossal proportions in the 1970s, when it appeared, at least in developed countries, to begin to level off. No other commodity reveals such an astonishing pattern.

We have mentioned the apparently innate predilection that human beings have for sweet substances but this only explains the increased consumption of sugar by the rich, since until about 1800, sugar was never cheaper than more nutritious alternatives. After 1800, it increasingly became a basic part of the diet of all but the very poor. To explain this we need to return to the characteristics of

Dr Johnson taking tea with the Boswells

One explanation derives in part from its early pharmaceutical history. The refinement of sugar by the Arabs eventually produced a pure white crystalline substance, sugar as we know it today. The discovery of this parallels the alchemists' search for gold. Sugar was celebrated as the elixir of life, the purest, and therefore the healthiest, of all foods. Thus, conspicuous consumption of sugar by kings and princes was a manifestation not simply of wealth but also of their potency. When sugar became more widely available in the seventeenth century, the middle class began to imitate such status displays, and sugar became an essential ingredient of ceremonial food for occasions like weddings, baptisms, funerals, Christmas, and so on. At the same time, its consumption as a sweetener of drinks like coffee, tea and cocoa which were first drunk in England in the 1650s, increased. At this time, there was only a limited awareness of the dangers of sugar consumption; that it damaged the teeth was already recognized, but the discovery of maturity-onset diabetes by Thomas Wallis in the Restoration period, which he identified by the sweet taste of the sufferer's urine, was the first serious challenge to the widespread notion that sugar was a pure and fundamentally healthy substance. Commodity capitalists, however, were not going to abandon the sugar trade or stop promoting sugar's alleged benefits when it was so profitable. Besides, notions of healthy eating were inevitably undermined by the shortage of alternative foodstuffs on the market which might have provided a cheap and adequate substitute. In such a situation, the anti-sugar lobby's arguments carried little weight; indeed, they were shouted down by the sugar interest, which argued that more and more sugar could and should be produced to satisfy the ever-increasing demand of the English population. Colonialism from that date went hand in hand with the 'modernization' of the English economy, and cheap sugar was, for industrialists and traders alike, the fuel of this development.

sugar once again. Although it is inadequate as a food, it is a remarkable provider of calories. It is clear that in nineteenth-century England, for example, tea with sugar was widely treated as a food by the working class; they spent their money on tea and sugar often in preference to other, cheaper foodstuffs.

This takes us back to the observation that for the rich, sugar was a luxury which was added to the diet, providing flavouring for sweetmeats, cakes and other delicacies, but for the working class its use was quite different. In almost every society meat, being scarce, has been consumed in greatest quantities by the rich; in poorer households it has been consumed in much greater quantities by men than by women. The working class diet was largely grain-based (whether millet, maize, rice, wheat, or oats), and here sugar has played a crucial role, because as an additive it can make even the most tasteless gruel palatable – just as it can make the bitterest unripe fruits edible. Thus, even in the poorest economies it had a crucial role to play. Its early use in certain ways mimics the use of spices and salt, but it does not explain the eventual preference for sugar over all other additives.

The liquor which carried sugar in Britain was, increasingly, tea. The phenomenal rise in tea consumption from 1700 onwards (almost all of it obtained from China until the 1850s), shows equally an increasing sugar addiction.

'Native cane mill',
Jamaica, 1890s

After the success of the 'free traders', in the early nineteenth century, who campaigned for the removal of all tariffs, the price of sugar fell, and working class consumption rapidly expanded. This was actively encouraged by the free trade lobby, which insisted that cheap sugar was good for everyone and that demand should be encouraged and expanded; if working class people could be encouraged to consume more sugar, they would work harder to buy the sugar, which would both increase the market and increase production. Such arguments won against a deeply-rooted cultural prejudice that the poor should not be encouraged to imitate the behaviour of their 'betters'. After the free traders abolished sugar duties altogether in the 1870s, manufacturers developed other uses for sugar in jams, jellies and marmalades; it was then that bread and jam became the basic diet of the poor in England and Scotland. Sugar was also widely used as molasses and syrup, and in the production of condensed milk, custards, chocolates and all other sweets. It was even marketed (by Tate & Lyle) as a substitute for honey, the company produced Golden Syrup with a picture of Samson and the Lion, a biblical allusion to honey, on the tin.

Sugar is a basic constituent of alcohol. Rum appears to have been invented from the distillation of sugar by the Dutch during their brief occupation of Brazil; rum rapidly became almost as important a commodity as sugar itself. The production of rum on the Caribbean islands follows that of sugar itself. By the 1780s, despite the bootlegging of rum between the Caribbean and the

North American colonies, two million gallons yearly were being exported to England. Even the generous rum ration issued to sailors (half a pint a day) left large quantities for sale and consumption. Sugar was also used in the brewing of beer after the 1750s (beer was also at this time promoted as a healthy drink for the English working class). This rapid rise in consumption signified a remarkable victory for the free traders. Mercantilism had argued that the market was limited and that therefore it was in the interests of the state to control production, but the free traders had apparently proved that it was in everyone's interest to increase supply until it equalled demand.

These consumption patterns were soon to be followed elsewhere in varying degrees. By about 1900, the consumption of granulated sugar peaked in most 'developed' societies, but since then, more and more sugar has been consumed in processed foods, soft drinks and alcohol. Thus, although our apparent consumption of sugar has declined, our real consumption has escalated to an alarming extent. This has, in part, been made possible by sugar's remarkable quality as a bulking agent. Cheap sugar can be added to more expensive ingredients to produce bigger cakes and thicker jams. Consumption of sugar is closely related to the consumption of fats, since one of sugar's particular qualities is the ease with which it can be combined with butter, lard and various oils to make cheap, edible products. The average US citizen now consumes about three quarters of a pound of fat and sugar per day, and the figure for England is not much lower.

One further pattern of sugar consumption still needs to be explored. The manufacturing and marketing of sugar-based foodstuffs with sugar as a preservative ingredient has radically altered the ways in which people eat. The increasing use of high-calorie, low-cost snacks has done more than anything to destroy the pattern of regular eating habits. Pop and crisps (or rather sugar, salt and monosodium glutimate) become meal substitutes for more and more people all the time; throw in ice creams, fast food batter, sweets, biscuits, and alcohol, which are also used as meal substitutes, then add the vast quantities of the white bread, jams, cakes, peanut butter, tinned soups and fizzy drinks which constitute many people's basic diet, and one begins to realize just how dangerous a commodity sugar really is. Clearly many of us are eating and drinking ourselves to death – all because of sugar.

SUGAR TODAY

Although consumption seems to have peaked, and may even be declining, in richer countries, in poorer countries it is still rising by between two and four per cent every year. About 75 per cent of the 100 million tonnes of beet and cane sugar produced annually is consumed in the producing countries, and almost all of the sugar traded internationally is cane sugar. The main exporters are Cuba (26 per cent of world total), Australia (12 per cent), the Philippines (7 per cent), Brazil (6 per cent), Thailand (5 per cent), and South Africa (4.4 per cent). The main importers are the United States (19 per cent of world total), the USSR (17 per cent, almost all of which it imports from Cuba, under a guaranteed trade agreement), Japan (11 per cent), Canada (4 per cent) and China (3 per cent). The EEC is both a major exporter (8 per cent) and importer (9 per cent); this is a ludicrous situation, which arose for two reasons: the granting of quotas to Britain's old cane-producing colonies, and massive investment in sugar beet by EEC countries.

Around 5 per cent of the price of a bag of sugar goes to the farmer who cultivates and harvests it; 5 per cent goes to the owner of the plantation, 8 per cent to the millowner, 9 per cent to the state selling agency, 12 per cent to the trader, 18 per cent to the refiner, 20 per cent to the wholesaler and 22 per cent to the retailer. Thus, the profit pattern has remained more or less constant since sugar was first marketed in Europe.

Sugar cane is still produced by labour-intensive methods; 60 per cent of the cane is grown on plantations owned by the same companies who own the mills, and the 5 per cent of the final price which goes to the growers represents less than a subsistence wage. Sugar workers are still perhaps the most ruthlessly exploited group of labourers in the world. In places like Brazil with a mass army of unemployed, wages for seasonal labour on the cane fields are between $2.25 and $3.50 per day. The workers have no hospitals and schools, the unions were crushed by the military government in 1964, and workers have no welfare payments when unemployed. Furthermore, although sugar workers were once encouraged to grow their own food crops, the extension of cane cultivation has deprived most of them of their vegetable plots.

In the Dominican Republic, wages rates for most of the immigrant Haitian workers are even lower (about $2 a day). They live in appalling conditions, and are often cheated out of what little they earn. The only reason that immigrants go there is that there is no work in Haiti, which has a 65 per cent unemployment rate and widespread starvation. As in Brazil, the sugar workers' union was crushed in 1967, when a US transnational, Gulf and Western, put pressure on the Dominican government to ban the union and impound its funds. The union leaders 'disappeared'; almost certainly they were murdered. At the same time, real wages have fallen by around a third over the past 15 years and food prices have continued to rise:

> When a worker with a wife and five children earns $2 or less per day, the outcome is predictable. Flour costs 20 cents per pound, and the family consumes three pounds for breakfast. There is not enough money for meat and beans. One cane worker reported that his children wake him in the morning complaining of hunger, and school for the children is impossible because of the expense of uniforms, pencils and paper. (Gatt-fly, p. 6)

These low wages are not confined to Third World countries. In Louisiana, cane workers earn half the average wage, and women doing marginal work earn between $300 and $500 a year. But worst of all are conditions in the Philippines. The big US sugar corporations shifted to the islands to take advantage of cheap labour and the viciously repressive labour legislation of ex-President Marcos (who like President Aquino and most other wealthy Filipinos, owned vast sugar plantations). Here sugar workers earn as little as 30 cents a day, which is

Filipino sugar workers on strike: 'Equal pay for men and women'

about the price of a kilo of rice. And they earn it working 14 hours a day, seven days a week:

> On Christmas Day, the local priest saw Francisco and his companions working in the fields, and invited them to a little party in his house. Four times the foreman came to send them back to work. (Gatt-fly, p. 11)

Most cane workers are employed by the sugar transnationals. Tate & Lyle is probably the biggest. Once, it owned extensive plantations in the Caribbean and Africa, but sold them after the countries gained independence, to concentrate on shipping, refining and trading. Apart from its complete monopoly of cane refining in Britain, it has over 150 subsidiaries in 30 countries. About half its profits are now made from sugar trading, and a sizeable

COMMODITIES

percentage of them comes from managing sugar estates for foreign governments.

Booker McConnell, another vast corporation, started as a plantation company in Guyana before slavery was abolished. The profits from sugar were then invested in mills, engineering and land; Booker McConnell came to control almost every aspect of the Guyanese economy. After the independence of Guyana in 1967, the Guyanese government nationalized Booker's interests, but was compelled to pay $40 million 'compensation'.

Other transnationals include the Great Western Sugar Company, the biggest sugar beet refiner in the US, which, incidentally, is controlled by the notorious billionaire Nelson Bunker Hunt, the man who attempted to corner the world silver market and the US soya bean market. Gulf and Western, with its banking and insurance interests and its zinc, tobacco and film companies, largely controls both the Dominican and the Florida sugar cane industries. Lonrho owns estates in Swaziland, Malawi, Mauritius and South Africa. Amstar, the largest cane refiner in the US, is followed by the California and Hawaiian Sugar Company, which through its 'Big Five' subsidiaries owns the best sugar land in Hawaii, as well as managing sugar projects in Brazil, Iraq, Iran, the Philippines and Equador. Interestingly, one of the 'Big Five', Theo. H. Davies, is now owned by the Hong Kong transnational, Jardine Matheson, which started off in the opium trade in the 1830s and has prospered ever since.

Throughout the twentieth century, the real price of sugar has steadily dropped. At various times, producer countries have tried to establish an international sugar agreement, though always without success. The problems facing cane sugar producers have also been exacerbated by the development of high fructose corn syrup (HFCS), which is obtained by crushing maize stalks. At the moment, it is only available in liquid form, but it now provides 20 per cent of the sweeteners used by the massive US soft drink industry. Tate & Lyle jointly owns the two biggest HFCS refineries in Europe, but development of the industry is limited by EEC legislation which protects beet growers.

The world now produces about eight million more

... international markets." Cuba's sugar deal with the Soviet Union has long been a factor in the country's economic salvation. With world prices at US3¢ a pound of crude sugar, ruin would be inevitable. By a sliding scale which adjusts Cuban prices to domestic price rises, the Soviet Union pays nearly 50 cents a pound. As an efficient sugar producer would have to invest 13 cents a pound, "we would be making a gift of nearly 10 cents a pound to western buyers if we were selling to them," Torras said. Last year, Cuba bought sugar cheaply on the world market to meet its Soviet quota. A similarly adva...

tonnes of sugar than it consumes. This glut has caused the price to drop from £291 a tonne in 1980 to £105 a tonne in 1983, causing acute distress in cane-producing countries. Today, the free market price of sugar is lower than the cost of production. Most producer countries have attempted to protect their sugar industries by subsidies, which does nothing to solve the problem since world overproduction serves to keep the price low.

After gaining independence, most Caribbean and African countries nationalized the plantations. The profit from sugar, however, comes from refining and marketing; with a world glut, these countries have no profits to invest in refineries or to buy new agricultural technology. On the other hand, sugar is attractive to developing countries because it provides both agricultural development and industrialization in tandem Cane has to be milled within 24 hours of cutting, and milling is an industrial process requiring capital and technology. In order to industrialize, these countries are forced to take loans from foreign banks on International Monetary Fund conditions; they are told to hold down wages, to control trade unions, to disband co-operatives and to hire in 'experts'. Thus, the old sugar companies are invited back, but this time as managers and controllers of the most profitable part of the operation. Challenged by corn syrup and artificial sweeteners like saccharine and aspartame and faced by declining consumption of sugar in Western markets with increased public awareness of the dangers of sugar consumption, developing countries have had to create local markets and new uses for sugar.

When Britain joined the Common Market in 1972, it was asked to adopt a set of highly protectionist trade agreements which would have excluded many Third World products, including cane sugar. But to protect its colonial interests, Britain argued that quotas from its ex-colonies be admitted to Europe. Under the Lomé Convention, Britain was permitted to import 1.14 million tonnes of cane a year. While the quota price is high (currently about £264 a tonne, against a world price of £110), the amounts allowed in are tiny. Zimbabwe, for example is allowed 25,000 tonnes under the Lomé Agreement. This is less than a twentieth of its total output, and the same proportion holds for other ex-colonies.

Countries like Barbados, Trinidad, Fiji, Guyana, Mauritius and Jamaica, are still critically dependent on cane as a major cash crop. But with the world price so low, there are no profits from sugar which could fund the diversification of their economies. At the moment, they depend on sugar exports to pay for essential food imports; thus, they cannot begin to contemplate cutting sugar production.

Cuba, after the revolution in 1959, did manage to diversify its agriculture, concentrating on rice, citrus fruits, dairy products and vegetables. This, however, was linked to the large-scale appropriation of the best agricultural land; Cuba was not crippled by the compensation debts which other less radical developing countries have paid to their old colonial masters. At the same time, faced with a US economic blockade, Cuba entered into a sugar agreement with the USSR; today, more and more of Cuba's land is being brought back into sugar cultivation, and Cuba's output is as high as it was in the hated days of Batista's regime.

In Jamaica in the 1970s, Michael Manley expropriated Tate & Lyle's plantations and handed them over to work-

ers' co-operatives. The land they took over, however, was worn out, the machinery was old and there was no money to invest in modernizing the industry. Western banks refused to advance loans, and when the obsolete machinery broke down, there was no money for either spares or replacements. In 1980, Manley's socialist agrarian programme was suspended when he was toppled by Seaga's right-wing government assisted by the CIA. The IMF encouraged Western bankers to resume their lending to Jamaica, but on certain conditions: that the co-operatives were disbanded (without compensation to the workers), that Tate & Lyle were invited back as managers (for an initial payment of £900,000, with a guaranteed £500,000 per year fee thereafter), and that the most political workers were laid off. With a union which is merely an arm of the Seaga administration, wage rates are now down to around £4 per week, and the surviving workforce is being reduced to the desperate expedient of burning the canefields and mobilizing strikes. Today, working conditions on the Jamaican plantations are as bad as any in the Third World.

In Zimbabwe, the situation for sugar workers is little better, despite Robert Mugabe's attempts to improve the conditions of agricultural workers. The large estates are all owned by foreign companies; the largest, Triangle, is actually owned by a South African transnational. When it was established by a failed cattle rancher Murray MacDougall, in the 1930s, a forced labour system, *chibaro*, was introduced. Villages were compelled to provide labour to construct the Kyle Dam to irrigate the land, and the Shangaan people who grazed cattle there were forcibly evicted:

> I was born in 1925. It was Tsovani's land until the coming of the European. Then I worked for a European called Maware. The farm was sold to him by the British government. How it was sold we do not know because the white men sold it between themselves. (Tsovani, Chief of the Chiredzi Area, Interview from the *Commodities* series, 1983)

Pensions were promised but only paid to those few workers who were employed full time. Most employees are employed for short periods during harvesting and therefore receive nothing when they are old. They are compelled to return to their 'communal lands', the poorest land which was allocated to them by the British after the richest lands had been sold to the highest bidders. An ex-plantation worker described their situation:

> We cannot look after our children, we cannot find soap, it is difficult to get food, water is scarce. The school for our children is very far away, those who go to school go with nothing, but there is nothing for them here. We have to live, what can we do? (Interview from the series, 1983)

The major problem facing cane growers throughout the world is competition from beet producers. This is compounded by the EEC's sugar policy, which is both a scandal and an absurdity. Countries like Britain, which are not ideally suited to beet agriculture in the first place, receive massive subsidies to grow beet. The million tonnes of sugar produced, most of it in East Anglia, provides half of Britain's current requirements, but yields there are much lower than those of the best beet growing areas of France and Italy – these alone could supply all of Europe's needs. Europe, through this policy, produces three million more tonnes of beet a year than it consumes, so the surplus is dumped on the world market, causing misery in the Third World cane-producing countries, who are forced to sell their own sugar at less than cost price. At the same time, under the Lomé Convention, the British customer pays a subsidy on the cane sugar imported from Britain's ex-colonies. The actual quota is so small that all but two of the cane refining factories in Britain have been forced to close in the last ten years. Thousands of jobs have been lost in Liverpool and London, while the British consumer is forced to pay subsidies twice over for what is the cheapest foodstuff in the world.

In general, there has been some progress in making the industry more efficient. New experimental canes have been established, the bagasse (the fibre waste left after crushing) is used both as a fuel and to make paper and boards, and mixed with molasses it provides a useful animal feed. Cane waste can also be used to make plastics and various chemicals.

Of course, sugar's terrible for kids' teeth, but luckily we've learned how to make them new plastic ones out of cane waste...

One possible solution to the problem of over-production is the use of sugar in the manufacture of cane alcohol. This is a relatively simple operation involving fermentation and distilling. It can be used in the manufacture of ether and vinegar, but most important, it can be used as a fuel substitute for oil or coal. When oil prices rocketed in the 1970s and sugar prices fell, the most industrialized cane-producing countries, led by Brazil, invested heavily in the process, aiming for complete self-

sufficiency in the production of motor fuel. When oil was over $50 a barrel, this industrial shift was economic and profitable, especially to those countries which lacked oil deposits. But now that oil has dropped to $15 a barrel, the shift back to oil from cane alcohol is certain to take place. It also needs to be remembered, in the face of the rhetoric about the Third World solution to oil debts, that sugar murders the soil. The deforestation of vast tracts of the Amazon jungle to extend cane cultivation to produce fuel alcohol is already having disastrous ecological effects. All this to produce a substitute for oil, of which the world still has abundant reserves!

To destroy forests and to use the richest agricultural land in the production of expensive fuel alcohol and nutritionally dangerous foodstuffs like sugar is not going to solve the problems of agricultural workers in developing countries. They remain the victims of their governments, which (advised by foreign 'experts' who still make profits out of sugar) continue to promote sugar related industrial development. But this industrialization is doubly costly. Not only do foreign loans need to be raised to start production, but, because of the world sugar glut, it has to be subsidized by governments in developing countries. The surplus is then dumped on local markets, and is being increasingly marketed as soft drinks and processed foods.

So ironically, after four hundred years of sugar slavery, the West is learning to wean itself from sweetness, while the Third World is increasingly being seduced into sugar dependency.

(*left*) **Company store, Triangle Sugar Estate, Zimbabwe**

71

Tea Fortunes three

Tea is a mild and amiable drug with a complex and often violent history. It is the most widely drunk non-alcoholic beverage in the modern world. In some countries, like Russia, China, Japan, England, India and Libya, it is the national non-alcoholic drink. In others, like Sri Lanka, Kenya, Indonesia, Argentina, Malawi and Bangladesh, it is the most important cash crop, though the workers who cultivate and pick it see very little of the profits.

Tea is, and always has been, a catalyst of social, economic and political change. The American Revolution, for example, was sparked off by riots over a tea tax; the Opium War was fought for tea; the great civilizations of India and Sri Lanka were destroyed by mercantile forces which then transformed them into tea plantations; and tea fortunes made many people millionaires. Tea is also an essential commodity in the tale of the English East India Company, the most successful and remarkable of all great monopolies, a company which not only provided fortunes for its investors and agents, but which itself became an imperial power on a world scale and conquered a country almost as large and once as rich as Europe. And at the other end of the chain, we need to remember that from the 1850s, the English working class was fed cheap tea and sugar, and further fortunes were made from the profits of their industry.

Although tea is a drug, it is a not a dangerous drug, except to those few people who are susceptible to its effects and who experience something approximating to drunkenness if they drink tea to excess. For most people, tea is innocuous and indeed mildly beneficial, if consumed in sensible doses. Furthermore, given the dangers of drinking unboiled water in many parts of the world and the cheapness of tea, the tea habit has almost certainly saved millions of lives in countries where water-borne diseases like typhoid and cholera are endemic.

We know very little about the early history of tea, but the Chinese were probably drinking tea (which they called ch'a) when Boadicea and her warriors were drinking river water and Christ was turning water into wine. The first discourse on ch'a, *The Ch'a Ching* (*The Book of Tea*), was written by a mandarin, Lu Wo, who died in 805 AD. In his encyclopaedia, Lu Wo discusses the many different kinds of qualities of tea, and the processes of preparation of the leaf of the shrub, now botanically identified as *Camillia sinensis*. In its wild state, this beautiful shrub has been known to reach 100 feet and to grow for hundreds of years. However, for the production of ch'a, the trees were cut down; the shrubs growing in their shade were pruned, and after four years the leaves and buds were plucked. The shrubs then produced increasing amounts of useable leaves and tips for about 20 years, and then they slowly declined until they were cut for firewood, usually after 40 years. Nowadays, a shrub growing in optimal semi-tropical conditions with plenty of rain and sun and a well-drained soil can produce about five pounds of tea per year. Different hybrids, soils, climates and altitudes also determine the eventual taste of the infusion.

73

Cocktails! they're all the rage, but no cocktails for me A stimulant, and harmless, is a cup of Twinings tea.

Once plucked, the leaves can be dried, cured and drunk in many different ways. For two thousand years, the Chinese have produced and drunk various types of green tea made by a repetitive, labour-intensive operation. The young leaves and buds are first carefully picked, then quickly heated over a fire in a pan ('tatching'), then rolled and rubbed in the hands, spread out, sifted, tatched again, tossed in baskets, spread out, sorted and tatched again, and finally packed in chests to reduce evaporation, before being taken to market. Green tea needs to be brewed fairly quickly if it is not to deteriorate, so in order to preserve it better, the Chinese changed the process and allowed the leaves to ferment before curing began; then they were processed like green tea, though with further tatching at the end. This produced 'black tea' which contains three times as much caffeine by weight as green tea. It is also a more astringent brew – this was the kind of tea first sold in large quantities outside China.

By the eighth century, tea had become part of the internal Chinese tax and finance system; by the tenth, the

(*right*) **Transporting bales of tea by river sampan**

government was sponsoring tea production in Hunan. By 1200, tea was already a major item in inter-province commerce, and by 1400, Hunan farmers had begun to specialize in its production to such a degree that they were obliged to buy their vegetables at local markets. Thus, cash crop monoculture was established early, long before the arrival of Europeans. By 1600, tea was, with silk, the major item in the China-Manchuria trade.

Tea first arrived in Europe in significant quantities in the late seventeenth century. At that time, most of China's tea was grown in the hills around Fukien, Kiangsi, Chekiang and Anhwei, as a state-licensed monopoly, and its export was controlled by favoured Chinese merchants called the hong, operating out of Canton. It was the hong who first sold tea, silks and porcelain to European 'barbarians' or 'foreign devils', as they were termed by the Chinese. Europeans were not allowed into China; they were not even permitted to learn Chinese. Thus they could not hope to control cultivation of such a lucrative commodity, and they appeared doomed to dependence on the hong.

It was only slowly that 'tea' (the Amoy dialect word for ch'a), and the taste for tea filtered out of China. The Portuguese had been permitted to establish a trading factory on Macao, an island near Canton, from where they brought back silk and other commodities in exchange for silver and copper. Yet they did not immediately trade tea or even drink it in significant quantities, since what was being merchandized was not the beverage drunk in China. Indeed, it was not certain exactly what was being sold, nor how these dried leaves were to be brewed and consumed. Although there were plenty of theories about tea, the real question was, could it be made palatable and marketable? Unsurprisingly, given the astringency and caffeine content of black tea, it was first sold and celebrated in the West as a medicine. Early on, it was mixed with other 'medicines', like honey, sugar and lemons in Portugal, and with milk and sugar in Holland after 1610, when it was first brought back from Canton by the Dutch East India Company.

It was in the form of these medicinal sips that tea first arrived in London in the 1650s, where it was first drunk

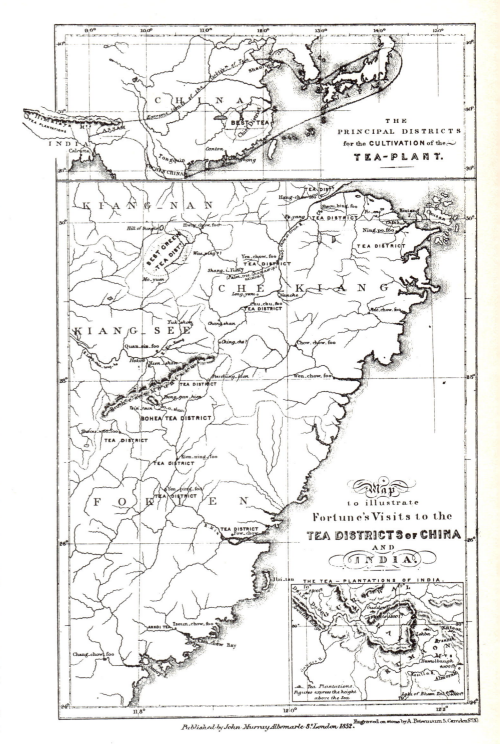

THE PRINCIPAL DISTRICTS for the CULTIVATION of the TEA-PLANT.

Map to illustrate Fortune's Visits to the TEA DISTRICTS of CHINA AND INDIA.

THE TEA-PLANTATIONS OF INDIA.

Published by John Murray Albemarle St. London 1852. Engraved on stone by A. Petermann 5. Camden St N.

in the Cromwellian coffee houses. But tea's particular qualities as a beverage were not easily recognized in such an atmosphere, for it was competing with wine, spirits, tobacco, coffee and chocolate on the mercantile menu, all of which dull the tea drinker's palate.

A more refined mode of drinking tea arrived in England when Charles II, to consolidate the Portuguese alliance, married Catherine of Braganza in 1662. She arrived with her dowry, which was Bombay and Tangier (if the English could hold onto them) and her tea-chests. The king neglected her and she found solace in tea. As a bribe, the directors of the East India Company gave her regular presents of tea; the Court ladies imitated her, and the taste for tea spread to bourgeois housewives like Mrs Pepys and thousands like her. However, at 50 shillings a pound, tea did not spread far beyond the Court; tea drinking and brewing became a high status ceremonial which only the richest and most refined ladies, allegedly, understood.

Throughout the eighteenth century the cost of tea fell and the taste for it spread. The bourgeoisie was soon commenting on the habits of tea-drinking servants who aped their betters, though the tea the poor drank was adulterated with all manner of dangerous additives including iron filings and lead; also most of the tea they consumed was smuggled to avoid the very high taxes on tea. By the nineteenth century, European demand had encouraged the wider cultivation of ch'a; Chinese merchants were advancing money or rice to hill farmers to expand production. Processing, which initially had been done by the farmers themselves, and subsequently by itinerant professionals, was, in the case of black tea, finally undertaken in factories controlled by the hong in Canton. These factories were very large, often employing several hundred workers for re-roasting, sorting, packing and blending; and the quality of tea they produced was high because the hongs' profits depended on the prices the 'barbarians' were prepared to pay for their drug.

Nothing, however, angers a monopolist more than to be confronted by a rival monopoly; in the case of tea, the hongs' monopoly was absolute. Traders did not even know what the tea plant looked like; popular wisdom and the opinion of experts like Linnaeus held that there were two species of tea plant, green and black. No one outside China and Japan had ever seen a tea bush, and no one knew how the leaves were processed – nor did the Chinese have any intention of telling them. Furthermore, the hong controlled the price of tea. Elsewhere, Europeans plundered and traded on their own terms; they bought cheap, attacked trading rivals, and sold in markets where they enjoyed a monopoly. But tea was only available in Canton, and the Canton price was high. In the early days, the Chinese would only accept two commodities, silver and copper, in exchange for tea. Europeans attempted to trade other things but they were rebuffed. In 1793, the Manchu Emperor informed George III, whose government was worried by the increasing drain of silver into China, 'As your Ambassador can see for himself, we possess all things. I set no value on objects strange or ingenious, and have no use for your country's manufactures' (Morse, vol II, p. 248). For this reason, Europeans had to trade other commodities around the Asian coast in order to get silver and copper, which they then exchanged for silks, porcelain and tea. But the British addiction to tea was so great that the drain of silver out of London was threatening to undermine the whole balance of payments. Some other commodity to exchange was urgently needed, and eventually an alternative was found: opium.

The Chinese had been cultivating and smoking a mild form of opium for several hundred years. Various imperial edicts had attempted to control the habit, but the officials of the Manchu dynasty never seriously attempted to enforce these laws. When European merchants first brought Persian opium into Canton, they discovered a chink in the Chinese wall. Although illegal, they could sell it to the easily bribed hong; since Persian opium was far stronger and more psychoactive than the Chinese variety, the hong were prepared to pay high prices for it. But as the demand in Canton went up, the price in Persia went up. The solution, discovered by the British, was to control the cultivation of opium elsewhere, and the place where they cultivated it was Bengal.

THE ENGLISH EAST INDIA COMPANY

In order to understand the history of opium and tea in India, one has to picture the subcontinent before European merchants arrived with their well-armed ships and their empty promises. In 1500, India was a prosperous collection of states, ruled in similar ways by different overlords, divided by mountains, forests and rivers, and subdivided by religions, languages, castes and traditions. It was relatively underpopulated at the time; large tracts of the country were forest, menaced by snakes, tigers and wolves, so there was not much incentive for swift expansion. However, in the populated areas, life was relatively orderly and prosperous. Around 500 AD, India's great irrigation system was begun, a system which guaranteed water during droughts and which controlled flooding during the monsoons, and upon which the lives and prosperity of millions of peasant farmers depended. One of the recognized responsibilities of all Indian overlords was the maintenance of this system. The peasants, who were taxed to pay for it, were otherwise relatively unregulated by their overlords. They organized themselves into communities, the 'village system', within which everyone had allocated roles, responsibilities and certain privileges, as well as enjoying communal ownership of land. In many areas, crafts flourished: metalwork, jewellery making, musical instrument making and others. The craft, however, which particularly interested European traders was cotton manufacture, in which the Indian craftsmen were unsurpassed.

This was the India first encountered by the English East India Company fleet in 1608. The English East India Company (EIC) had been established by royal charter in 1600, but it was underfunded, and, initially, much less successful than its powerful rival, the Dutch East India Company. When English ships attempted to trade in the Spice Islands they were driven out by the Dutch. When they landed in Surat in India in 1608 and attempted to trade with the local merchants, they were challenging a long established Portuguese monopoly, and the Portuguese immediately attacked them. But the Portuguese were not popular in India. Between 1500 and 1600, they

East India House, built c. 1740

had come to control the trade of much of the Indian coastline, ousting the Arabs, building forts and factories. They had also coerced the Indian merchants into accepting their trading terms. The Indians, therefore, welcomed any competitors prepared to challenge the Portuguese monopoly; because competition between the buyers also brought higher prices.

However, when the English arrived, they had little to offer. Their woollen cloths were ridiculed by the Indian merchants who dressed in cottons and silks and for whom wool at most was a material for rugs and carpets (which anyway they could obtain in abundance from Persia and Arabia). So their trading overtures were rejected. Sir Henry Middleton, commanding the EIC's sixth voyage in 1611, was attacked by the Portuguese. Then, having been refused permission to trade by the Mughal official, he stormed off into the Persian gulf and collected merchandise by piracy, which did little to reassure the Indians when they contemplated trade with the English. But when the Portuguese attacked the English fleet in 1615 and the English resoundingly defeated them, the situation changed. One thing the Indian princes lacked was a coastal fleet, and when they witnessed the engagement between the two European powers, they were happy to support the stronger and to use the

Battle between
British and Dutch
ships, Sumatra, 17th
century

English as a kind of naval auxiliary fleet, in return for which they allowed them certain trading privileges and the right to build factories along the coast.

An important difference between the English and the Dutch companies was that the English East India Company only claimed a monopoly of trade between Asia and England; its agents were paid small salaries which they were expected to supplement by trading on their own account along the coast ('country trade'). In the process, some agents became extremely rich. John Pitt, the father and grandfather of two British prime ministers, started off as a country trader working for the East India Company. Like many others, he returned to England to invest his profits in property and political power. The Committee of Directors back in London also made handsome fortunes, but the shareholders made very little, not least because of the notorious corruption of the company's agents and directors. Furthermore, in order to retain its monopoly the company had to make bigger and bigger bribes. On occasion, scandal broke. In 1693, for instance, it was discovered by a parliamentary committee that not only was the aristocracy in on the game, but so also was King William, to the tune of £10,000. Since one of the fundamental issues which united the mercantile opposition was its hatred of monopolies, the government was compelled to open up the India trade to competitors. All the interests combined to create a new company, the EIC, in the early eighteenth century, and it was this company which conquered India.

In the seventeenth century, the Mughal Empire in north India had already begun to decline, and as its central authority weakened, various local rulers formed alliances with foreign traders in order to hold on to their power. By 1750, the EIC was established as a naval and military force acting for different princes in many parts of India; and, as has often happened, the mercenaries eventually became the masters.

The British usually achieved this by backing a claimant to a disputed throne and putting him on it by force of arms. This was not difficult. Even in defeat, the British could take to their ships, and from their ships they could recapture the territories they had lost. When they were victorious, however, and had settled their puppets on their thrones, the British were there to stay. They then demanded protection money, so that their Indian puppets were compelled to grant them land revenues to pay for the standing armies of native soldiers led by company officers.

Hitherto, local land revenues had been fixed at about a third of the value of all produce, and a significant amount of those taxes had been spent on maintaining the irrigation system and on public works. After the arrival of the British, all that changed. The cost of the armies (or rather the alleged cost of the armies, because the EIC pocketed most of the taxes), increasingly bankrupted not only the princes, but their subjects. EIC merchants stepped in and lent the princes money at high rates of interest. The princes' debts got bigger and bigger, the taxes paid by the villages got higher and higher; when they could no longer pay, the company's soldiers went in and seized anything they could find, taking the peasants' food stocks, tools and homes. The company also destroyed the infrastructure upon which the prosperity of India was based. At first, the most profitable trading commodity to both Indians and Europeans had been Indian cottons, which, beautifully woven and dyed, could be traded in Africa and the Americas and sold at high prices in England. From the 1700s, the company began to advance money to the India producers to increase production, and so by the 1780s hundreds of thousands of Indians had been drawn into cotton growing and manufacture. Dacca, the centre of this industry, was a city comparable in size and wealth with London. But once established, the company lowered the prices paid to native weavers, until eventually the weavers starved. Having advanced them trifling sums of money, the company then seized the weavers' looms as collateral. The survivors were then compelled to work in the EIC's factories. They were transformed from artisans to wage slaves, but the native industry was now utterly destroyed. In 1835, the Governor General of the company reported: 'The misery hardly finds a parallel in the history of commerce. The bones of the cotton-weavers are bleaching the plains of India.' (Mukherjee, p. 304)

In 1750, the English did not control large territories in India – they collected revenues from their puppets but did not legally control the land. Indeed, they could not legally own the land, since from time immemorial, land in India was held in common. So the next phase in the conquest of India was to transform its laws and labour force into those of a plantation economy. Disregarding traditional systems of land tenure, the English increasingly claimed landowning rights over the tracts of land ruled by their puppets, and by taxing native manufactures and produce, whilst paying them very little for what they did produce, they drove natives out of their villages onto the plantations.

One could map out stage by stage the encroachment of the British into India, but that is hardly necessary. The long term ambition, the conquest of India, had been set out in a company document in 1689, but initially, the British could only proceed slowly, since the operation had to be financed by the company's plunder of India, and that took time. The EIC was also competing with the Portuguese in Goa, the Dutch in Sri Lanka, and the French in the south – the Carnatic. By 1750, the EIC was secure in three areas alone, around Bombay, Madras and Calcutta, but it enjoyed one significant advantage over its rivals: its tax-collecting operations, particularly the *diwani* (the right to collect land taxes) of Bengal. The company, by guile and compulsion, had transformed the *diwani* into a rich source of revenue, most of which was embezzled by its agents; but some was used to arm native soldiers, and was crucial in the success of EIC armies against other native rulers and against the French. The Carnatic Wars (1746–57) fought between the British and the French were decisive. After the battle of Plassey in 1757, the British controlled half of India, with its soldiers, territory, subservient puppet rulers, forts, revenues, factories and ships. Although it took another hundred years to mop up the rest, the company eventually got what it wanted.

Until about 1800, the EIC's operations were largely parasitic; it sucked one ruler dry, one kingdom dry, and then moved on. What was left after the plunder was very little; desolate farmlands, broken-down irrigation systems, broken spinning wheels and looms, and the corpses of the peasants. Famine, hitherto almost unknown in India, began to occur and reoccur with terrifying regularity, and by the 1770s, the company was in serious trouble. The plunder was being remitted to England by various routes, but it benefitted only the agents, and the agents had killed the legendary bird that laid the lucrative eggs.

This situation outraged the British government and company shareholders (most MPs in Britain were in fact EIC shareholders). They were not particularly concerned about the deaths of millions of Indians, but they were upset about the collapse of the India trade. From the 1770s, the government, in return for substantial loans to the company, regulated its operations more closely, appointed its governors and attempted to restore some

kind of order in its Indian territories. The EIC, however, remained as the official government of British India.

At the same time, the source of the company's trading profit was largely tea and silk traded through Canton. Obviously some of the Indian plunder, the gold, silver, jewels, silks and cottons, when sold in Europe, provided the bullion with which tea was purchased in China; but as the plunder dried up, the drain on silver increased. The company dabbled for a time in the West Indian slave trade but failed to compete against the Liverpool merchants. It was then that a country agent suggested opium cultivation. After Plassey, the EIC had seized Bengal, where opium was known to grow well, so it advanced opium seeds and money to peasant producers there and paid them reasonable prices for their opium. Other peasants were attracted by the prices, and soon the company was in control of a flourishing opium industry. The Governor General, Warren Hastings, gave it his blessing and in 1784, dispatched two cases of opium to Canton.

OPIUM AND THE OPIUM WAR (1839—1842)

At the same time the EIC annexed Benares in Northern India and extended poppy cultivation there. Initially, it made huge profits from this move, but the extension of cultivation lowered prices; native producers soon learned to adulterate their opium and sell it to independent traders, so the cost of opium to the company went up and the profits on its sale went down. In 1800, the company attempted to corner the market; it began to supervise the production of opium and to buy competitors' stocks. In ten years, opium had increased in value from $50 a chest to $1,500 a chest. But the high price attracted interlopers, and by the 1820s it was clear that the company could no longer fix the price because of increased competition. So it began to increase production, thereby maintaining its total profits, albeit at reduced prices.

That the company traded in opium, although well known, was often denied, since opium was known to be a poison. The trade was alternatively sometimes defended on the grounds that properly used, opium was also a medicine. When this defence was ridiculed, the response

was that it was only sold to the degenerate Chinese, who were not human anyway. But few people quibbled; they knew their supply of tea depended on the trade. The British government raised ten per cent of its tax revenue from tea, and eminent figures who might have questioned the morality of the opium trade, men like Thomas Love Peacock, Charles Lamb, James and John Stuart Mill, were all beneficiaries of the company and had no intention of rocking the boat.

When a parliamentary committee questioned one of its agents in 1832, he merely acknowledged that the company grew opium in Bengal and that it was sold in Calcutta, arguing that the company could not be held responsible for its export to China. But other witnesses admitted that the trade went on and that opium was actually carried in company chests even if was not traded by the company. The company's star witness was James Mill, the free trade ideologue and father of J.S. Mill, who had worked for the company and who knew that it owed its profitability and chance of survival to opium. When challenged as to whether it was morally right for the company to continue to trade opium, he argued that the issue was not moral but economic, and asserted, as a free trader, that the government had no right to restrict trade at all. He also pointed out that opium was being produced not for profit but for revenue (a specious distinction), and that the burden fell not on British subjects but on miserable Bengali farmers; rather than tax the British for the government of India, it was cheaper (and fairer) to immiserate the natives, and to continue to produce and sell opium in Bengal.

The issue was even debated in the House of Commons;

Opium den, Canton

it took opium from them at minimal prices, in lieu of land tax, leaving them with nothing more than the means of subsistence. But the critics of the EIC were, in the end, defeated. The accepted sophistry was that it rested with the Chinese to stop the traffic by suppressing the consumption of opium, and that prohibition of the trade would be disastrous to the finances of India. This was true: opium was by now the basis upon which the British in India financed their conquest of the rest of the subcontinent.

But distant parliamentary debates and the illegality of its operation hardly bothered the company's agents in Canton. It was not until 1839, when the EIC's factories in Canton were raided by the Chinese Viceroy, that its involvement in the opium trade could even be publicly demonstrated. But by then it was too late.

After the importing of opium had been banned by the Chinese in 1800, British traders had attempted to smuggle it in through Macao, but the Portuguese demanded a cut and the English had no intention of sharing the profits. Besides, by 1820, the company's increased production of opium in Bengal had created an opium glut and the merchants were expected to promote sales wherever they could, irrespective of Chinese prohibition. In the 1820s, two country traders, William Jardine and James Matheson, decided to run the trade entirely from the sea. They moored their warehouse ships, which were essentially floating forts, off the Chinese coast, and supplied these ships with Bengal opium. Chinese skiffs took off the opium, which they paid for with silver; the Chinese customs junks which attempted to interfere were blasted out of the water.

By the 1830s, Jardine and Matheson had moved their operation into Canton because they were having problems handling over 40,000 chests of opium a year. How much opium got into China at the time will never be accurately known because, after all, it was a smuggling trade. The total was at least ten times greater in 1839 than it had been in 1800; moreover, the Chinese were now paying more for illegal opium than they were receiving from the British traders in return for their tea.

The situation was clearly getting out of control. In

one radical member, James Silk Buckingham, vigorously attacked the company's record. He said that the EIC claimed

'the high prerogative of being the guardian of the laws, and the preserver of the morals of the people over whom they ruled, and punished with extreme severity any infraction of their own regulations, [and yet] they cultivated opium for no other purpose than for smuggling it into China against the laws and edicts of the empire; and, as has been truly said, of poisoning the health and destroying the morals of the people of that country . . . If the traders of China could be supplied with British manufactures in payment for their goods, instead of this deleterious drug, a wholesome and reciprocally beneficial commerce would be created, instead of the mischievous and demoralizing traffic which now does injury to both.' (quoted in Inglis, p. 87)

Buckingham also quoted from Robert Rickards' surveys of India, which showed that British rule in India, far from benefitting and protecting the native populations, was actually responsible for their misery and poverty because

Canton, the British Superintendent of Trade, Captain Charles Elliot, was ambivalent in his attitude to the drug. He realized that the balance of trade depended on it, but he also realized that it threatened the existence of the British tea trade with China. In the circumstances, it is not surprising that he vacillated. In 1837, skirmishes broke out between country traders and the Chinese authorities, who began burning Chinese smuggling skiffs. As the violence escalated, British traders became better armed and more adventurous. Canton (with its taxes and controls) was increasingly bypassed by British traders, and this threatened the whole basis of the Canton tea/opium trade. Elliot was alarmed and urged Lord Palmerston, the British Foreign Secretary, to control the British in China, but already Jardine had returned to England and had secretly persuaded Palmerston to provide money, and naval and military support for the British smugglers. Elliot was merely expected to hold the fort until this secret expedition arrived.

In 1838, alarmed at the opium plague, the Emperor consulted his mandarins and dispatched one of them, Commissioner Lin, to Canton to stop the trade. Lin arrived in March 1839, and immediately ordered all foreign merchants to surrender their opium. They played for time, but eventually delivered it to Lin, who publicly destroyed it, having promised compensation to the merchants. Lin then sent a letter to Queen Victoria,

asking her to outlaw the trade:

'It appears that this poisonous article is manufactured by certain devilish persons in places subject to your rule. It is not, of course, either made or sold at your bidding, nor do all the countries you rule produce it, but only certain of them. I am told that in your own country opium smoking is forbidden under severe penalties. That means you must be aware how harmful it is. But better than to forbid the smoking of it would be to forbid the sale of it, and better still, to forbid the production of it, which is the only way of cleansing the contamination at its source. So long as you do not take it yourselves, but continue to make it and tempt the people of China to buy it you will be showing yourself careful of your own lives, but careless of the lives of other people, indifferent in your greed for gain to the harm you do to others; such conduct is repugnant to human feeling and the way of heaven.' (quoted in Waley, pp. 29–30)

Lin's is a long letter and it was never delivered to the young queen, but it shows how a Chinese philosopher

(*top left*) **East India Company ship destroys Chinese junks, Opium War, 1841**
(*top right*) **British troops capture Chuenpee, 1841**

had a greater understanding of the problem than any contemporary British rationalist. But reason never defeated capitalist greed. Even before Lin composed the letter, Palmerston had dispatched two men of war, two frigates, two river steamers, and 7,000 soldiers to China, with a list of Chinese ports which were to be coerced into accepting the English principle of free trade. From then on, it was obvious that the Chinese would be defeated. Two thousand years of isolation had rendered them incapable of war with a capitalist power. British gunpowder, arms and steam-driven ships gave the aggressors an absolute advantage.

In May 1839, Canton fell to the British. The Chinese paid $6 million to the British as a compensatory bribe to withdraw. The British were not satisfied; in August 1841, the expeditionary force sailed north, sacking one coastal town after another, capturing Ting-hai and Ningpo in October. The next year, it sacked Shanghai in June, and then proceeded up the Yangtze River to take Chingkiang and Nanking in August. It was clear then that nothing could prevent it taking Peking. The Emperor was forced to capitulate. At the Treaty of Nanking in 1842, Britain was ceded Hong Kong as a trading base, with the right to trade in five other ports; it was also given an indemnity of $21 million for the loss of the opium trade.

From Hong Kong, which rapidly developed as a mercantile and banking centre, men like Jardine and Matheson continued to trade opium with impunity. After the wars, Chinese tea exports continued to boom and ships from other countries traded opium for tea just like the British. The first three American millionaires, in fact, all made their fortunes out of the China trade, which after the coercion of the Chinese became increasingly profitable and stable. High prices were maintained by the expanding demand for tea in Europe and the US; the carrying time was halved by the great China clippers, the fastest and most beautiful trading ships ever constructed; fortunes were gambled on their races; and opium continued to flood into China.

A less romantic but more significant consequence was the financial settlement which followed the opium wars.

Before Hong Kong was established, all bills of exchange were drawn on London, so enormous amounts of paper money were circulating in the Pacific, particularly around Canton. This began to worry the London banks, because when a ship returned from the east with millions of pounds in bills, it caused a run on the banks. Once Hong Kong was established, it made sense to run the operation from there. Local banks were set up by London bankers, but they were independent operations which greatly facilitated the flow of credit. Traders and smugglers running up the coast preferred to have bits of paper which could be forwarded to their widows in England if they died or their boats were sunk, and traders could sell their opium for bullion which they then deposited in the Hong Kong banks in exchange for bills. The tea buyers could go and buy that same bullion and use it to buy tea on the mainland. Officially, the Chinese were content since they were not suffering a net drain of bullion, and the tea merchants were happy because they had the bullion to buy the tea. The country traders with the same bill of exchange which they got in Hong Kong could spend some of it on Bengal opium and forward the rest back to England. And merchants like Jardine and Matheson could return to England, where they became Members of Parliament and supported Palmerston. The profits from opium lasted legally until 1910, when, finally, the US and China forced the British government to intervene and stop the trade, which had killed millions of Chinese and enriched a handful of 'foreign devils'. Hong Kong had become the entrepot of the opium trade; thus one final legacy which Jardine and Matheson bequeathed to Hong Kong was the greatest heroin problem in the world.

TEA AND THE BOURGEOISIE

At this stage, we need to go back in time to look at the development of tea drinking outside China. There are many ways in which tea can be prepared and consumed. It can be flavoured with scents like jasmine, rose and the carcinogenic oil of bergamot, or with fruits, honey, sugar and milk. It is even boiled and mixed with fats to make a soup in Outer Mongolia. In general, wherever it was adopted by a new consuming group, it was fetishized in various ways; particular methods, utensils and manners mediated its early consumption. The tea habit and tea addiction had spread through Persia by the seventeenth century and to central Asia by the eighteenth. But it was European addiction which determined the future pattern of cultivation.

So rapidly did European demand for tea increase that by 1700, 17 million lbs of China tea were being exported to Europe each year, mostly to Holland, Portugal and England. The early history of tea outside China was characterized by innumerable ill-informed controversies concerning its alleged qualities. Its defenders claimed that it

> corrects indigestions . . . it is a very famous cephalic [i.e. a cure for all head ailments] adds a wonderful strength to the animal spirits . . . opposes the megrim [migraine] and wonderfully comforts the memory and other faculties of the soul. (Ovington, 1699)

An anonymous pamphlet of the 1690s claimed that it made

> 'the body active and lusty . . . it helpeth the headache . . . it removeth the obstructions of the spleen, it is good against the stone and gravel, it cleaneth the kidneys, it taketh away the difficulty of breathing, it vanquisheth heavy dreams, easeth the brain and strengtheneth the memory.' (quoted in Ukers, 1935, p. 84)

In short, like sugar and coffee it was a universal panacea to its defenders. Dr Johnson, for example, sprang to its defence speaking as

> 'a hardened and shameless tea drinker, who has for many years diluted his meals with only the infusion of this fascinating plant; whose kettle has scarcely time to cool; who with tea amuses the evening, with tea solaces the midnight, and with tea welcomes the morning.' (quoted in Boswell, *Life of Johnson*, vol. I, p. 313)

Johnson also considered that it was 'a liquor not proper to the lower class of people'.

The dangers of tea (probably composed by hacks working for the brewers and wine merchants) were spelt out in various pamphlets: 'It is a drug . . . not less destructive than opium . . . it attenuates and depauperates the blood and may bring on any disease.' But no amount of criticism was going to undermine such a profitable trade. Tea was drunk in salons and levees, and the aristocratic order of the day ritualized the consumption of various types of tea at particular times with specific side dishes: breakfast tea with fish and toast, morning tea with dried fruit, low tea with bread and cakes, and high tea with meat and vegetables. Tea accompanied music and conversation, poems were written in its praise, and novels were plotted according to its rituals. By the end of the eighteenth century, only cranks condemned it.

Brewer's satirical cartoon defending high tax on tea

The exorbitant tax on tea (120 per cent of the wholesale price) may have pleased the government, but it did not, of course, please the consumers. Smugglers bringing tea from Dutch ports or loading off ships at sea began to supply the market. In the 1720s, 250 customs officers were assaulted, six were murdered, 230 ships were confiscated and 2,000 smugglers were prosecuted. In Sussex alone, towns were beseiged, battles were fought, customs houses were burned down and innumerable atrocities committed in the smugglers' war with the Exchequer. Parliamentary witnesses suggested that as many as 20,000 people were engaged in tea smuggling in Kent and Sussex alone, and it was suggested that three times as much tea was imported illegally as reached customers through the official market. Parts of London like Stockwell and Leather Lane became notorious for nocturnal meetings between smugglers and crooked dealers, a situation which was only ended by the Commutation Act of 1784, which reduced the duty on tea and trebled the legal tea trade in less than five years.

This smuggling had an indirect influence on another major political event, the American Revolution. So great was the volume of tea smuggled, that in the early 1770s, the East India Company found itself with four times more tea in its warehouses than it sold in a year. To get rid of the surplus, it persuaded the government to pass an Act in 1773 permitting the company to re-export tea to America. The tax on sales was to be remitted to the British government. The Americans might well have ignored this, since they smuggled everything they needed, including tea, but the issue of 'taxation without representation' sparked off attacks on British ships carrying tea, like the Boston Tea Party, and then war with Britain between 1775 and 1781, followed by American Independence at the Treaty of Versailles in 1783.

TEA IN INDIA

In the 1830s, the British began to annexe the remaining independent hill states of Bengal. Fighting was fierce and protracted and revolts in subjugated territories were frequent, so it was not until 1873 that the British controlled the province that came to be known as Assam. The motive for expansion in India was simple: profit. But how to make the money there was less obvious.

The charter granted to the East India Company by the British government in 1833 was obviously influenced by the collapse of the Caribbean sugar trade. Without slavery, other forms of plantation agriculture were needed, and the new charter allowed Europeans to purchase land within company territory. Since labour was scarce, the

Raj first abolished slavery in its Indian territories, but not for philanthropic reasons; the emancipated slaves, without land or protectors, were compelled to work on the plantations at subsistence wages.

The Assam Company, which henceforth controlled the development of plantation agriculture in the area, was established in 1839. Tea, which was eventually to dominate Assam, was not yet exploited, though, ironically, it grew wild in Bengal. Up-country agents had been sending back samples and seeds to Calcutta since 1823, but the company's experts initially denied that this was tea. A Tea Committee was established in 1834, and by 1839 eight chests of ill-prepared and empirically cultivated local tea had been produced. But without expert advice and skills, the experiment did not look promising. In 1848, a botanist, Robert Fortune, was dispatched to China and ordered to find out what he could about tea. He travelled in disguise, made four trips into China and returned with all the information that was needed, as well as smuggled seeds, 12,000 plants, tools and a skilled workforce. Five years later, once the Chinese had taught the British their skills, they were dismissed and told to find their own way back to China. From then on, tea growing outside China was largely a British monopoly.

To attract British planters to Bengal and Assam, the 'Wasteland Rules' were framed, which granted land on 45 year leases to those who had capital. Naturally, native farmers lacked capital, so all the wastelands were purchased from the company by European settlers. To attract even more planters, these concessionary rates were improved in 1854 with the promise of 99-year leases at lower rents. Would-be planters flocked to Assam in their thousands, valuable timber was cut and sold, forests were cleared, and the land not needed for tea was rented to starving natives, tied like serfs to the soil. Under the system, the smaller the area of land farmed the greater the land tax, which meant that natives who paid three rupees an acre for their land were ruined while the planters who paid no land tax prospered even more.

In the early days of the Assam tea company, Chinese workers were paid 15 rupees a month, but once the industry was established, natives were paid on average

three rupees. This rose to four rupees after a wage revolt in 1857, though the magistrates arrested the strikers and whipped them on the grounds that any stoppage of work before the expiry of a contract was illegal. In the 1850s, tea from Assam was first sold on the English market. These astringent teas caused considerable surprise when it was discovered how well they sold. From then on, Assam tea with sugar was drunk in ever-increasing quantities. The profits from tea cultivation speeded up change in the Indian economy. The first railways in Asia were constructed to open up the tea plantations, steam-driven rolling machines were introduced, and paddle steamers chugged up the Bramaputra.

The 1860s were boom years in Assam. Planters were no longer interested in making any pretence at legal procedures. They stole native grazing rights, seized traditional tribal lands and blocked local routes, thus depriving peasants of their access to traditional markets. Often, they sold native lands to other planters over the heads of the peasant cultivators.

At this time, white planters were competing with the public works department and the railway companies for native labour, where natives could earn on average seven rupees a month. The planters were only paying them four rupees and making fortunes, but rather than raise wages to attract more labour, they introduced the inden-

ture system. The recruits were shown a table of piece rates in Calcutta and promised a life of ease and prosperity on the estates. Once there, they were forced to work nine hours a day, six days a week in slavish conditions, at abysmal piece rates, until the expiry of their four-year contracts. Even if they picked more tea, the planters paid them the same by merely raising the price of the rice with which they supplied their 'coolies' (thus effectively lowering wages and increasing profits).

By the mid-1860s, labourers were being recruited from outside Assam, packed into railway trucks (ten per cent died en route) and taken up to the plantations. Men, women and children were enticed, kidnapped and traded like cattle. Absconders were hunted down, publicly whipped and tortured like runaway slaves. Once on the estates (or 'tea gardens' as they were euphemistically called) the life expectancy of the workers was even less than that of slaves in the Caribbean; about half the labour force died within three years of arrival.

(*right*) 'Sifting tea in Assam', 1890s

By 1860, tea was being grown on 60 per cent of the plantation land, and Assam was producing a million pounds of tea a year. But production was still limited by shortage of labour, so the Raj planters petitioned the government to raise the land tax in order to flush the last peasants onto the plantations. Only one section of the labour force remained, those peasants growing opium

COMMODITIES

who had originally been encouraged to grow it by the British. In 1860, the government banned peasant production of opium while increasing production of opium on its own plantations. The peasants, who were addicted to opium (having been encouraged to grow it for years), were not only deprived of their single cash crop, but were forced to buy government opium at twice the old price. And to pay the price, they had to indenture themselves to the British tea companies.

Overall, the population of Assam doubled in the years between 1825 and 1870. All the work was done by native labour and financed by British capital, though a few missionaries were allowed to establish Christian schools for the natives and public schools for the Raj. British planters enclosed Assam, as the English aristocracy had enclosed England, and turned it into a plantation for tea-drinking Britons. The Raj had only an economic interest in India and made no attempt to adapt to its culture or traditions. The British went out to make their fortunes as soldiers, planters and agents, and once there, they transformed local traditions and institutions into easily managed and controlled units. The planters were idle enough to have plenty of leisure to play polo and cricket, bridge and billiards, to invent snooker and tiffin; while India became a nation of coolies so that ladies and gentlemen in Britain could sip tea, and reflect comfortably on the greatness of their empire and their Queen.

The final 30 years of the nineteenth century saw an

Tea planter's residence, India, c. 1885

shareholders 15 per cent dividends throughout the period. The railways, by now stretching all over the sub-continent, could bring labour in from remote areas, particularly from the poverty-stricken south. By 1900, there were half a million tea plantation workers. Conditions were appalling. Even civil servants on occasion protested. Sir George Campbell described the labour system as 'slavery' and Sir Bampfylde Fuller described it as the 'keeping of beasts in a menagerie'. The contract was itself described in a 1901 debate as

> 'a transaction by which, to put it rather bluntly, a man is often committed to Assam before he knows what he is doing, and is thereupon held to his promise for four years, with a threat of arrest and imprisonment if he fails to perform it. Conditions like these have no place in the ordinary law of master and servant. We have made them part of the law of British India at the instance and for the benefit of the planters of Assam.' (quoted in Guha, p. 41)

(left) coolies on a Ceylonese estate, c. 1880

Another administrator, Sir Henry Cotton, was forced to retire from his post of Chief Commissioner in 1902 because of his open criticism of the planters. In his autobiography published in 1911 he described the system thus:

> 'I knew of cases in which coolies in the fourth year of their agreement were not paid the higher rate of salary to which they were entitled. In other cases, rice was not provided at the statutory price and the subsistence allowance prescribed by law was not paid to sick coolies or pregnant women. Advances were often illegally debted against coolies, and labourers were thus bound hand and foot to the garden service. In some instances, only a few *annas* (or pence) found their way into the hands of a coolie as wages in the course of a whole year.' (quoted in Guha, p. 44)

The system worked, not because the natives were stupid, but because if they went on strike they were imprisoned; if they escaped they could be arrested without warrant,

enormous growth in the Assam tea industry. Tea acreage increased six times to 340,000 acres in 1900, and tea production increased from £12 million to £134 million in the same period. Although much of the processing was mechanized, neither then, nor even today, was there machinery which could replace human fingers as pluckers of tea. Since women's labour was, and is, cheaper than men's, from then on tea production was synonymous with the exploitation of women.

The opening of the Suez Canal in 1869 also cut transport costs. Tea cost 11d a pound to produce in 1870 but only 3d in 1913. Since it retailed at more than two shillings a pound, the profit margins were enormous. Between 1900 and 1914, 'the golden age of Assam tea', Assam was supplying half the world's market. Since the plantations, agency houses, fleets, and broking houses were all in British hands, the value of tea to the British economy was immense.

At this time, there were seven hundred miles of railway in Assam and Bengal alone. Coal was being mined locally, oil was being barrelled, and 14 sawmills provided the millions of chests necessary for the transport of the tea. Only part of the capital came from Britain. Most of it was provided from the profits of the system itself, which despite reinvestment still paid

COMMODITIES

and flogged and tortured by the planters. Neither did the coolies, once on the plantations, have any freedom of movement. They were not permitted to go to neighbouring tea gardens or even to neighbouring villages, and their daughters could not marry out of the plantation without the manager's permission. Most were locked into their hovels at night. The whole scene reminded Bampfylde Fuller of Uncle Tom's Cabin: 'I came across notices posted at river ferries and railway stations describing runaway coolies and offering rewards for their apprehension.' (Guha, p. 45) Although the workers were effectively enslaved, they had small plots of land on which to grow their food, with estate managers acting like Caribbean planters, taking native women as concubines, and ruling as local magistrates to their own advantage. Even after the legal right of planters to arrest runaways was abolished in 1906, the situation did not change. Nabin Bardaloi, an Indian small planter and reformer reported in 1919 that:

'A tea garden is like a small town by itself, with the barracks for labourers and the stately bungalows of the managers and their assistants. Nobody, not even the policemen can enter this kingdom without the manager's permission. A manager can assault a labourer, insult him, take girl after girl from the lines as his mistress, yet there will be none to dispute his actions or his authority. It is only at sometime when the manager's cruelty surpasses all bounds that the labourers set upon him and assault him. Had it not been for fear of Britishers and the guns and pistols they possess, and the fact that at their beck and call all the constabulary and magistracy of the district would come over there and punish the labourer, rioting would have occurred pretty frequently in these small domininions.' (quoted in Guha, p. 106)

Despite this, even though they risked their necks, wage agitation and strikes became increasingly common throughout the period. Strikers and runaway workers were supported by other Indians, and the solidarity thus built up became a crucial factor in improving conditions on the plantations. At the same time, the struggle continued outside the plantations, and the planters, to keep the Communist unions out, recognized the reformist, anti-strike, pro-government, Assam Tea Workers' Union. By the 1930s, however, it was clear to the British planters that they would have to go elsewhere. They stopped planting new bushes, allowed the estates to run down, and moved on to East Africa, if they could afford it.

After Independence in 1947, Assam was retained by India, and much of Bengal became East Pakistan (Bangladesh after 1971). The British were forced to sell their controlling interests in the estates to Indians, mostly Mawari traders from western India. Since the 1950s, the price of tea has dropped steadily. The tea bushes at the time of Independence were old, and estates were often exhausted. The Plantation Labour Act of 1951, which legislated for improved conditions, was everywhere ignored, partly because the labour force was not from Assam, illiterate and low caste and thus unorganized and incapable of fighting for its rights. Productivity has increased since the 1960s, though wage rates have dropped by 10 per cent. Today, only 10 per cent of the children attend schools and many are blind because they are malnourished. Hookworm, caused by poor sanitation and lack of footwear, is universal, as is anaemia which is caused by hookworm. Most of the tea workers suffer from malnutrition, tuberculosis, pneumonia and digestive diseases.

BRISK TEAS AND BRISK MONEY
Sri Lanka, now the biggest tea exporter in the world, began tea cultivation in the 1870s. The island, which had once comprised two separate kingdoms, the Tamil in the north and the Sinhalese in the south, had been occupied by the Dutch in 1621, and then by the British in 1815, who took over and expanded the Dutch coffee plantations. In the 1870s, a quarter of a million acres of coffee was destroyed by blight. Planters were bankrupted and land was extremely cheap. The government then began to promote tea growing, influenced by the success of the experiment in Assam.

LIPTON'S TEAS.

ONE OF LIPTON'S TEA-GARDENS CEYLON

Tea Merchant.
BY SPECIAL APPOINTMENT
TO HER MAJESTY.
THE QUEEN.

FINEST THE WORLD CAN PRODUCE
1/7 PER LB.
NO HIGHER PRICE.
RICH PURE & FRAGRANT
1/- and 1/4 PER LB.

LARGEST SALE IN THE WORLD

Chief Offices : City Road, London.   Branches and Agencies throughout the World.

Thomas Lipton, a Glasgow grocer, arrived in Sri Lanka in 1871 while on a world cruise, and bought dozens of the plantations at knockdown prices. He was an interesting man for a number of reasons, not least his obsession with 'cutting out the middleman', in the process demonstrating the financial advantages of 'vertical integration'. By taking over all the operations – management, processing, transport to the coast, shipping, blending, packaging and marketing, Lipton was able to cut the cost of tea to the consumer from 2/6d to 1/7d a pound. He also promoted his tea in a series of imaginative advertising campaigns, under the slogan 'From the tea garden to the teapot', as well as selling the first of all brand label teas under the poetic but meaning-less name of 'Orange Pekoe'. Lipton made a fortune from this move, and other companies quickly attempted to imitate his methods.

Brooke Bond was founded in 1861 and went public in 1892. Two Yorkshire brothers, the Tetleys, broke into the American market in the 1880s. Lyons was founded in 1886, opened its first teashop in 1894 to expand sales, and in 1920 was operating the largest tea packing and blending plant in the world. Ty-Phoo was first marketed as an invalid tea in 1905. All eventually were bought out by larger companies, but already by 1914 the monopoly of tea by a handful of British companies was complete.

In Sri Lanka as in India, Europeans paid no land tax, benefitted from public works schemes like roads and rail-

91

Muster of Coolies
MONERAKANDE ESTATE, CEYLON

LIPTON SERIES

Lipton's publicity photo spells out the company name with workers in formation, 1890s

ways, and received assistance in procuring labour. Low caste Tamil Hindus from the famine-stricken area of south India were recruited. As elsewhere, there were European superintendents, high caste Indian office staff, and gang leaders or *kangany*, who recruited, organized and paid the workforce, ran the truck shop, and lent the workers money. The labourers were housed in 'lines', which were (and are) like army barracks, divided into ten rooms (each 10′ by 12′) often with two or more families living in a single room. Being low caste, low paid, isolated on estates in the highlands, with no political voice, the estate Tamils were effectively enslaved on the plantations. Between 1841 when recruitment started, and 1849, a quarter of the Tamil population died:

> The miserable gangs of coolies of 1843 and 1845, with one or two women to 50 or 100 men, strangers in a strange land, ill-fed, ill-clothed, eating any garbage they came across . . . travelling over jungle paths sometimes with scarcely a drop of water to be found anywhere near for miles, and at other times knee deep the greatest part of the day in water, with the country all around a swamp, working on estates just reclaimed from the jungle, or in jungles about to be converted into estates, badly-housed and little understood by their employer. (Tanner, p. 10)

A further problem faced the Tamils. They were Hindu in a predominantly Buddhist country, and being low caste their plight was ignored, even by the long-established Tamil population on the north coast of Sri Lanka.

Before Independence in 1948, the British government had a contract system which obliged Sri Lanka to export goods at predetermined prices which were well below world market prices. This meant that commodities like rubber, coconuts and tea (which were, and still remain, the main cash crops of the island) were being sold for little more than the cost of production. Haunted by the spectre of nationalization, the tea companies, as in India, stopped planting new bushes and maintaining the estates, and attempted to increase production so that they could repatriate the profits, knowing that they would not be permitted to repatriate capital. Thus, at Independence, all the estates were run down and many had been abandoned. Had it not been for the Tamils on the estates, who had nowhere else to live or work, the tea industry in Sri Lanka might well have collapsed.

Although unionism spread after the 1940s and strikes were common on all the estates, the fact that women were paid lower wages than men for the same work was never challenged. At Independence, all estate Tamils were given the vote. Anger which should have been directed at the British was displaced by the majority Sinhalese against the defenceless Tamils. The estate Tamils lost their vote in 1949 on the grounds that they were immigrants. In 1964, the notorious Sirimavo-Shastri pact agreed that all estate Tamils would be 'repatriated' to south India. This was amended in 1974 by Mrs Bandaranaike and Mrs Ghandi, who agreed to the forcible repatriation of 525,000 estate Tamils, with 375,000 receiving Sri Lankan citizenship. As a consequence, 150,000 estate Tamils remain 'stateless' and they still provide a pool of cheap labour, a people without political rights in a country in which they and their ancestors have lived for 100 years. So far, 300,000 Tamils have been 'repatriated' to India – a country they have never seen, where they have no land, no work and no families.

Low tea prices in the 1960s and food shortages caused appalling misery in both Sri Lanka and India. In 1973, a Granada TV World in Action programme aroused widespread awareness of the conditions on Brooke Bond estates in those countries, where old people and children were dying of malnutrition. Brooke Bond claimed in its defence that the estates were making no profits (but that year, Brooke Bond worldwide showed a profit of £16 million). Even so, Brooke Bond's tea sales dropped

significantly, and the company was forced to improve conditions. This also speeded up the nationalization of foreign owned estates.

In 1972, a land reform and nationalization programme was announced by Mrs Bandaranaike's 'socialist' government, though foreign companies, as always, demanded 'compensation' (though why they should have been compensated for ruining the soil and ruthlessly exploiting Tamil labour for more than a hundred years, was not explained). More than 60 per cent of the tea estates were nationalized. The repatriation of many estate Tamils, however, created an acute labour shortage, which was made up by Sinhalese men and women. More than half the estate workers are now casual labourers – women

Tea weighing, Sri Lanka, 1980s

tend to go to the estates, men to the cities. Until 1984, men were paid more (35p per day) than women (30p per day). In that year, strike action on the estates won equal pay – even so, there is still a clear sexual division of labour on the estates, with almost all the plucking done by women and the supervisory jobs being held by men. 'Free housing' still means the nineteenth century 'lines'. 'Free schooling' means 60 children to a class with no books or equipment, often being taught in a foreign language – Sinhalese. Few children attend, anyway, because the schools are often miles from the estates and because the girls start work at the age of ten. Few women can read or write, or even read the scales on the weighing machines. There are 'dispensaries' on the estates which supply little more than Disprin. Hospitals are miles away and most women only see them when they are giving birth. The final indignity inflicted on the workers, is that when they die they 'are actually buried beside the paths, between the bushes where they have toiled all their lives'. (Selbourne, 1983)

Violence against the Tamils broke out in 1956. Hundreds of Tamils were killed and 25,000 fled to the old Tamil kingdom on the north part of the island. Violence erupted again in 1977, when Hindu temples were sacked and widespread rape, assault and murder was reported. In 1981, the government-controlled police force went on the rampage in Jaffna, the ancient Tamil capital, burning the market, Tamil newspaper offices and Jaffna Public Library – which contained an irreplaceable collection of Tamil historical and cultural artefacts. The President of the Ghandhiyam Society, which worked for Tamil refugees, was murdered in prison in 1983 along with more than 50 other Tamils. About half of the 140,000 Tamils who remained in the area around Colombo lost their houses and 100,000 people fled to refugee camps; officially, 350 died in the streets, but since the government censors all information, the figure is probably closer to several thousand.

Disenfranchised, murdered, assaulted, imprisoned, exploited, made to speak a 'foreign language', a religious minority discriminated against in education and employment – the plight of the Tamils is an extreme case of the plight of all labour that is commodified and shipped into another country to grow crops for foreign capital.

THE CUP THAT CHEERS

Picture once again the popular image of the tea picker – a smiling face, dressed in traditional costume, adorned with jewellery, working in the sunshine in one of the most beautiful landscapes in the world. The reality, however, is quite different. Women are restricted to the lowest paid jobs like plucking, sifting and weeding. Officially, they are allowed to begin work at the age of ten as 'child labour'. Many, however, begin work when they are younger, because their parents are too poor to afford schooling.

The smiling face in the picture will also be completely responsible for looking after her family. Often, she will be the sole breadwinner. The eight hour day she officially works, does not include walking to the 'tea garden'. If she is lucky, she will be an estate worker and will get up at 4 a.m. If she lives in the village and is 'casual' she will rise at 3 a.m. She fetches water, often from a distant source, makes a fire, prepares breakfast and a midday meal, feeds her man (if he is there) and her children when they wake. She takes her children to school or to the crêche, before reporting for work at 7 a.m. The work she does all day is monotonous, repetitive and backbreaking. Because there are two monsoon periods in Sri Lanka, she often works in pouring rain with no protective clothing except, perhaps, a fertilizer bag over her head and shoulders (which she must pay for), and with her hands bandaged because of sores caused by pesticides.

At the noon break, she waits in line to have her tea weighed. Then she goes to the crêche to feed her baby, often suckling the baby while eating her meal, before returning to work at 1 a.m. Three hours of monotonous drudgery follows, sometimes more if the tips are flourishing. She then carries her basket to the weighing shed, where she sorts it for twigs or coarse leaves. She may wait there with other workers for up to an hour. If she lives on the estate it may take an hour to get home, if she lives in a village it can easily take twice as long.

Once home, she collects firewood and fetches water, makes a fire, prepares a meal, and nurses her baby before feeding her other children and her man. Sometimes men and children help collect wood, and daughters from the age of nine are expected to help with the children and the housework. She is unlikely to be in bed before 10 p.m.

An estate woman can expect six hours of sleep, a village woman as little as four. Unmarried women rarely know about contraception, and often they are left with the entire responsibility for any children they conceive. The smiling picker, if a mother of several children, will be sterilized through 'family planning' schemes which aim to terminate fertility rather than control it. Women are paid 500 rupees (about £15) if they are sterilized, men are paid half that for a vasectomy. Thus men compel their women to have the operation.

The smiling woman will have gynaecological problems and stomach disorders due to insanitary conditions and lack of unpolluted drinking water. In the highlands, women have tuberculosis, colds, chest pains, pneumonia and other respiratory problems. Since the hospitals are remote, they rely on Disprin for all their ailments. Although maternity wards are available in local hospitals, they are often only reached with difficulty. Maternity benefit is normally collected by the men, who often drink it away or use it to settle their gambling debts.

Village women are liable to be laid off at the end of any day, and to be left without any income for long periods of time. Often, because they are so poor, they agree to work overtime. But, by a mean device, they receive a declining rate of return for every basket they bring in over the norm. The norm takes no account of seasonal variation in the harvest, so in lean months women have to work harder to reach the norm. Bonuses in lean months are also lower, so they have to work even harder to earn even less.

Plantation work, under these conditions, is little more than slavery. The workers are permanently in debt and are forced to buy food from shops owned by the plantations.

> It is a particularly captive form of wage slavery, and the barracks in which the workers are housed symbolize their captivity in the very conditions of existence. They are nothing more than cells – [though] I think that many cells are probably more liveable places than line rooms, since the rooms are windowless, airless and floorless and water runs down their frontage. In their inner rooms . . . it is actually impossible to see the people in them. It is not even possible to see people's eyes, so strong is the blackness in which the men, women and children live. (Selbourne, 1983)

THE RUBBISH IN THE TEA BAG

Tea was first planted in Kenya in 1924, but expansion only began in the 1950s when British companies switched investment from India and Sri Lanka to East Africa, to take advantage of lower taxes. Kenya is not ideally suited to the production of quality tea. But in the postwar period, lower quality teas were promoted by aggressive advertising campaigns directed at the working housewife, and used as 'filler' in packet teas and tea bags, so the astringent, high caffeine and tannin content teas of East Africa began to take up a bigger share of the market.

After Independence in 1963, the government left the transnationals alone. Smallholders were encouraged to grow tea as a cash crop; half of Kenya's tea is now grown on plots less than an acre in size. The African-owned estates are bigger. But the industry is still dominated by transnationals like Brooke Bond and Finlays, with their 100,000-acre estates. Because these are sited on the best tea growing soils, are partly mechanized, use pesticides and fertilizers, and benefit most from the government-sponsored, foreign-financed, irrigation schemes, production per acre on them is twice that of the smaller estates.

Conditions are better than they are in Sri Lanka; there are dispensaries, hospitals (which do not, however, provide maternity care), stores with goods at government-controlled prices, and compulsory primary schooling. However, many workers still live in lines, with whole families in a single room. Earnings are higher (51p to 82p a day), but even so, a family of five spends all its income on food; malnutrition and pneumonia are still common. Few workers belong to unions, because strikes are illegal and unknown. In order to control an inflation rate of 20 per cent, the government set wage increases at 10 per cent, which suits the transnationals, since they control external marketing and cream off the difference.

In Malawi, there is a dictatorship where trade unions are banned. Estate workers earn 15p a day (the price of a loaf of bread). Most of the estates are still owned by companies like Booker McConnell and Brooke Bond. One for example, the British owned Ruo Estates Holding, has assets of £1.8 million and showed overall profits of £400,000 in 1978, though its 4,000 workers, many of them young children, receive no share of this. Workers receive 'free meals' (maize porridge), with fish on pay days to entice them back for another week. Skin complaints, ulcers, malnutrition, influenza and pneumonia are common. A third of the children die within a couple of months of birth. Adults can expect to be dead at 40. There are 'schools' with a couple of teachers for several hundred children. The children dress in rags and have no shoes, while the companies protest that they are not permitted to pay higher wages for fear of offending Banda's tyrannical government.

All this has to be seen in a context of current world overproduction, which means that even those countries with the will to pay their workers better are unable to do so because the world price is so low. The only way of improving the world price on a long term basis would be to have an international tea agreement which would restrict production. Such an agreement was attempted in the 1930s to carve up the market between Dutch and British colonial producers, but it was not successful because of the world recession. In the 1960s, the idea was revived but without success – in part, because of consumer country opposition, but also because of competition between producer countries. While it is in the interest of the old established producers to adhere to quotas because they cannot increase production, it is in the interest of new producers, particularly in East Africa, to increase production by extending cultivation. This overproduction means that the price paid at auction, whether in Mombassa, Colombo, Calcutta or London, although reflecting occasional cyclical highs, has continued to decline in real terms against the dollar and sterling. The only teas to obtain good prices are the high quality teas, like Darjeeling, for which there is always a market; there is continuous overproduction of lower grade teas.

International trade and the British market are still controlled by four British companies – Brooke Bond, Cadbury Schweppes, Allied Lyons and the Co-operative Wholesale Society. All compete on the high street, producing cheap teas which are sold as 'loss leaders' on supermarket shelves. Only Brooke Bond and the Co-op still own estates abroad; the others rely on world overproduction of tea, which enables them to buy it at auction at low prices.

Unilever, through its subsidiaries Brooke Bond and Lipton's, now controls 35 per cent of the world tea market, 60 per cent of the packet market in India, and 40 per cent of the British retail market. Brooke Bond's

becomes ... ... note in the company accounts.

Unilever owns 39 subsidiaries in the UK. These employ around 69,000 people, producing food, plastics, animal feeds and toiletries, and working in the company's packaging and transport businesses. The contribution of individual subsidiaries to the company's financial well-being makes a small mark in the overall picture: the British subsidiaries are included in the report and accounts as part of 'European Community countries'.

market shelves. Oxfam allegedly markets Third World tea in Britain, but few people have ever seen a packet.

Finally, in the post-revolutionary China of Deng Xiaoping, the tea industry has developed in two directions. Peasants have been encouraged to produce the finer traditional teas and are permitted to sell any surplus above their quota on the new open markets. The other trend, promoted by the Chinese government which needs foreign capital, is to produce black 'filler' dust for export to the West.

Thus the circle is now complete: India was used to undercut China, Africa was brought in to undercut India and Sri Lanka, and now cheap black tea dust, is mass produced in Yunan Province, to buy dollars and sterling, by women who work in conditions of dreary monotony for some of the lowest factory wages in the world.

policy of 'vertical integration' has also enabled it to profit from the low price of tea, since it controls everything from the plantations to processing, packaging and advertising. It also owns broking houses, which means it makes an additional profit on commission sales to other companies. It employs 22,000 workers in India, 12,500 in Kenya and several thousand in Tanzania and Malawi. Over half the estate workers are casual and therefore they do not qualify for housing and medical care. Most workers are affected by hookworm and anaemia, and three quarters are malnourished. Few children receive free milk and supplementary food, and only 12 per cent go to the company school. Yet 'conditions', according to the company, 'are always improving'. In 1978, its estate workers were earning around 46p a day, its British workers about £60 a week (£20 below the national average), while the chairman, Sir Humphrey Prideux, was earning £25,000 plus dividends on his shares. That is to say, even after tax he earned more in a week than Brooke Bond pickers earn in a year.

Some countries, like Zimbabwe, have attempted to bypass the transnationals by packing and marketing their own brand name teas, but they are starved of capital to develop their industries. They have also been blocked by the transnationals who refuse to sell their tea on super-

Tea tasting, Sri Lanka, 1980s

Coffee Empires

*Economic history and the division of labour in society
is brought about by the exchange of commodities, and
based on the antithesis of the countryside and the city.*
Karl Marx, *Capital*, vol. I, ch. 14, section 4

The division of labour between the countryside and the city is the historical basis of economic development. As industry evolved in the towns and cities, labour was drawn from the land, while the labour force which remained was forced to produce more foodstuffs and raw materials to support the urban population. The historic divisions between town and country in European societies therefore anticipated the divisions between the 'developed', European powers and the producers of raw commodities in the Third World. At the same time, the commercial and manufacturing sectors always attempted to accumulate surpluses in order to develop their industries, and to raise their living standards. Insofar as they controlled the mode of production they paid as little as they could for raw materials and charged as much as they could for finished goods.

For this reason, throughout history, the terms of trade have increasingly moved against the producers of raw materials – whether individual peasants and farmers or Third World countries in general – because the price of products like tools, machinery, manufactured and processed goods, has steadily increased relative to the price of raw commodities. Peasants in Third World countries, therefore, have been compelled to work harder and to grow more cash crops for export, in order to sustain the flow of capital and goods from the 'advanced' economies in the West.

In this context, the story of coffee is exemplary. Because it can only be grown in tropical and subtropical climates, it is a cash crop of immense importance in the Third World, where 20 countries depend on it for over a quarter of their export earnings, and ten for over half. The annual value of the world coffee crop in 1985 was $15 billion (exactly how much of this gets back to the growers, we shall see). As an earner of foreign currency, coffee is the second most valuable commodity after oil. Over 60 per cent of it is produced in Latin America; 30 per cent, mostly unwashed *arabicas* and some *robustas* is grown in Brazil. About 15 per cent, higher quality mild, washed *arabicas* comes from Colombia. Although coffee was first established in the Americas as a plantation crop, today more than 60 per cent of the world's coffee is produced by peasant labour on smallholdings.

As we have seen, the development of early colonial agriculture was firmly controlled by the core powers. They selected the crops, transported the labour, and ran the operation from start to finish. In the case of sugar cane, the early links between the tropical growers and the northern consumers were broken when substitutes that could be grown in temperate climates were discovered. But in the case of a handful of crops like coffee, tea and cocoa, production in temperate climates has never supplied a substitute; thus, potentially, they remain one of the few bargaining counters in the Third World's trade with its old masters.

The ability, therefore, to bargain over commodity prices (and to win), or to industrialize, are the two tactics open to Third World countries if their dependency on the 'developed' industrial economies is to end. But, histori-

COMMODITIES

(*top right*) Bagging coffee, Colombia, 1980s

come from existing exports, or from loans based on the security of commodity exports. If profits are low, Third World countries are forced to depend on loans from foreign banks and governments, who thereby establish a lever over them.

This kind of financial and market control, neocolonialism as opposed to direct colonialism, first developed in Latin American countries during the 1820s, when they fought for independence against their colonial overlords, the Portuguese and the Spanish. In 1823, the American President, James Monroe stated that 'the American continents . . . are henceforth not to be considered as subject to future colonization by any European power'. The Monroe Doctrine (as this position was called) suited Britain well. It meant that Britain had an ally in keeping Latin America open to British trade; Britain's command of Atlantic trade after the Battle of Trafalgar in 1805 meant that no other European power was better poised to seize the commercial opportunities which an independent Latin American offered. In 1825, Canning, the British Foreign Secretary (and significantly, MP for Liverpool) recognized the new republics of Argentina, Mexico and Colombia, as well as Brazil, under its constitutional Emperor, Pedro I.

Thus, increasingly, Latin America came under the influence of British banks which by 1914 still controlled over 60 per cent of foreign investment in the continent. Countries like Argentina, Uruguay and Colombia provided beef, minerals, coffee, and so on; the British provided credit, and a commercial and industrial infrastructure. Foreign loans were also provided by French, German and US bankers. Throughout the twentieth century, the situation has changed continuously. The Wall Street crash of 1929 and the Great Depression crippled Latin America. The prices of its commodity exports dropped and supplies of foreign capital dried up, creating massive problems both in the countryside and the cities. During the Second World War, most Latin American countries, cut off from northern markets and suppliers, were forced to industrialize. Most of the capital needed for this came from the profits of existing agricultural and industrial enterprises within Latin America, but

cally, this struggle against dependency has been limited by certain factors. Mineral extraction has generally remained under the control of the core powers, because they had already developed their technologies, and because they already controlled the market for processed minerals. Other commodities like cotton were increasingly brought under white control; first, Indian looms were smashed, then slaves were taken to the southern states of America to grow cotton for British mills. Other crops, like tobacco, can also be grown in temperate climates which undermines the bargaining power of tropical producers. Most vegetable products deteriorate in transit. Since the core powers have always controlled transport links (shipping, railway systems, ports, and cheap air freight) as well as preservation methods (whether by the use of sugar, salt, refrigeration or canning), they have come to control the marketing of most Third World perishable commodities as well. Because of this, Third World countries have increasingly attempted to diversify their economies. Most have an early history of supplying a single commodity which, when prices fell, bankrupted planters and merchants and undermined the whole economy. Also, plantation agriculture, like mining, has always been a finite operation. Eventually, the soil and the mineral deposits are exhausted. The capital to diversify, however, can only

increasing amounts came from the US. After the war, the shift from agriculture to manufacture paralleled the large scale movement of population from the countryside to the cities. Latin American countries became increasingly dependent on imported industrial equipment, consumer goods and foreign capital, creating, in the process, massive debt problems, which we look at in more detail in chapter seven.

Coffee production, inevitably, has been affected by these developments, as we shall see. But first we need to look at what coffee is, and to explain how it arrived in Latin America in the first place.

THE ORIGINS OF COFFEE

This little fruit is the source of happiness and wit.
Dr William Harvey, 1657, quoted in Jacob, p. 48

The historical popularity of coffee is, in part, due to its delightful taste and aroma; but coffee also contains caffeine, a powerful drug. In some ways, coffee is like alcohol: its effects and taste are immediately attractive to many adults and like alcohol, it plays an important and often essential role in most people's patterns of drug abuse. Both drugs, of course, are often used together – alcohol as a downer and coffee as an upper. Coffee was also the first drug introduced to Europe, capable of extending the working and waking day almost indefinitely. To the consumer it has always been expensive – even coffee produced by plantation slaves in Brazil was never cheap – but it is a drug for which northern addicts, since 1650, have been prepared to pay high prices. Clubs and institutions were created for the consumption of coffee, and in many instances, those institutions came to have a profound influence on economic and political events: insurance companies, commodity and stock exchanges, and a daily press emerged from the London coffee houses – The French Revolution, the Boer War, and the Alaska gold rush were all speeded up by coffee.

Coffee is not an easy crop to grow. Like sugar, it murders the soil, and like sugar it requires well-drained and irrigated, virgin soils with constant manual hoeing, weeding, watering and protection from pests for the first

year. The berries (or cherries, as they are usually called), from which the coffee bean is obtained are first picked after three years, but the bush does not peak until the sixth year. Thereafter, production slowly declines for about 40 years, at which point the bush is finished. Harvesting, separating the ripe red cherries from the green berries and twigs, is a skilled and arduous task. The coffee bush is also extremely vulnerable to climatic shifts; one year, a bush may produce four and a half pounds of coffee, the next year less than half a pound. There are two main types of coffee. *Arabica*, native to Ethiopia, is a mild coffee which now supplies 70 per cent of the world total. *Robusta*, native to the African equatorial belt, is now mostly grown in Africa and Asia; it gives a lower quality coffee, but yields more soluble, or instant coffee, per pound of raw green beans.

FROM THE LEVANT TO THE COFFEE HOUSE

Coffee, like sugar, was an Arab invention. In 575 AD it was being cultivated in the Yemen, where the Arabs used it as a food and a medicine. It was not until the fourteenth century that the processes of extraction of the bean from

Arab trader, 17th century

A

VOYAGE

TO

ARABIA Fœlix

Through the

EASTERN OCEAN and the *Streights* of the RED-SEA, being the Firſt made by the *French* in the Years 1708, 1709, and 1710.

Together with

A Particular Account of a Journey from MOCHA to MUAB, or MOWAHIB, the Court of the King of YAMAN, in their Second Expedition, in the Years 1711, 1712, and 1713.

Alſo a Narrative

Concerning the Tree and Fruit of COFFEE. Collected from the Obſervations of thoſe who made the laſt Voyage; and an Hiſtorical Treatiſe of the Original and Progreſs of COFFEE, both in *Aſia* and *Europe*.

Tranſlated from the FRENCH.

To which is added,

An Account of the CAPTIVITY of Sir *HENRY MIDDLETON* at *Mokha*, by the TURKS, in the Year 1612; and his Journey from thence to *Zenan*, or *Sanaa*, the Capital of the Kingdom of *Yaman*, with ſome Additions, particularly relating to that Country and the *Red-Sea*.

LONDON:

Printed for E. SYMON, over-againſt the *Royal-Exchange*, in *Cornhill*, 1732.

the fruit ('hulling'), as well as drying, roasting, grinding and finally brewing with boiling water, were all combined to create coffee (from the Arabic word *qahwah*) as we know it today.

Given the prohibition of alcohol within the Moslem empire, the taste for coffee spread very rapidly after it had arrived in Mecca around 1400. Fifty years later it was being drunk everywhere in Arabia; prices were so high that coffee production was increased over much of the Yemen. Thence, it was taken by pilgrims to distant parts of the Moslem empire. Arab princes recognized the value of this lucrative drug and prohibited the export of seeds, so production remained confined to the Yemen, while the roasted berries were sealed in medicinal caskets – which is how coffee first reached Europe from the Levant.

Wherever coffee went, it was greeted with criticism and praise while the theologians and pharmacists debated its qualities. Theologians were worried that coffee might be as pleasurable as alcohol and wanted to ban it. Pharmacists wanted to sell it, and celebrated its alleged benefits. It was prohibited almost everywhere soon after it arrived, but soon legalized so that import and purchase taxes on it could be levied.

Arab coffee was very strong and was drunk black. Sugar was added surprisingly late, in Cairo in 1625, thus creating a different drink and a different combination of potential addictions (sugar and caffeine). In 1600, an English traveller to the Levant, Thomas Biddulph, commented on the extraordinary Arab addiction to coffee:

'Their most common drink is *coffa*, which is a black kind of drink, made of a kind of pulse like pease, . . . which being ground in the mill, and boiled in water, they drink it as hot as they can suffer it, which they find to agree very well with them against the crudities [indigestion].' (quoted in Purchas, vol. VIII, p. 266)

The way that people combined coffee with other drugs also aroused Biddulph's interest: 'Some of them will also drink opium, which maketh them forget themselves and talk idly of castles in the air, as though they saw visions and heard revelations.' (ibid)

Coffee was also associated with sex and hedonism, according to another traveller, George Sandys:

'Many of the coffee men keep beautiful boys who serve as stales [prostitutes] to procure them customers.' (quoted in Purchas, vol. VIII, p. 146)

But this combination of drugs and other pleasures was not to reach England. Coffee arrived alone, probably brought in by Dutch merchants. It was first sold as a medicine and praised by that maverick genius Dr William Harvey, who in his will left 65 pounds of the miracle bean to be shared once a month by the fellows of the College of Physicians in London.

The speed of coffee addiction is well attested by its arrival in mercantile England. It was brought back from the Levant by a London merchant, along with his Greek servant, Pasqua Rosee. Pasqua made an excellent cup of coffee and the merchant was inundated with friends at the hour he was known to drink coffee; to recover his privacy, he lent Pasqua money to open a coffee house in 1652. One of the wittiest and most interesting free thinkers of the period, Sir Henry Blount, frequented this establishment and defended coffee against all critics: 'Drunkenness [Sir Henry] much exclaimed against, but when coffee first came in he was a great upholder of it, and hath ever been a constant frequenter of coffee houses' (Aubrey, p. 132).

But Sir Henry Blount was a well-known rogue and a rake who had been 'called to the bar for spreading abroad that abominable and dangerous doctrine that it was far cheaper and safer to lie with common wenches than ladies of quality'. So from the beginning, coffee was associated with licentiousness –while tea was associated with civility and chastity.

Coffee was also, this time correctly, associated with sedition. Sir John Harrington, the radical political genius, presented and tested his republican models of government in a London coffee house, the Turk's Head, until he was arrested and taken to die in the Tower of

London coffee house,
late 17th century

London after the Restoration of the English monarchy in 1661. The 'free and open society of ingenious gentlemen' at the Turk's Head was witnessed one evening by Samuel Pepys as he waited for the tides to turn.

Coffee houses fulfilled a number of important functions, not least, given the shortage of small change in Commonwealth England, the tokens issued by the coffee houses were widely circulated around the City.

Coffee's first influential defender in England was a

judge with medical pretensions, Walter Rumsey, who published *A Defence of Coffee* in 1657, insisting that coffee dissolved corns, corrected convulsions, fits upon the temples of the posterior [syphilis], as well as 'cooling those blisters upon the liver that's procured by excessive drinking'. He also defended it on the grounds that

> whereas formerly apprentices and clerks used to take their morning's draught in ale, beer, or wine, which, by the dizziness they cause in the brain, made many unfit for business, they use now to play the goodfellows in this wakeful and civil drink. (Rumsey, p. 9)

At the Restoration there were already a dozen coffee houses in London; ten years later, there were at least 100. In 1674, the English brewers, worried by this Levantine import, stirred up the debate with a spurious pamphlet, *The Women's Petition Against Coffee*: 'At these houses meet all sorts of animals, whence follows the production of a thousand monstrous opinions and absurdities'. Furthermore, it alleged, the men had lost interest in sex:

> 'The dull fellows want a spur now, rather than a bridle . . . the occasion of which . . . we can attribute to nothing more than the excessive use of that newfangled, abominable, heathenish liquor called coffee, which has so eunacht our husbands, and crippled our gallants, that they have become as impotent as age, and as unfruitful as those deserts whence that unhappy berry is to be brought.' (*The Women's Petition Against Coffee*, quoted in *Old English Coffee Houses*, 1954, p. 11)

In 1675, Charles II rashly attempted to suppress the coffee houses because of 'the idle and disaffected persons therein' who published 'diverse false, malicious and scandalous reports . . . to the defamation of His Majesty's Government, and to the disturbance of the peace and tranquillity of the realm'. But the proprietors quickly pointed out that they had already paid duty on their coffee, and that if the trade was stopped, the spendthrift monarch would lose his excise. The king relented, and withdrew his ill-considered proclamation after 11 days.

For the next 100 years, coffee houses were at the centre of English intellectual life. Dryden pontificated for 40 years at Will's in Covent Garden; 'the worst conversation I ever remember', was Swift's comment on the place. But Defoe was more impressed:

> Here is the best of conversation till midnight, where you will see the nobility sitting familiarly and talking with the same freedom as if they had left their quality and degrees at home. Here a stranger tastes with pleasure the universal liberty of speech of the English nation. (Defoe, *A Tour Through the Whole Island of Great Britain*, 1724)

Steele launched the *Tatler*, once an intelligent newspaper, at Will's in 1709, moving to different coffee houses like The Grecian, Sir Isaac Newton's haunt, when covering more intellectual matters. Pope's favourite coffee house, Button's, was frequented by the editors of the *Guardian*, and by Addison and Steele when they started the *Spectator*. From such establishments, the taste for coffee percolated into society, though society women remained wedded to tea. Street sellers, using coffee house dregs and various adulterants, sold it with sugar and milk to all and sundry, and grocers roasted and packed it for wealthy customers. One factor though, always limited its appeal. Few people in England ever learned the secret of making a drinkable cup of coffee. The magazine *Punch* ran a joke in 1902: 'Look here, steward. if this is coffee I want tea; but if this is tea, then I wish for coffee'. Even today, this is echoed by victims of the British indifference to the art of coffee making.

FROM THE LEVANT TO AMERICA

The coffee bush is without doubt one of the most beautiful shrubs with which Nature has beautified this land. When spring comes, Zephyrus blows away the mists and then the mountains offer to the eyes and soul the joyous image of an Earthly Paradise. For flowering coffee bushes are the most seductive sight. Their white flowers contrast with their green leaves, and the sugar in their nectar summons a myriad butterflies, gold,

silver, emerald and ruby hummingbirds, and diligent bees, from the ancient forests, to share that which the Universal Mother, beautiful Nature gives to all her children.
Tussac, *Flora des Antilles*, 1808

Initially, the coffee monopoly of the Arab merchants was as restrictive as the tea monopoly of the hong. Even so, coffee was smuggled out of Mecca and grown in Mysore in the sixteenth century, though these bushes only supplied the Mughal princes. Elsewhere, traders were still dependent on Arab suppliers or Venetian middlemen, who had been selling coffee in Italy since 1600. It was from Alexandria, Constantinople, Beirut, Mocha and Acra that the English and Dutch first obtained their coffee. The Dutch managed to smuggle a coffee plant out of Mocha, the only port on the Red Sea in which they were permitted to trade; it was cultivated under glass in Holland in 1616 and in Sri Lanka after 1658. But coffee is a difficult plant to cultivate, and these experimental plantings were not initially successful. More important was the planting of coffee by the Dutch on Java in 1696. From there it was taken to Timor, Sumatra and the Celebes, and by 1720 these islands were suppling the Dutch with most of their coffee. In 1706 they transplanted seedlings to the Amsterdam Botanical Garden, the source of the first plants to be taken to the Americas.

The French also experimented with the bean, but predictably failed in Dijon, when they discovered that the plant could not survive frosts. It was a Dutch plant sent by the States General to Louis XIV in 1714 which provided the seeds of the French coffee industry. The next year, these seeds were planted in Réunion off Southern Africa and cultivated with slave labour. From that plant too, came the seedlings which were transported in an epic voyage in 1723 from Bordeaux to Martinique by an ambitious courtier, the Chevalier Gabriel de Clieu. The ship on which he sailed was pursued by pirates and almost shipwrecked. The ship was becalmed and water was rationed; then de Clieu gave his own drinking water to the dying seedlings, before they arrived, parched, in the Caribbean. Myth suggests that

one of these seedlings was the ancestor of all Latin American bushes, though since coffee was established in Haiti and San Domingo ten years earlier, this is probably nonsense. But Martinique was important in demonstrating the possibilities of coffee growing. By 1800, there were 19 million coffee bushes on that small island alone. It was these plantations which were seen and praised by F. de Tussac, the French botanist, who stressed the economic advantages of coffee growing:

De Clieu watering his seedlings

It is, after sugar, the most profitable of crops, and one can produce it with only a few black slaves – indeed it is the only tropical agriculture which could be undertaken by whites, for the climate in the mountains where it is grown is like that of Europe. But an insurmountable obstacle which fashionable philanthropists and opponents of slavery have not considered is that the price of a white man's wages in the Caribbean far exceeds the price of a cup of coffee. If we want cheap coffee we must have slaves. (Tussac, 1808)

COMMODITIES

It took time for the Martinique plants to propagate, and until the 1740s most of Europe's coffee still came from Mocha. The Dutch had destroyed half the coffee crop in Java in 1738 in order to hold up prices, but Britain, 'the nation of shopkeepers', wanted to expand markets. East India Company ships carrying pilgrims from India to Mecca loaded coffee at Mocha. At the height of the early coffee boom, over 30 ships a year, half of them British, were loading coffee there for the London market.

By 1700, there were over 2,000 coffee houses in London, paying small fortunes in rents to astute landlords. By now, the conversation had shifted from republican politics to commerce:

(*right*) Lloyd's coffee room, 1798

> The city coffee houses have been for some years filled with people whose fortunes depend on the Bank [of England, the] East India [Company], or some other stock. Every new fund to these, is like a new mortgage to a usurer . . . Here around the Exchange are to be found merchants, sharks, speculators and others of that type. (Swift, 'The Conduct of One's Allies', in *Works*, vol. VI, p. 53)

It was in Garraway's, where tea was first sold in England at 50 shillings a pound, that the Hudson Bay Company held its sales by an inch of candle (the 'candle auction'), and where the South Sea Company scheme was first floated for gullible gamblers. Lloyds, founded in 1688 in Tower Street, was the market for secondhand ships, though it was not until 1730, when the landlord first issued his famous List, which gave all the shipping news, exchange rates and prices, that it became exclusively reserved for insurance brokers. The Virginia and Maryland, where slaves were auctioned, became the Baltic Exchange after 1744. Jonathan's, 'the general mart of stock jobbers', became the Stock Exchange in the eighteenth century, and the Jerusalem was the base of the East India Company speculators.

The early coffee houses attempted to control gambling, but gambling was fundamental to the discourse of merchants and speculators alike. Before long, particular coffee houses in London became gambling clubs where aristocrats like the Earl of Carlisle could lose £10,000 in a night's play. By 1800, coffee was the most popular non-alcoholic drink throughout most of Europe, Scandinavia and the Americas. It was at this time that the enlightened despot, Gustavus III of Sweden, hearing the interminable arguments about the relative dangers and benefits of tea and coffee, determined to settle the question. He ordered that two condemned criminals awaiting execution should be reprieved; their sentences were mitigated. One was ordered to drink vast quantities of coffee, the other of tea. The College of Physicians was to dissect them after they had died and to pronounce judgement on the dangers of the drugs. But the experiment did not work. One by one, the physicians died; the judge died, and the king was assassinated. Both criminals lived to a ripe old age.

After that date, no one attempted again to ban coffee, and it was not until the twentieth century that the dangers of coffee drinking were clearly established. Although relatively harmless to most people in small quantities (four cups a day), large doses of caffeine produce palpitations, high blood pressure, sleeplessness and probably cancer of the pancreas. The dangers of coffee are also enhanced when it is used with tobacco. But compared to some other drugs like opium, heroin, valium and cocaine, the side effects of coffee are not particularly

after the abolition of slavery. The slave trade to Brazil continued until the 1850s and slavery was not finally abolished there until the 1880s. As sugar cane growing became less profitable, the more 'progressive' Brazilian slave owners, particularly in the States of São Paulo, Rio and Paraná, which offered rich *terra roxa* soils and an ideal climate for intensive coffee agriculture, moved into coffee. The coffee blight in Sri Lanka in the 1870s gave a further boost to Brazilian production. The building of railways in the 1890s into the Brazilian interior, particularly around São Paulo opened up vast territories for coffee production. This development, financed by British capital, encouraged further British investment in the Brazilian coffee industry, making it, by 1900, the most efficient and cost-effective coffee growing area in the world.

Brazil is an enormous country of eight and a half million square miles, which is twice as big as Europe. Eighty per cent of its land area is cultivable. It has vast reserves of oil, gas, hydroelectric power, iron, diamonds and bauxite. Half the world's hardwood forests cover two thirds of the country. It is a leading producer of coffee, sugar, soya beans, tobacco, corn, cotton and bananas, as well as being the major rice growing area outside Asia. It is now the leading Latin American producer of cars, ships, steel, aeroplanes, cement and computers. Its population of 135 million is increasing rapidly; yet a quarter of the population is malnourished and poverty abounds, particularly in the cities. The depredations of the land have also created severe ecological problems not simply for Brazil, but potentially for the planet as a whole. Coffee, in many ways, was the motor of these developments.

When the Portuguese first attempted to settle Brazil in the 1520s, there were perhaps two million Indians living there. Today, despite ostensible government policy to protect them, the last survivors are being hunted out and shot. Officially, 200,000 are said to survive, but the figure is certainly much lower than this. Indians were pressed into service to collect brazilwood dyes and brazil nuts, or to work as slaves on the new sugar plantations, but they escaped or died in servitude. So, over the next

(left) **Satirical print of Frederick the Great, who attempted to suppress coffee drinking in Prussia: he orders a lackey to remove a wall poster depicting him as a grinder of coffee beans**

terrifying. Used carefully and prepared properly, coffee is an admirable component of civilized life. Beethoven had 60 beans to a cup, 20 times a day; Balzac worked 18 hours a day on four pints of thick, black coffee; both these men died in their fifties, but Voltaire drank more than either of them, and died aged 84.

THE ARRIVAL OF COFFEE IN BRAZIL

Between 1850 and 1950, the words 'Brazil' and 'coffee' were almost synonymous; for the whole of that period, Brazil was supplying between a half and 70 per cent of the world market. Brazil rose to importance as a coffee producing country when the Caribbean began to decline

COMMODITIES

Coffee harvest, Rio de Janeiro, view overlooking Sugarloaf Mountain, mid-19th century

three hundred years, up to four million African slaves were shipped in. As in the West Indies, mortality was very high and the birth rate very low; only one and a half million slaves were emancipated in the 1880s, when slavery was finally abolished.

The Portuguese first settled in the north east and Bahia, the first capital of the country, was established in 1549. In 1693, gold was discovered in Minas Gerais, and labour flooded in. Diamonds were discovered soon afterwards. The ensuing boom yielded £200 million in the eighteenth century and soon, the area around Rio de Janeiro had overtaken the sugar-growing north east in importance. In 1763, the capital was transferred to Rio. In 1807, the Portuguese Regent abandoned Portugal after it was invaded by Napoleon, and was escorted to Rio by the British fleet, where he established his court. In 1822,

encouraged by the British, Brazil declared itself independent of Portugal and the Regent was proclaimed Emperor. The old Portuguese monopoly of trade with Brazil was abolished and Brazilian ports were opened to other nations, which effectively meant the British free traders. The empire lasted until 1889, but real power in the country remained with the landowners, while the trade and finance system was largely controlled by the British.

As Tussac observed, coffee was a valuable crop, but it was established slowly for several reasons. First, coffee beans lose their fertility though not their taste soon after harvesting, so they need to be germinated and transplanted quickly. The second problem was that coffee growers guarded their bushes and secrets very carefully, so seeds had to be obtained by stealth. The final problem

108

was that coffee production, like sugar, requires a lot of capital in the form of labour.

Despite these handicaps, coffee was established in Brazil by the 1730s, and by 1740, the Portuguese Crown felt sufficiently sure of this source of supply to prohibit the import of coffee from outside the Portuguese empire. Coffee growers in Pará were favoured by a royal edict which allowed them immunity from normal taxes and tithes until the end of the century. By 1750, the region was exporting over 60 tons of coffee to Lisbon a year. But the equatorial climate and the soil in north east Brazil were generally unsuited to coffee, and production shifted south in the 1760s to the area around Rio, which remained the main growing area in Brazil until the 1860s.

THE RIO CYCLE

A lot of capital was needed for a *fazenda* and interest had to be paid at around 15 per cent per annum. The farmer could only begin to pay it off after four years when the first berries were harvested. The great house, mill, warehouse and slave *senzalas* or shacks had to be built, the forest cleared, subsistence crops planted, and coffee bushes started. All the *fazendas* were established near rivers, both for water and for milling power. Fruit trees were planted as windbreaks, and subsistence crops were grown between the coffee seedlings until the bush was three years old. The next stage was the most capital intensive, the shelling of the cherry. Traditionally, this was done by pounding the cherries manually with rods, separating the shell and then the parchment from the bean. The mill, although expensive, greatly speeded up the operation and left slaves to concentrate on traditional tasks.

Sorting was done by the women slaves, the children and the old slaves. Each was expected to sort four *arrobas* (1 *arroba* = 12.5 kilos) a day. Coffee was taken to Rio by mule and boat and sold for cash which paid for more slaves, tools, salt and cotton. As with sugar, high prices encouraged the owners of large *fazendas* to concentrate on coffee production and to neglect subsistence crops. Initially, these were available cheap on local markets, but as more farmers moved into coffee, attracted by the high

prices, the price of coffee fell and the price of other foodstuffs rose. Even so, coffee continued to attract farmers. Cleared forest could be sold for timber, and young coffee plantations could be intercropped with rice, maize and beans during the first four years of growth; when fully productive the coffee bushes only required six annual hoeings, though they did require a large labour force during the harvest.

Intensive coffee cultivation takes the organic matter and most of the mineral nutrients out of the soil; a coffee *fazenda* was only viable for 50 years so planters were always on the move. But coffee cultivation spread inland slowly, because the crop had to be transported by mule. Shortage of capital also restricted expansion. Often, it was the sugar planters whose plantations were declining but who owned slaves, who could borrow money to establish coffee plantations. It was reckoned in the 1830s that £6,500 was needed to establish a 100,000 bush plantation. Of this sum, 70 per cent was spent on buying slaves. After the abolition of the slave trade by France and England and the discontinuation of the trade to Brazil in 1855, the cost of slaves steadily increased, so that by 1870 slaves cost four times what they had cost in the 1830s. Clearly, a planter who already owned slaves enjoyed a clear advantage over his competitors. The richest slave owners in early nineteenth century São Paulo kept between 150 and 300 slaves, but it was possible to start with less, and one of the advantages of coffee was that it demanded less labour than sugar production, and thus provided a higher return on capital.

London and its expanding trading empire was the early major European market for Brazilian coffee, though other markets like Hamburg and Le Havre were also important. As the population of the US increased, much coffee was marketed through New York. Coffee production increased 30 times in the period 1821–71, by which time Brazil was exporting a quarter of a million tons a year mostly to the US, where tea drinking was a sign of unpatriotic, pro-British sentiment. In the US, alcohol had not yet found its most lucrative market, and after the American Civil War (1861–65), coffee consumption soared.

COMMODITIES

In these years, a Brazilian coffee grower could expect to be clear of debt after ten years with perhaps 30 years clear profit after that, since a coffee bush can be profitably cropped for about 40 years. However, the Brazilian slave-owning planters were living on borrowed time and they knew it. Slaves, since the beginning of the slave trade, had escaped into the hinterland, and by the 1880s slave riots and attacks on planters were commonplace. The crisis came to a head when army officers, fearing mutiny after a series of slave massacres, petitioned to be exempted from slave-catching duties. Once the army's coercive influence had gone, the remaining slaves were effectively free, because banks would not advance credit to planters whose main collateral was slaves.

Coffee production was always linked to events in distant markets. The boom 1840s in Europe, before the revolutions of 1848, saw an intensification of Brazilian production. Although the slave trade to Brazil had been outlawed by the Emperor in 1831, the ban was not enforced – not least because the judges were heavily involved in the trade. The boom brought 370,000 more smuggled slaves into Brazil to grow coffee on the *fazendas* of Rio State. After the official ending of the slave trade in 1855, the coffee business expanded again because slaves became more valuable, and the planters who were in debt because they owned the most slaves suddenly found they had the best collateral, and expanded slave-based production everywhere. The scale of these plantations was unprecedented, even compared to the *latifundiae* of ancient Rome. In Vassouras by 1836, there were plantations with 800,000 coffee bushes, exporting 300,000 *arrobas* of coffee each.

However, oscillations in northern markets continually undermined smooth expansion of the industry. High prices attracted new farmers; then after six years, a glut caused the price to fall again. Since the seven-year coffee cycle never quite matched the boom/slump cycles of northern capitalism, Brazil's agrarian development was particularly unstable. Even before the ending of slavery, the shortage of labour forced *fazenda* owners to devise new ways of attracting labour: some slave owners compelled their female slaves to breed; an *agregado* system was established which allowed plantation workers to cultivate a patch of land as part of their wage; other plantation

Italian indentured labourers, Brazil, 1890s

110

workers were offered land and capital as an incentive; and share-cropping was introduced. In the 1840s, an influential planter and politician, Nicolau Vergueiro, petitioned the government to subsidize the recruitment and transport of indentured workers from Germany and Switzerland. But after they had completed their indentures, these poor immigrants often received nothing, because fares and alleged debts were subtracted by the landowners. One of them, a Swiss schoolteacher, Thomas Davatz, published a scathing indictment of the system on his return and asked:

> Would it be exaggerated, in the face of all these facts, to say that the *colonos* [foreign indentured workers] are subjected to a new form of slavery, more advantageous to the bosses than the real one, since they receive Europeans at much more modest prices than they do Africans. (Davatz, p. 219)

For landowners accustomed to dealing with slaves it required considerable adjustment for them to treat their workers on contractual terms. Davatz cites a common remark among planters to their *colonos*: 'I bought you, you belong to me'. Planters came to fear *colono* revolt quite as much as slave uprisings, claiming that the *colonos* were agents of foreign governments, subversives and 'communists'. Finally, the word about conditions in Brazil got back to Switzerland, and the recruitment of indentured labour was stopped.

For the next three decades, planters had to recruit freed slaves and impoverished peasants from the north east and to introduce a system of cash payments by result. Some of these labourers even ended up owning small farms; slowly, planters began to realize that free labour was just as profitable and easier to manage than slave labour.

THE SÃO PAULO CYCLE

By the end of the 1880s, with slavery finished, planters prevailed on provincial governments to re-adopt the system of subsidized indentures, but this time from Italy. A hundred thousand Italian immigrants a year arrived until the turn of the century. The contracts often went to British companies, who shipped immigrants in British ships to British-built ports, whence they were shipped into the interior on railways built and financed by the British. From this period dates the massive expansion of production in São Paulo State. Coffee prices were now much higher and coffee production increased dramatically. In the 1890s, 350 million new coffee bushes were planted; the annual harvest of São Paulo State rose in ten years from 170,000 tons, to more than half a million tons.

Again, word got back to Europe about the working conditions and the Italian government prohibited indenture recruitment in 1902. The appalling conditions and derisory wages were in part caused by falling coffee prices after 1896, largely caused by overproduction, and provincial governments briefly discontinued subsidized immigration. Even so, until the First World War, about 50,000 poor Spaniards and Portuguese labourers arrived in Brazil each year; between 1908 and 1941, 200,000 Japanese workers were also brought in to grow rice and later coffee. From that time, the characteristic racial mix of Brazilian society was well established, and there was no longer a serious labour shortage in the country. Indeed, given that land and capital were controlled by a very small sector of the population, there was increasingly a labour surplus, which in part explains the dramatic mobility of labour which is a characteristic of twentieth-century Brazil.

COFFEE MONEY

The profits from sugar provided the capital for the first coffee plantations in Brazil; slaves provided the collateral. There were numerous ways, however, in which foreign, and particularly British, capital played a crucial role in the development of the coffee industry. The role of British capitalism is explained by several factors: firstly, the traditional alliance between Portugal and Britain which dated from the Commonwealth Period; secondly, the diminishing returns from investment in Caribbean sugar with the development of beet and the ending of slavery; and thirdly, the capital surplus which resulted from Britain's eighteenth-century domination of world trade.

When Brazil achieved independence from Portugal in

COMMODITIES

1822, the British were already poised to take advantage of the new opportunities. Direct investment in the estate system itself was rare, possibly because financiers wished to avoid offending abolitionist sentiments at home; but equally likely, because investment in plantations was already recognized as being both more risky and less profitable than investment in trade and the transport and industrial infrastructure. In 1824, Brazil contracted a £3.686 million loan from British bankers in order to 'compensate' the Portugese for the loss of their colony and to finance Brazil's war with Uruguay and Argentina. In the 1860s, there were further loans to finance Brazil's war with Paraguay, since it was in Britain's interest for Brazil to secure its frontiers, as an area of British investment, and to lock Brazil into an indebted relation with the metropolis. Another early instance of British loan-mongering was a round of negotiations in the 1840s, in which the future coffee harvests of Bananal, at that time the major coffee producing area in Brazil, were demanded by London bankers as collateral for a loan to the Brazilian government.

The coffee business also attracted and depended upon investment in transport. British capital financed the Don Pedro II and São Paulo railways in the 1850s and 1860s, it built the docks at Santos and Rio, laid the underwater cables across the Atlantic linking Brazil, London and New York, as well as developing the power industry around São Paulo in the early 1900s. British engineers and contractors carried out much of the work. Such projects and hundreds like them elsewhere provided a major stimulus to British industry, as well as providing more capital both as interest and wage remittances for further investment and surplus accumulation at home. (The penetration of British capital into Latin America is also vividly reflected in the rapid spread of football, taken by English and Scottish workplace teams everywhere in the subcontinent).

Coffee profits also allowed the Brazilian national bourgeoisie to buy political power and influence, and to invest in light industry, shoe and textile factories and railways. Coffee financed the rapid expansion of Santos. In 1870, Santos was a small port exporting $10 million

(*right*) Santos—São Paulo railway

worth of coffee a year. By 1892, its exports were worth $40 million, and by 1912 its coffee exports were worth $170 million. Coffee also underwrote the even more rapid development of São Paulo, today one of the world's largest cities, with 17 million inhabitants. In 1872, that city's population was 23,000 and by 1920 over half a million; meanwhile the whole state increased in population from three quarters of a million in 1870 to over 4 million by 1914.

The infusion of foreign capital into the coffee business was initially effected by various intermediate commercial agencies, such as banks and import/export houses, in ports like Rio and Santos. These houses dealt mainly with the commissionaires, who themselves acted as middlemen offering credit, tools and supplies to prospective and established coffee growers. In return, they received interest on the loans and the right to handle the coffee produced, for which they received a three per cent fee.

Thus, the commissionaires acted as bankers to the planters, and from the 1880s to the 1929 Wall Street crash they came to monopolize the coffee sector. Many, though not all, operated with loans raised on foreign money markets, and thus it was that foreign capitalists secured a further foothold in the Brazilian economy. The commissionaires' and planters' interests were linked, since they both benefitted from increased production and rising coffee prices; marriage between the groups was common. This local capitalist elite eventually became the nucleus of the Brazilian national bourgeoisie responsible for Brazil's industrialization from the 1900s onwards.

The commissionaires were also linked, though with contradictory interests, to the import/export houses, most of which were established and controlled by foreign traders, whose interests were those of the metropolitan powers. These trading houses wanted to increase production but to keep the price of coffee low. This they did by continually raising the amount of the Brazilian milreis, which they were prepared to take for dollars or sterling. (In effect, they systematically devalued the milreis). This meant that they received more for industrial and manufactured goods which they imported into Brazil and paid less for the coffee which they took out. But they had to be careful. If they paid too low a price for coffee they would bankrupt the planters and thus lose their market for imported goods as well as the coffee upon which their coercive power depended.

Between the commissionaires and the exporters there grew up an intermediate class known as *ensacadores* (the sackers), a name derived from their humble function of mixing blends of beans and sacking them for final shipment. In the sixteenth and seventeenth centuries, the price of coffee did not fluctuate wildly because production and trade was controlled by the Arabs, who could fix the price in relation to the goods and services which they themselves wanted in exchange for their

Workers bagging coffee for an *ensacador*, Brazil, c. 1900

coffee. But once coffee was produced outside the Yemen, its price to traders was determined more by supply and demand; high prices encouraged planters to shift to coffee, and the windfall profits from high prices provided capital for extended production. Since coffee bushes take six years to mature to full production, coffee prices move in seven-year cycles (the one-year time lag allows producers to gauge what is happening). In short, high prices attract new growers; after six years more coffee reaches the market; the price falls; marginal producers go bankrupt; no new coffee bushes are planted; and after seven years, the price rises again due to the shortage of coffee.

Historically, this system benefitted financiers, since they could claim the land and slaves of bankrupt producers when prices were low and the profit from high interest rates when prices rose. Green coffee, however, properly prepared, can be stored for several years without deterioration as long as efficient warehousing is available; it was this profitable service which was provided by the *ensacadores*. With pronounced oscillations in the cash value of coffee in the nineteenth century, and the increased speed of communications afforded by

Bill poster in a 19th-century coffee ad

since all benefitted from a rise in coffee's export price; but at other times, because they made a living from exploiting price fluctuations, they undermined the stability of coffee agriculture.

After reaching a high point in 1893, the price of coffee fell back to less than half that in 1897; it remained low for ten years. Due to a glut of coffee produced by a rapid expansion of planting, there was little possibility of a shortage which might have driven prices up again. Since coffee was abundant and everything else increasingly in short supply, the value of the milreis dropped catastrophically. Coffee growers had to produce more coffee in order to earn less from it. The value of the milreis dropped again. The big landowners who had lost their slaves without compensation turned on the monarchy and the military took over in 1889. The king abdicated and the new government issued paper money to cover its deficits, creating an orgy of extravagant consumption and speculation; inflation spiralled.

Before this occurred, foreign traders and financiers had begun to copy the *ensacadores*. They also invested in warehousing and attempted briefly to buy directly from the producers, bypassing the *ensacadores* and the commissionaires. But such manipulation of the economy by foreign interests was not popular with the Brazilian bourgeoisie. In 1903, the newly-established Republican regime saw the advantages of institutionalizing the warehouse system by establishing state-controlled warehouses, thereby increasing state revenues and placating the coffee interest, upon which it depended for political support. Forced onto international money markets to raise loans, the Brazilian government negotiated a £10 million 'funding loan' in 1898 from a consortium of foreign bankers led by the Rothschilds. The bankers agreed to bail the government out, but only on certain conditions. The government had to cut public spending and revalue the milreis. This was popular with the coffee interest because it raised the price of coffee despite the world glut. But the government itself was now acting as a buffer between producers and buyers. It had to finance the loan from its trading operations and it had to warehouse vast quantities of surplus coffee at con-

steamships and cable links after the 1870s, *ensacadores* began to operate as major speculators on the coffee market because they could control the supply of coffee by hoarding it in their large warehouses and releasing it when the price was right. Unfettered by the financial links which bound commissionaires to planters, and trading houses to foreign bankers, the *ensacadores* by 1900 had control of the coffee market in Brazil. They drove up the price by creating shortages, and bought cheap when stocks were abundant. On occasion, their interest corresponded to those of the planters and commissionaires,

siderable expense. Despite this, Brazil had discovered, after almost a century of free-wheeling economic liberalism, the advantages of a controlled economy.

The funding loan and its corrective measures were successful enough to encourage individual state governments to look for other ways to stabilize coffee prices. In 1906, the governors of the main coffee-growing states (São Paulo, Rio and Minas Gerais) signed the Taubaté Agreement which raised foreign loans in order to buy up excess coffee to maintain world prices. Interest on the loan, fixed at 6 per cent, was to be paid by a tax on every bag of coffee exported from Brazil. Thus, increasingly, local and national governments came to control coffee agriculture in the country.

However, the interest had to be paid out of the profits of the system itself. This was fine as long as the price held up, but it was catastrophic once the price fell. State warehouses solved several problems, but they could not solve the problem of the fluctuating milreis, the unit of Brazilian currency, which itself was largely determined by the export price of coffee. Until 1929, however, no one anticipated the problems. The stability of the system encouraged farmers to expand production and to move into new areas. At such boom periods, coffee agriculture could pay quite well. A family might earn 600 milreis a year tending 10,000 coffee bushes, and workers were usually entitled to grow corn, manioc, beans and vegetables on smallholdings which they could sell on local markets. Even so, the labourers were at the mercy of the planters. They often spoke a different language, they shopped at the company store and paid company prices. Police could not enter the plantations, co-operatives and unions were not permitted, and strikes were rare.

By 1929, the natural limits of production had been reached in São Paulo State. Then the Wall Street crash of 1929 rocked the coffee business to its foundations; it

Coffee drying, plantation in Rio province, 1880s

destabilized international trade and exchange rates, and cut luxury consumption in northern markets. Brazil's coffee earnings (70 per cent of its total foreign earnings) dropped by a half. The first coffee growers to go bankrupt were the owners of the large plantations established in the boom 1890s. Forty years later, their coffee bushes were old and the soil was finished. Their plantations were parcelled up and sold to smaller farmers, who turned to other crops. The planters themselves turned on the government in the half-hearted Paulista Revolt of 1932; the government, to placate them, agreed to absorb most of the losses resulting from the enormous over-production of coffee in Brazil. A minimum guaranteed price was paid for excess stocks, and the loans contracted for this purpose were serviced by a 20 per cent tax on coffee exports. The surplus was then burned or used as fuel. Between 1931 and 1944, four and a half million tons of coffee (enough to supply the entire world market for three years) was destroyed, often being used to power the same trains which carried the harvest down to Santos and Rio.

The military government of Getùlio Vargas, which seized power in 1930, marked the end of the domination of Brazilian politics by the coffee interests. However, the military government continued to bail out the ailing coffee economy. It also sponsored research into new methods of preserving coffee, and it developed instant coffee in co-operation with Swiss scientists from Nestlé. The advantages of this discovery to Brazil might have been considerable. For the first time, a producing country had developed the technology to roast, pack and preserve a marketable coffee. Hitherto, all these operations, and the profit which accrued from them, had been carried out by the big roasting companies or by the grocers in consuming countries. However, because it was Nestlé which patented the process, Brazil was unable to build its own instant coffee factories until the 1960s. When it did, foreign coffee companies refused to handle Brazilian instant coffee, since they had no intention of losing control over the most profitable part of the operation.

FROM PLANTATION TO PEASANT AGRICULTURE: THE PARANÁ CYCLE

Coffee in Brazil, given the low price, was starved of capital. Planters went bankrupt and capital was diverted to new uses, particularly to light industrial development around the largest cities. During the Second World War, coffee prices were pegged, which made large-scale coffee planting even less attractive. The plantations which survived the Depression and the war were quite different to the vast *fazendas* of earlier years. The typical operation which emerged struck a balance between capitalist interest and cash incentives to growers. Companies were formed with British and Brazilian capital to establish colonization schemes in new areas – particularly Paraná State. These offered a new generation of Brazilian farmers outright ownership of small plots of land, whose cost would be paid for by future harvests. The companies reaped the rewards of its investment since they owned the local transport system, the drying facilities (which by now were essential to the efficient large-scale production of coffee), the company store, the local brickyards, the local bank and so on. Capital was concentrating its activities on the most lucrative part of the operation, leaving the labour-intensive, unprofitable part to small farmers. Increasingly, therefore, small-scale peasant family production of coffee in Brazil took over.

In post-war Europe and the US, coffee consumption expanded way beyond its pre-war levels. Most significant was the development of instant coffees, which substituted convenience for quality. Manufactured and marketed by transnationals like General Foods, Nestlé and Allied Lyons, and backed by expensive advertising campaigns, instant coffee soon came to occupy a large sector of the British and US markets. More sophisticated coffee drinkers, however, remained resistant to this invention. At the same time, Italian coffee, coffee bars, hip jazz and student culture took proper coffee into traditional tea drinking markets. And coffee triumphed, being more speedy and macho than tea.

PART FIVE

THE HANGMAN'S MERCY

I

THE condemned man did not eat a hearty breakfast. He pushed the food aside and asked for more coffee. He also demanded his daily allowance of ten cigarettes. They offered him one cigarette and told him that this did

..... and Julia had

...... She was still angry. He picked up the morning paper, and the first item he read—his glance was drawn to it as if by a magnet—was a small announcement that Starling would be executed at Farways Prison that morning. He threw the paper down. He looked at the clock. Five minutes to nine. Five minutes to go. He found that he had no appetite. Pushing away his plate, he reached for the coffee pot. Julia frowned. At two minutes to nine he closed his eyes and prayed ...... It was a prayer for Don Starling

In 1952, as a consequence of the post-war boom, coffee accounted for up to three quarters of Brazil's total foreign earnings; by 1965, it had dropped to less than a half, with sugar, minerals, other commodities and, in particular, light industrial products all increasing in importance. A

record harvest of three million tonnes in 1968 led to coffee mountains, a fall in prices, further bankruptcies, and, since the government still had to buffer the operation, higher taxes on coffee and everything else. Today, following Brazil's 'miracle growth' in the 1970s, with its emphasis on industrialization and diversification, coffee accounts for less than ten per cent of Brazil's export earnings. Even so, Brazil still supplies about a third of the world's coffee.

In 1964, a military government took over and imposed strict controls over the economy while shifting government spending to roads, power schemes and so on. The military created a climate in which the Brazilian bourgeoisie could develop its own industry, (particularly the construction and car industries), and simultaneously control the conditions under which foreign transnationals could both invest in and profit from their Brazilian subsidiaries.

In the 1970s, with the influx of massive amounts of foreign capital, as the holders of petrodollars sought out safe and profitable opportunities for investment, the Brazilian economy achieved annual growth rates of nearly ten per cent, which were unprecedented in Brazil and almost unrivalled elsewhere in the world at the time. Protected by government controls over the repatriation of profits by foreign companies, free enterprise 'flourished' and the cruziero (the new unit of Brazilian currency) was allowed to float. It went down against the dollar, real wages dropped, prices of imports and inflation rose, and the coffee price fell, while speculators moved into dollars and shifted vast fortunes out of Brazil into Swiss banks.

Fragmented in their holdings and heavily indebted to the banks, coffee producers no longer had any political clout. Instead, they suffered the ignominious fate of providing some of the revenue which kept the military in power. Paraná coffee growers became involved in the illegal, untaxed export of coffee out through Paraguay. Then, in 1970, leaf rust, which blighted the bushes, first arrived in Latin America. A frost in 1972 reduced the crop by a half, followed by a worse frost in 1975, which killed half of the bushes.

Planting a coffee bush, Colombia

lems, preferring to leave to an elected government the task of repaying the foreign debts it had incurred.

Yet even today, 64 per cent of the export price of coffee is taken by the government, leaving only a third of its value for the growers, exporters, and other intermediaries. The frosts, partly caused by the cutting down of forests south of Paraná which allowed the cold winds from the Pampas to blow north, have been followed by excessive rains which rotted the coffee, and finally by a severe drought in 1985. However, with northern buyers losing confidence in Brazil as a dependable seller of good coffee, and with marginal coffee producers continually going under, coffee is no longer synonymous with Brazil, even if it is a key to an understanding of its past.

COFFEE IN COLOMBIA

Colombia, like Brazil, is potentially one of the richest countries in the Third World. It produces a third of the world's emeralds, is the second largest gold producer in Latin America and has the largest open-cast coal mine in the world, as well as significant reserves of bauxite, oil, gas, copper, silver, platinum and uranium. It is a big country (440,000 square miles), with large, remote, unexploited and sparsely populated territories. Even so, since 1964, more than half the population (now 28 million) lives in the towns and cities, and a quarter of the population lives in conditions of absolute poverty.

At first sight, coffee might seem a solution to Colombia's problems. A fifth of the cultivated land now grows coffee, and coffee accounts for over 60 per cent of its official foreign earnings. More than 300,000 families, or three million people, depend on coffee for their livelihood. People say in Colombia, 'When the coffee price is high we have schools; when it's low, we starve'. Coffee profits have certainly financed the building of roads and the provision of electricity in rural areas. Coffee is well suited to the amply irrigated, well drained and mineral rich soils which lie between 4,400 and 6,600 feet on the Andean slopes. These produce abundant crops of high quality mild *arabicas*, which are traditionally grown beneath the shade of fruit trees. The emblem of the Colombian coffee industry is Juan Valdez, a smiling model

The wholesale price of coffee increased by 800 per cent – ironically, enabling Brazil to replant. The government began to encourage the replacement of coffee with soya and other food crops in Paraná State, which, because of its latitude, was the most frost-afflicted state. The government also subsidized the expansion of coffee in Minas Gerais and the planting of *robusta* coffee in the new areas of colonization in Rondônia, far to the west. With the development of high caffeine, high cost, low quality instant coffees, *robustas* could be used to bulk out the various blends. Poorer farmers formed co-operatives and attempted to put pressure on the government. Farm labourers joined illegal unions. The military finally resigned in 1985, incapable of coping with all its prob-

dressed as a smallholder – a romantic but not wholly inaccurate symbol, because, since the 1930s, much of the Colombian crop has been grown by peasant family units.

After the Spanish conquest, Colombia (then part of a vast territory which included Equador and Venezuela, called New Granada) was ruled from Spain by colonial administrators, the *peninsulares*. The Catholic church was granted about a third of the land, the Crown retained large tracts, and some was granted to the indigenous Indian population as reservations. The rest was held by the *criollos*, the white descendants of the *conquistadores*. As elsewhere in the Spanish empire, little attention was paid to developing cash crop plantation agriculture. Subsistence agriculture continued to be practised by the Indian population, who were also forced, through the *encomienda* (forced labour) system, to work on the haciendas for the *criollos*. The main export of the colonial era was gold – the miners were Indians and a few African slaves.

Colombia remained underpopulated and undeveloped. Its slow development was in part due to the mountainous terrain and the thick equatorial forest which covered most of the country. Its main arteries were its rivers, particularly the Magdalena. Gradually, a merchant class emerged through its control of the inevitable contraband trade with the US and Britain. With illicit trade came republican ideas from North America and France. Independence was proclaimed in 1811, and power was seized by the *criollos* with the support of the British and sections of the slave and *mestizo* (mixed race) population who believed the *criollo* promises that independence would bring land reform.

Following independence there was indeed 'land reform'. The white elite of merchants, oligarchs and planters increasingly parcelled out Colombia among themselves, through a series of measures that appropriated Crown and Church lands. In the 1850s, the Indians' title to many reserved lands was also taken from them and those on reservations near *criollo* settlements were compelled to pay rent in kind to their new landlords. *Mestizo* squatters who were initially encouraged by the government to colonize and develop unused lands

FEDERACION NACIONAL DE CAFETEROS DE COLOMBIA

(left) Juan Valdez, personifying the National Federation of Coffee Producers

were either evicted or forced to work for *criollo* planters. In 1850, the slaves were 'freed', but without land they were compelled to work in the mines or on the land for the *criollos*. The few attempts at large scale farming, growing crops like cotton, anil (for indigo dyes), quinine and tobacco were never very successful, because of the transport problem and fluctuating world prices.

The development of the Colombian interior did not really start until steam navigation was introduced on the

Magdalena River in the 1870s. Coffee was planted to the east of the Magdalena around Santander, and further south around Bogota. These plantations were established by hacienda owners who had links with the trading houses, and merchants who were always looking for new cash crops. Some haciendas had their own *peons* or peasant workers, who were effectively tied to the land since they had nowhere else to go, and were therefore compelled to work for whatever wages they were offered. Often these *peons* worked side by side with free labourers who had smallholdings of their own, but who paid the rent by day-labouring for the landlord. Another widespread arrangement was share-cropping, where the peasant gave an agreed share of the crop (generally half) to the landlord.

From the point of view of the capitalist landowner, however, labour was always a problem since peasants had little incentive to work for landlords if they could find land to work of their own. This search partly explains 'the Antioquia colonization'. Antioquia was settled after the 1850s, when the pressure of population growth and evictions drove peasants off the fertile valley bottoms and highland plateaus (where, since pre-colonial times, the majority of the population had been concentrated) in search of new land. At first these *colonos* grew subsistence crops, but around the turn of the century, merchants in local towns encouraged them to experiment with coffee. In 1885, Colombia was exporting 200,000 sacks a year from the area east of the Magdalena; by 1935 it was exporting three million sacks – almost all the additional coffee came from the area of Antioquia colonization.

At this time, mild Colombian coffee sold at a premium on northern markets and, gradually, more *colonos* moved into the central cordillera, cutting down virgin forest and planting subsistence crops, and later coffee on the mountain slopes. As coffee cultivation became more attractive, land acquired an exchange value. Under the laws of the 1850s, the colonizers were entitled to any unused land which they made productive. These laws, however, included a clause which allowed inheritors of title deeds (granted to *criollo* ancestors by colonial viceroys centuries earlier), a ten year period in which to develop the land before it could be appropriated – though few had ever done this. But when peasants went to register their claims (if they ever did) they were informed that the land they had occupied was already owned, mostly by speculators who had bought the deeds from the titular owners. The peasants who opened up the land were thus deprived of the product of their labour. The last decade of the nineteenth century was a period of massive violence known as 'the War of the Axe and the Official Paper'. The land speculators were often merchants and coffee middlemen; as coffee became more valuable, the speed of colonization increased and the merchants, growing rich on coffee exports, began to finance further colonization schemes, advancing money for tools and supplies against a percentage of the future harvest. In addition to their own share, they also bought the *colonos* share. They hulled, bagged and warehoused the coffee, and then sold it to export houses, as well as selling tools, sugar, salt and seeds to the *colonos*. Inevitably, since the price of coffee fluctuates, the *colonos* tended to get into debt, so even that land still owned by *colonos* fell into the hands of large landowners or companies, even though the smallholdings were (and still are) mostly worked by family units.

The development of the Colombian coffee industry was complicated by Colombia's political history, which has been characterized since the 1850s by the domination of two political parties, the Liberals and Conservatives. Between 1899 and 1902 there was a violent civil war, which was in part financed by the sale of Panama to the US and which resulted in the opening up of Colombia to US capital. The US, at the same time, had become the principle export market for Colombian coffee, as well as becoming clearly established as the sovereign power in the Americas providing investment capital (with political strings). US companies bought oil rights on the Magdalena river, and the United Fruit Company established banana plantations on its banks.

Similarly, Colombian coffee interest became dependent on even bigger merchants in London and New York, and on foreign financiers who lent them money to build docks, railways and to import machinery for

120

hulling, washing and skinning the berry. After the Civil War, a group of Colombian merchants, angered by the encroachments of US capital into the country, tried to establish themselves in New York to cut out US middle-men. At first they were successful because the Brazilians were controlling exports in their attempt to stabilize the price of coffee. Therefore, initially, the American roas-ters had to buy from the Colombians. But the price of coffee fell after the war, when Brazil could no longer protect its price and dumped its excess stocks on the market. The Colombians could not find the cash to buy up cheap surplus coffee to protect the New York price, let alone cover the losses on the coffee which they held in stock, and in 1921 they went bankrupt.

In 1927, the Colombian National Coffee Growers' Federation ('a private company with a public interest') was formed, in an attempt to improve the coffee expor-ters' bargaining position on the world market and to override the political divisions of Liberals and Conserva-tives, whose infighting was damaging the whole economy. The Federation's long-term aim was to adopt the Brazilian system of buying up cheap, surplus coffee, warehousing it and then selling it when prices improved, with a tax on exports to fund the operation. In the short term, they were unsuccessful because of the price collapse in 1929. In the 1930s, in co-operation with the Brazilians and other Latin American producers, Colombia attempted to compel the coffee-importing countries to raise the price of coffee. But Britain, for strategic reasons, had already begun large-scale coffee production in its East African colonies and the Dutch had increased production in Indonesia. Thus both these core powers could buy their coffee elsewhere, and this pioneer Latin American attempt to form a producer cartel failed.

It was in the 1930s, with the price of coffee low, that big growers got out of coffee, because it did not even pay to harvest the crop. Agrarian unions and peasant leagues were formed, partly seduced by the Liberals' 1936 land reform promise, which made occupancy and exploita-tion of the land the legal basis of tenure. Peasant land invasions meant that peasant production grew more and more important in Colombia. Peasant growers produced more coffee, even though the price was lower, because coffee was their only cash crop; the only way they could get more cash was by growing more coffee; thus Colom-bian production increased as did Colombia's share of the total world market. But inevitably, Colombian merchants retained control of the export market.

During the Second World War, the US government introduced a guaranteed price scheme for Latin American coffee-growing countries, to dissuade them from aligning with the Axis powers, Germany, Japan and Italy. In Colombia, the responsibility for administering the price control mechanism fell on the Federation, which established, in co-operation with the government, the National Coffee Fund. The aim of the fund was to stabilize the coffee price by buying up surplus production (as in Brazil). One might assume that this would have brought stability to Colombia, but instead it heralded an era of increasing conflict. Between 1946 and 1958, around 300,000 people were killed in the Colombian countryside in a conflict known as the *violencia*. The roots of this violence lay in the recession of the 1930s, when the bigger landowners gave up coffee production and the peasants invaded their land, or else neglected to pay their share-cropping percentage to the landlord (because it was practically worthless). In the post-war boom, landlords began to demand their paper rights and to evict squatters. The *violencia* was complicated by the fact that the Colom-bian bourgeoisie was split, with the Conservatives and

Peasant insurgent army, Colombia

Liberals fighting for control of the economy. They disagreed over the relative importance of the agrarian and industrial sectors, the role of foreign capital, and over the modernization of agriculture and land reform. The peasants, in this essentially feudal country with its traditions of landownership and party loyalty, became caught up in the struggle and turned on each other. Village was divided against village. Assassins, known as *pajaros* (birds), roamed the countryside, hiring their guns to either party, 'persuading' peasants to give up their land. Many peasants moved into the cities hoping to escape the violence and to pick up work in the new factories.

The hopeless violence of the 1940s was translated into more potent guerilla movements – the FLN under Camillo Torres, the FLP and the FARC. In 1953, the military took over, giving way in 1957 to a new constitution in which Liberals and Conservatives would alternate in power. After the Cuban Revolution, the Colombian military was funded by the US to hold down 'Communism'. The military became a beneficiary of the 'Alliance for Progress' (1961), an economic programme designed to promote the Americanization of Latin America. (Elsewhere in Latin America, this definition of 'progress' meant about ten years of right-wing, American-backed dictators.) A major clause of the Alliance for Progress required that the Colombian and other governments introduce agrarian reform. Accordingly, Colombia established the INCORA, the National Institute of Agrarian Reform. In ten years, the INCORA succeeded in handing over 6,000 title deeds to peasant producers. However, at that rate the land transfer to two million landless peasants would have taken 3,000 years!

Gradually, the coffee interest triumphed over party divisions. The National Coffee Fund stabilized the domestic price. Whereas initially, only the big landowners had been members of the Federation, it was now in their interest that peasant producers become part of the system; membership, although not granted individually to small growers, was granted to delegates from peasant co-operatives. As the Federation itself grew richer, it took on a leading role as a coffee exporter and banker to the whole Colombian economy. It experimented with new strains of coffee, bought its own fleet of merchant ships, started to make freeze-dried instant coffee, provided access to credit facilities for the purchase of machinery, fertilizers and pesticides, and gave technical advice and assistance to growers. It also represented the Colombian coffee interest abroad, both as a direct coffee exporter and as the Colombian representatives on the International Coffee Organization, which now regulates not only the international coffee trade but also demands that exporters regulate domestic production.

Thus, although the Federation is committed to buying export-quality coffee at a guaranteed price, it also has to restrict production, which it does by refusing to give credit for technical development to growers without extant title deeds (which, as we have seen, has been the peasants' principle grievance for the last 100 years). The INCORA has largely failed to redistribute land, either because the compensation valuation cannot be agreed, or because landowners have argued that they are using the land and therefore it is not liable for expropriation (often on the basis of the improvements the squatters have made). A Colombian peasant, Antonio Castellanos, defined the nature of their plight :

> We came here six years ago because we didn't have homes or work. Here the Peasants' Union was helping people. We formed ourselves into groups and invited others to join us. People came every week to build the houses, sow the crops and to work for the collective. We grew coffee saplings and sold some, and with this we got enough to plant our own plots of food. And all the time we were day-labouring and starving. But we're not going to be able to go on living from coffee. We've got blight and other diseases, we don't earn enough to buy insecticides, we don't have title deeds so we can't get credit. Now we shall have to return to subsistence crops in order to survive. (Interview from the *Commodities* series, 1983)

Following the bonanza of 1976–80 (due to the Brazilian frost), many Colombian coffee growers modernized their production methods by introducing new coffee strains, using more fertilizers and pesticides, and using electricity for depulping and drying. Colombian production grew from 7 million to 13 million sacks per year. However, Colombia's export quota is now less than 10 million. The surplus is warehoused at considerable cost to the Federation, which has consequently embarked upon a diversification programme with central government support. The only beneficiaries are peasants with title deeds.

With so many peasants unable to make a living from coffee, it is hardly surprising that the value of marijuana and cocaine exports from Columbia is twice that of coffee exports. Coca bushes grow well in Colombia, but it is primarily as an entrepot on the cocaine route from Peru and Bolivia that Colombia earns money from cocaine; and Colombian marijuana, was, before sensemilla (itself developed by high tech agronomists in California), reckoned to be the finest marijuana in the world.

Trading networks for drugs, similar to those established for coffee, have also emerged. Colombia, always protectionist, runs its own cocaine operation. Middlemen in the towns and cities refine the coca base; they pass it on to intermediaries and the cocaine is then flown into Miami. Sometimes it turns up in Colombian carnations (another cash crop intensively grown around Bogota). The operation is financed by a handful of untouchable Colombian businessmen.

The military promotes the convenient notion that the Colombian drugs trade is run by a 'communist' peasant league, thus justifying its receipt of funding from the US State Department. More convincing reports suggest that the drugs trade is run by the military itself, in association with a few corrupt oligarchs. Whatever the case, one thing is clear at the end of the day – Colombian peasants are very poor, despite the fact that they cultivate three of the most sought-after drugs in the world.

(*left*) Satirical poster: 'Gringo problem, Colombian solution'

For Thomas Hobbes, money was 'a commodious measure of all things else between nations', and in his gigantic metaphor of the state, *Leviathan*, money was the blood of the beast,

> whose veins receiving the blood from the several parts of the body, carry it to the heart; where being made vital, the heart by the arteries sends it out again, to enliven, and enable for motion all the members of the same. (Hobbes, 1651, ch. 24)

Sir William Petty, a friend of Hobbes and like him a materialist, preferred a different physical metaphor:

> Money is but the fat of the body politic, whereof too much doth as often hinder its agility, as too little makes it sick . . . as fat lubricates the motion of the muscles, feeds in want of victuals, fills up the uneven cavities, and beautifies the body; so doth money in the state quicken its action, feeds from abroad in time of dearth at home; evens accounts . . . and beautifies the whole; although more especially the particular persons that have it in plenty. (Petty, 1691, p. 14)

The word 'money' derives from the name of the goddess Juno Moneta, in whose temple coins were minted in ancient Rome. In general, throughout history, money has been identified with coinage and has been symbolized and embodied in commodities of value like silver and gold. To most of us, however, living within the commercial empire of the modern banking system, 'money' means coins of small metallic value, banknotes, cheque books, credit cards and (possibly) savings in a bank account or building society. Today, the material embodiment of money is generally of low intrinsic value, since money is, in essence, a token of an abstract idea.

We call gold and silver, whether in the form of pure metal or coin, 'bullion'. The value of bullion is directly tied to the market price of gold and silver. Spanish dollars minted with Aztec and Inca gold, the golden guinea – that emblematic memorial of slavery, first minted in London from West African gold in 1663 – and kruger-rands, minted in South Africa today are all bullion. Coins are known as 'specie'. Other forms of money, like banknotes, cheques and bills of exchange, are called 'fiat', because their value is guaranteed by fiat or government legislation.

The most commonplace function of money is as a medium of exchange. Local trade, in pre-modern societies, was largely through barter. Peasants exchanged their surplus produce for foodstuffs and manufactures often, we can assume, without money ever changing hands. However, once local markets became more sophisticated and were linked to distant markets, money, or something which had the properties of money, was necessary as a medium of exchange. Trade without money was either inconvenient or impossible, as was discovered by the early traders between Europe and Africa, with their floating warehouses of knives, guns, pewter and blankets. The peasants lacked money and the

COMMODITIES

African traders did not want it, which illustrates the problems of 'making a market' under primitive economic conditions.

However, we need to remember that a barter economy, where commodities are exchanged for other commodities without the mediation of money, survived for a long time and ran parallel to a money economy. Indeed, barter, as we shall see, still acts as a crucial medium in international exchange. Barter is also an essential medium of exchange in the poorest societies, where money is either scarce or unobtainable because outsiders have not thought it worthwhile to make inroads into areas where goods cannot be extracted, produced and transported at competitive rates.

Coinage, which is a particular form of money, was invented by the Lydians around 600 BC. Within three hundred years, it was in common use around the Mediterranean and through trading contacts it had been taken and accepted as far away as India, so convenient was it as a lubricator of exchange. Rulers, rentiers and tax collectors also quickly recognized the convenience of coinage over payment in kind, since coins, unlike most other commodities, were easily transported and did not lose their value. Thus, early on, peasants were forced to sell their produce to traders to obtain specie to pay their taxes. Slowly and inexorably, money filtered into the furthest corners of every economy linking peasants with markets and markets with governments.

Specie has other characteristics. It is convenient for it to have a high value to weight ratio, otherwise it would be too heavy to transport. It must also be made of a commodity which does not deteriorate. Gold and silver (the earliest emblems of money) do not oxidize and only deteriorate as they rub palms and other coins in merchants' bags. Therefore, they hold their value better than other metals like copper, (which is also too abundant to provoke acquisitive desire), and other commodities which deteriorate more or less rapidly through time.

The metals from which the earliest money tokens were forged also had to be obtainable with the primitive tools available; this precluded the early use of minerals like platinum, and aluminium. Thus, early on in human history these three metals, gold, silver and copper – stamped with the images of kings, emperors and tyrants – served well as a medium of exchange for most purposes. Gold was used for the most expensive transactions, silver for the middle range, and copper for the rest. Furthermore, once these metals became widely recognized and valued, they could be exchanged outside traditional trading areas. Before long, they had displaced traditional currencies almost everywhere in the world, from cowrie shells in Polynesia to coca leaves in the Andes.

A currency, then as now, is exchangeable only within a trading area where it is recognized. It therefore symbolizes the extent of a commercial empire. From the fourth century AD to the fall of Constantinople in 1453, the gold bezant was the dollar of the Byzantine commercial empire; the Venetian ducat and the Florentine florin were the dollars of the late Middle Ages; the Dutch thaler (from which the word 'dollar' derives) was the universal coin of the Dutch seventeenth-century trading empire; and sterling's empire lasted two centuries. Since the Second World War, the US dollar has been the core currency of the world.

Another property of money is that it is a notion of equivalence or a standard of value. Wherever there is superfluity, surplus production can be exchanged. Where there is exchange, there must also be some abstract notion of equivalence: three coconuts are worth ten yams, two transistor radios are worth one pig. Cowrie shells, cattle, coca leaves – as well as gold, silver, and copper – have all been used as money in this way at various times. But then it became convenient for that equivalence to be measured against a third commodity, which, being neither consumed, nor losing its value, could flow separately as money. It was thus, as a notion of value or equivalence, that money commenced its path towards abstraction, a development which also made possible more complex and wide-reaching spheres of exchange. Nevertheless, it is as a medium of exchange that the fundamental utility of money still lies; money still serves as a token which enables commodities to flow round the world.

Today, economic systems are so complex that almost anything can be turned into money, and money can be turned into almost anything. We should also remember that individuals and institutions control, or aspire to control, the way that money operates, for the power of money derives from its status as a universally desired commodity.

ABOVE : REALISATION THAT MONEY, ALTHOUGH A COMMODITY, CANNOT BE CONSUMED.

MONEY AS A COMMODITY

Money, that in former times was only used as a measure to value all commodities by, is become now itself a commodity.
Sir George Downing, 1661

The relation between money and all other commodities needs to be understood if we are to grasp the eventual primacy of money. For, although money is a commodity and has long been recognized as such, it is unlike all other commodities in that it cannot be consumed.

For most of us money is a medium for consumption. It allows us to buy things which we then consume. In order to obtain it, we either have to sell our labour – which, as Hobbes correctly observed, 'is also a commodity exchangeable for benefit as well as any other thing' (Hobbes, ch. 24) – or we have to sell foodstuffs, manufactures, or other commodities we might produce or own. Whatever the case, we begin with a commodity; we then exchange it for money in the market place; then convert that money back into commodities which we consume.

But the reverse of this series of exchanges works differently. For the above exchanges to take place (commodity–money–commodity), there have to be other people in the market who neither produce commodities for exchange nor desire commodities directly. They start with money and they finish with money (money-commodity-money). For those capitalists (as we call them), the object is not to own and consume commodities, but to use commodities as a medium of exchange which will bring them profit. Capitalists start with money, buy other commodities and eventually exchange them back into money again. They hope that their skills and luck will bring them a profit from the chain of transactions. They are basically making money out of money, while using some of their profit to buy the commodities which they wish to consume. But since it is they who use money as a commodity, it is they who control the market in this commodity, and therefore in all other commodities. This process is the essence of both mercantile and financial capitalism.

Money's potentiality has always been limited by certain constraints. So great is its power that governments have attempted to curb it – but it is no more easy to control the flow of money than the tides of the ocean, as innumerable reformers discovered. So money evolved in a context which was essentially limiting. Certain usages were defined as 'fair' and 'just', while other operations were defined as 'corrupt', 'illegal' or 'unacceptable'.

Take, for example, usury – the lending of money at interest – the earliest use of money as a commodity. The *Old Testament* is quite emphatic about its illegality: 'Thou shalt not lend upon usury to thy brother; usury of

127

money, usury of victuals, usury of anything that is lent upon usury'. Judaic law, however, specifies, 'unto a stranger thou mayest lend upon usury' (*Deuteronomy* 23). Such an injunction protected the faithful from the moneylenders, whilst allowing them to lend money to infidels.

Throughout history, the estimate of risk has generally been the final determinant of the rate of interest. At the same time, moneylenders, historically, have taken advantage of the borrower's degree of need; supply and demand applies to money as to any other commodity. In Ancient Rome the rate of interest fluctuated between one per cent and 12 per cent. During Charlemagne's reign as Holy Roman Emperor (800–814), moneylending was considered usurious only when 100 per cent interest was demanded.

The papacy needed moneychangers, since the taxes of Christendom which poured into its coffers were paid in specie of a bewildering variety of denominations. Jews, familiar with most of the traded currencies in the Christian and Arabic worlds, were therefore permitted to settle in Rome's ghetto. Since the Papacy was always short of ready cash, the Jews began to lend money. They

Banker at work, Germany, c. 1500

were not, however, permitted to charge more than ten per cent. On the other hand, after Pope Martin V annulled all ecclesiastical laws forbidding usury in 1425, Christians were permitted to charge what they liked, or rather whatever they could get on the money markets.

It should not, therefore, be assumed that Christians failed to take advantage of money. They were simply more circumspect than the Jews, more devious in the ways in which they disguised their usurious practices, and more contrite at the end of their lives when they were preparing for their imagined encounter with St Peter. Besides, the Pope, St Peter's heir on the Roman throne, was often the richest and greediest of princes. Even the bishops pawned their episcopal rings and vessels with Jewish moneylenders at low rates of interest. Indeed, the Roman Church in the Middle Ages was the chief propagandist of money, with its army of tax collectors and moneychangers drawing the coin of Christendom to Rome.

Historians have made too much of theological differences: Were Protestants keener capitalists that Papists? Did Jews invent capitalism? Were Christians more or less mercenary than the infidel? It seems, rather, that moneylenders offered a convenient (indeed, often essential) service on their own terms. It was left to theologians and moralists to adapt their ethics to those of the moneylenders as best they could. Increasingly, the power to legitimate financial practices shifted from the church to the state and then from the state to the marketplace, although the last two still tend to operate in collusion, albeit with contradictions.

SPECIE

The lack of specie in medieval Europe is easily explained. Although gold and silver mines were developed in Europe, particularly after the fifteenth century, there was still little gold and silver available with which to manufacture coins. Most of what did exist had to be bought into Europe by traders, usually through the Levant, and it had to be obtained by the exchange of other goods: wool, olive oil and so on. For this reason, historians have stressed the role of long-distance trade as a necessary precondition for the development of capitalism in Europe.

However, aspects of capitalism evolved early on outside Europe. The Banyan merchants in fourteenth-century India had bills of exchange, offered credit facilities, insured ships, and changed money. Likewise, the Kyoto merchants in seventeenth-century Japan played copper, silver and gold currencies against each other and used banknotes, bills of exchange and credit; they also advanced loans to the Shogun. But in both these countries, and elsewhere, mercantile capitalism did not advance beyond the margins of production. By contrast, in Europe, merchant bankers gradually came to control all the operations of the economy despite, or indeed perhaps because of, the general lack of specie.

CREDIT AND MONEY CHANGING

Without specie, something else was necessary in medieval Europe, if trade and manufacture were to expand and flourish. The substitute was credit. Now it doesn't take much imagination to realize that the giving of credit is risky; the borrower may default, the goods against which credit has been advanced may never materialize, or when they do materialize they may prove to be worthless in the marketplace. Thus credit evolved very slowly and the risk was balanced by high rates of interest. At a local level, merchants advanced credit to local producers, accepting their tools, land, future harvests or daughters as collateral: at a distance, however, they had to be more cautious. Merchants of one city could appeal to the corporations of other cities to ensure that debts were honoured, but foreign debts might never be recoverable. Thus, credit was largely confined to those who could be either compelled or trusted to repay the debt.

There are two fundamental aspects of credit. The first is that it generated a paper money market; the ownership of gold or silver, initially held on deposit in a moneylender's strong room, was symbolized by certain recognized tokens such as goldsmiths' receipts, merchants' bills of exchange, bank receipts, banknotes, and so on. As the ratio of paper money to gold and silver held on deposit

rose, the amount of token money in circulation thereby increased. Economic activity in general then increased, resulting in a growth of the money supply, even though the amount of gold and silver on deposit remained the same.

Given the risks, it was inevitable that credit for long distance, long term trade developed as a bond between reliable associates, between members of the same family or guild, or between traders with the same interests in different cities. Associates would advance agreed sums to an enterprise; when it was concluded, they would share the proceeds. The bill of exchange was first widely used by merchants who bought and sold produce at the annual fairs in fifteenth-century Flanders. The bill was essentially a promissory note which guaranteed payment at a future date. Since usury was frowned on by the Church, skilful manipulation of exchange rates could be used to conceal the high interest rates which gave the purchaser of the bill his profit when he resold it. It was also useful in that it enabled a merchant to travel long distances without having to carry large quantities of specie which could easily be lost at sea or stolen by bandits.

A further advantage of the bill is that it was often negotiable; it could be sold to a third party, who would 'discount' it for cash – that is, buy it at less than its face value before it was due. If the price was right, it benefitted both the buyer and the seller of the bill: the seller could raise immediate liquid cash which he could put to use, while the buyer would make his profit when he realized its face value with the original issuer. Bills could thus pass through many hands and be used to lubricate many different exchanges.

Another advantage of the bill, since merchants were also moneychangers, was that bills could be played against the coins of different value in circulation. Some coins were better than others; they were made of purer gold or were less worn. But a worn coin had the same nominal value as a new coin, and thus in the marketplace people were obliged to accept coins of a lower real value. Moneychangers, therefore, could also make a profit out of the difference between the nominal and the real value of coins. Their trick was to give specie of the lowest real

COMMODITIES

value in circulation in exchange for the bill or foreign coins which their hapless client was proffering. 'In any payment, reach out for the currency in lowest esteem at the time', advised a seventeenth-century money-changer's handbook.

Moneychangers could also take advantage of the fact that silver and gold had different values in different places. For example, silver was worth about a fifth of the weight of gold in China and India, whereas it was worth about a fifteenth of the weight of gold in most parts of Europe (which explains why the British used silver rather than gold when buying tea from the Chinese).

EARLY BANKING IN EUROPE

A further aspect of credit is that, parallel to its evolution, there developed institutions which made credit possible. Initially these took the forms of 'banks' – a word derived from the Italian for 'bench', *banco*, the table which moneychangers set up in the market place. Their significance lies in the fact that they initiated the shift of power from the sovereign state, which minted coins, to the financial and mercantile sectors.

The first banks were established in Italy in the thirteenth century. It was Lombard bankers from cities like Florence and Lucca who brought banking to London; 'Roman Pontifical Money Dealers' was their official title. But these merchant princes – men like Ricciardi of Lucca, and Bardi and Peruzzi of Florence – lost their fortunes when Edward I and Edward III of England defaulted on their debts in the fourteenth century. The Lombard bankers (whose name still survives in Lombard Street, London) apart from being tax collectors for the Papacy, also lent to the English Crown and operated as deposit takers, moneychangers, and moneylenders at high rates of interest – loans were often secured against future delivery of wool. They also issued bills of exchange which enabled English merchants to buy commodities through their agents in Italy, and Italian merchants to pay for wool in England. However, the Italian bankers' credit was always backed by bullion. They were not public banks, and they confined their territorial claims to their local cities and to the Papal throne.

After the collapse of the great Lombard banking houses, their role in England was taken on by local merchants, tax farmers, scriveners, and goldsmiths. Tax farmers advanced loans to James I and Charles I, which explains their unpopularity. Scriveners acted as middlemen or brokers, accepted deposits and advanced loans. Some, like John Milton's father, finished up with considerable fortunes. Goldsmiths also discounted promissory notes and bills and accepted deposits which paid interest and advanced loans at higher rates. Significantly, however, they advanced loans on credit; Sir Roger North commented, 'merchants keep their money with goldsmiths and scriveners, whose accounts show ten thousand cash, but they seldom have a thousand in specie'. (Richards, p. 18)

Many were bankrupted when Charles I seized all the bullion in the Tower of London in 1640; others followed when Charles II defaulted in 1672. The tallies, promising eventual repayment at specified future dates, were bought and sold, thus serving as paper money. However, given the Stuarts' lack of credibility, the tallies were accepted only reluctantly and at rates far below their face value.

EARLY MONEY MARKETS

Banking in sixteenth-century Antwerp was quite different from that in London, because it fulfilled different functions. Flemish, Italian and German bankers met in Antwerp and established a bourse (literally a 'purse', though it came to mean a money market). There, they traded money at a point where currencies and commodities from all parts of the world were beginning to be marketed. It was at this time that Antwerp bankers began to imitate the Genoese, and Antwerp bankers switched from dealing in other commodities to dealing in money:

> alterations in the traffic have forced them of Genoa to change their course of trading with wares, into the exchanging of their money: which for gain they spread not only into diverse countries where the trade is performed with merchandise, but more especially to serve the wants of Spain, in Flanders

130

and other places . . . and thus wheresoever the moneys live abroad, circuiting the world for gain; yet in the end the centre of profit is in their own native country. (Mun, 1664, pp. 52–3)

This shift of emphasis explains why it was, that even as early as the sixteenth century, certain individual bankers, like the Fuggers, had financial empires infinitely greater than those of their client governments. The Fugger empire extended from Antwerp to Lisbon, and from Yugoslavia to the Americas. The Fuggers even opened a branch in Chile in 1531, less than ten years after del Cano's first circumnavigation of the world.

The great advance over Italian banking, invented by Antwerp bankers, was the role of financial mediation. Antwerp bankers borrowed from anyone who had surplus cash, and lent it to rising princes and collapsing dynasties. Fugger himself became an intermediary for many small lenders, all attracted by the high interest that Spain was prepared to pay on its borrowing.

From there the Antwerp bankers began collecting taxes for their royal clients. This activity was notoriously difficult and dangerous; few people had specie and everyone resented paying tax. Furthermore, the Antwerp bankers lent 'long' and borrowed 'short'; that is, they mediated between borrowers who wanted more time to repay and creditors who wanted liquidity. Of course, they charged high rates of interest for performing this useful function.

Money markets became much more complex and sophisticated in Amsterdam. With produce flooding in from all over the world came money of every description – cowrie shells, conches, Chinese silver bars, pearls, diamonds, and coins from every part of Asia and Europe. There were over four hundred currencies circulating in the United Provinces in the seventeenth century, and there was a vast profit, as we have seen, from changing currencies.

It was also in Amsterdam that merchants first discovered that commodity trading could advantageously be linked with currency trading – indeed, the failure to take account of the relative value of coinages throughout the world would rapidly have led to bankruptcy. Therefore, Amsterdam commodity markets developed in tandem with currency markets and currency exchanges. Furthermore, currencies began to behave like commodities in the fluctuation of their values – unless, of course, the trader's currency happened to be a core currency, like the ducat or dollar, which was taken as a standard of value.

Finally, the opportunities to make money work as a commodity were unparalleled in Amsterdam. In 1621 Thomas Mun reckoned that money shipped out to India would yield five times as much value in the end; he based that calculation on his knowledge of Holland. The delirium of Amsterdam (for a capitalist) was the freedom of money. Other commodities were taxed, food and land were taxed but money was free – it could come and go as it liked. Admittedly, some of it had to be given away in bribes but much of it already was 'offshore', funding rival ventures in England, Scandinavia and France, nibbling at the oligarchs' monopolies, feeding the enemy and circling the world like a Genoese banker's gold. In late seventeenth-century Amsterdam and London, the idea that money was a commodity, although a recent discovery, was already taken for granted by financiers and other commodity traders alike.

CENTRAL BANKS

The function of all of the early central banks was to provide valid money in place of a motley assortment of coins of uncertain worth. The earliest central bank in Genoa was founded in 1407, and by 1600 there were others in Spain and Italy. Since the state banks paid out only good coin while melting down worn or debased coins and reminting them, they paid less than nominal value on bad coins.

The Bank of Amsterdam, which was founded in 1609, also performed this role, but with so many coins in circulation this proved difficult. Instead, the bank bought in coins and issued bank money; in other words, it accepted deposits against transferable bank notes. This bank money was often worth more on the open market than the coin against which it was backed, since it was easily transferred and widely accepted. The bank also oversaw the minting of Spanish silver for local and Asian trade. It charged fees for opening accounts and transfers – when creditors and debtors both had accounts in the bank, the latter facility greatly speeded up settlements, since money did not have to change hands. The effect of this was to speed up the circulation of coins and thus the money supply. The bank imposed high penalties for overdrafts as well as making a profit on playing its own paper money on the market. It was not, however, a lending bank or a discounting bank. For every guilder circulating as bank money, there was a guilder in the bank. It was, in short, a 'bullionist' operation with a 1:1 capital/lending ratio.

Increasingly, during the seventeenth century, English mercantile thinkers came to recognize that Amsterdam's banking system, with its four per cent interest rates was the pump of Holland's empire of trade. There were many proposals for an English central bank. But when it was finally founded in 1694, the Bank of England differed from earlier prototypes in many respects. It was founded as a private joint-stock company. The original share-holders were interested in profit, not public service; they advanced £1.2 million to the Crown for a payment in perpetuity of £100,000 per annum. The stockholders included City men, Huguenots, Jews, and English investors at home and abroad.

Hitherto, extraordinary revenue for wars had been voted by Parliament. Following the creation of the Bank of England, the Bank not only lent to the Crown but also acted as agent for raising money in the City and the country at large through bond issues, such as navy bonds and war bonds. This was, in essence, the origin of the national debt. Thereafter, the Crown was settled with a revenue derived from customs and excise which sufficed to pay interest on its loans. As trade increased, its revenue increased. Thus there was a shared incentive among merchants and monarch to expand trade. King William, a competent general, returned to Holland to lead the alliance against France, while the merchants pursued profits from Asia to the Americas.

The War of Spanish Succession, which finished in 1713, increased the British government's borrowing from £2 million to £6 million a year. Since the interest was guaranteed, buying and selling of bank bonds and rapid taking up of new issues was a crucial feature of the London money market. Although individual bond issues were repaid with interest, the national debt was always rising as new bonds were issued. It was assumed that the debt would one day be paid off. It never was – in fact, just the opposite. In effect, the government only had to continue to pay interest; it could continue to raise funds as long as it could repay the interest, and it could continue to pay the interest as long as it continued to pursue a policy of successful conquest and expansion abroad.

The Bank of England, however, experienced several major crises in its early days. The inflation which its note issue provoked led to runs on the bank in the 1690s. Only two years after it was founded, it was saved from defaulting by borrowing funds, at high rates of interest, from Dutch financiers. In 1707, speculators tried to organize a run on the bank by cornering the specie in circulation in London and then presenting £300,000 in banknotes for payment. The run on the bank and the panic which ensued were only checked when various nobles and Queen Anne advanced specie and bullion, which saved the bank from closing its doors and thus undermining confidence in its stability. Another syndicate took the lucrative £2 million lottery from the bank in 1711. It was also threatened by the notorious South Sea Company, which wanted to take over management of the government's debt. Because of this competition, the bank was forced to lend more money to the government at lower rates of interest. However, the bank survived the stock market mania of the 1720s, when innumerable speculative joint-stock ventures collapsed along with the South Sea Company. By 1742, it had been granted a monopoly on printing bank notes in England and its security was established.

By 1750, the Bank of England was already performing the key functions of all central banks: it was responsible for issuing banknotes; it had bailed out collapsing banks and finance companies, that is to say, it had already emerged as a lender of last resort – though this role was not consolidated until the Bank Act of 1844; and it was

the key factors in the development of Britain's military empire of trade.

The function of central banks as lenders of last resort was also often criticized. Hankey, a nineteenth-century Governor of the Bank of England, for instance, attacked this notion as 'the most mischievous doctrine ever breathed in the monetary and banking world' (Kindleberger, p. 92). He argued that bankers and directors, knowing that a bank or firm would be saved from the consequences of their folly, would be more tempted to indulge in wild schemes in their pursuit of high profits. However, the arguments of Walter Bagehot, another financial expert, prevailed: 'A panic is a species of neuralgia, and you must not starve it.' (Kindleberger, p. 91) The medicine was free lending by the bank at very high discount rates, with a guarantee from the government that it would indemnify the bank against losses.

Thereafter, in an increasingly complex financial world afflicted by speculative cycles, it was inevitable that centralized institutions should be empowered by governments to take responsibility for stabilizing and maintaining confidence in the financial system. But, as we shall see, when the aims of the central banks of different nations and currency trading areas came into conflict, international mechanisms had to be invented to prevent the collapse of the whole interrelated financial network.

(top left) **Satirical print on the South Sea Bubble**

The principle of core powers printing money to roll over a national debt survives, however. Today, albeit in a slightly different form, the US government runs a $120 billion budget deficit to finance its military and space programmes. Half of the deficit is funded by US treasury borrowing abroad, because of the high exchange rate of the dollar. As US military spending increases the debt

increasingly being relied on by the government to maintain confidence in the national currency, sterling. Once confidence in the system was established, once exchequer bonds and navy-bonds had become a byword for safe investment ('gilt-edged stocks'), the national debt could continue to be rolled over and over. Bonds could be sold on the market as long as confidence remained in the government. Money kept rolling in. After that, the monarchy was an irrelevance; the king might not speak a word of English (like George I), or be mad (like George III). It made no difference, money now ruled England.

Britain's system for rolling over the national debt was both praised – 'the standing miracle in politics' (Mortimer, 1769) – and constantly criticized in Europe on the grounds that it would fuel inflation and would one day lead to an almighty crash. In fact, it must be seen as one of

increases – money which might have gone into productive investment elsewhere is thus locked into the barren and terrifying technology of supremacy.

CORNERING THE MARKET

With the developing power of financial institutions and the corresponding collapse of the monopoly companies, merchant bankers came to control other commodities as well as money. The collapse of the monopoly companies also created a vacuum which was rapidly filled by bankers who controlled the market by financial methods. Perhaps the most bitterly resented of all such operations were attempts to corner the market by controlling the production or supply of a commodity. All that was necessary was sufficient finance and a large warehouse. When prices were low, goods were stockpiled; then when prices rose due to a dearth, the merchant could sell at any price he chose. In 1787, hoping to push up the price, the Hope banking dynasty attempted to buy all the cochineal in Europe. But there was more cochineal than they had bargained for; dyers found other supplies, the price of cochineal didn't shift and the Hope bank deservedly lost millions when it was compelled to unload its stocks and to sell cochineal for less than it had cost.

Attempts to corner the market on a large scale rarely succeed. Novices in the City of London are still shown a mythical tramp, sitting on the steps of the Royal Exchange. He is 'the man who once attempted to corner the pepper market', but who did not realize that the Sultan of Zanzibar had warehouses full of pepper. The Sultan was only too happy to unload them at the high price that the speculator had created in his attempts to corner the pepper supply.

The best-known recent example of cornering the market is the Texan oil billionaire Nelson Bunker Hunt's attempt to corner the silver market in the late 1970s. As he bought up increasing amounts of silver, the price of silver rose from $6 an ounce. As the price rose, the gross value of his investment rose, enabling him to borrow more money from the banks, to buy yet more silver. In 18 months the price rose to $44 an ounce by February 1980; the spiral was only broken when the US govern-ment threatened to offload its supply of strategic silver, and reached an agreement with Hunt so that he quietly withdrew.

CREDIT ON CREDIT

Today, credit is advanced on little more than optimism and bankers' confidence. Even a mortgage in which the house is collateral is based on the assumption that should the borrower default on interest payments, the building society could claim the property and sell it to liquidate the debt. But should house prices collapse (as they did in Amsterdam in the late 1970s and New York in the 1980s), building societies cannot liquidate their assets and confidence in the market generally collapses. Ultimately, credit has to be based on something more substantial, and historically it usually was.

An early example of the failure to recognize this occurred during the Siege of Tournay in 1745, when there was shortage of money to pay the garrison. The sum was borrowed from the canteen, and it was then returned to the canteen so that the garrison could be fed. This was repeated for seven weeks. The sum borrowed was seven times the total money supply; not surprisingly, when the food ran out, the garrison surrendered. The moral: credit had to have some physical collateral.

Sophisticated and extensive credit operations probably could not have evolved as they did without the prior stimulus of trade, particularly with the gold and silver-rich Americas. Often, the departure of the Spanish galleon fleet from Seville was held up whilst it waited for English and Dutch ships to bring corn, woollen goods and other supplies. These goods were either advanced to the Spanish on credit or paid for by German and Genoese bankers who were themselves advancing credit to the Spaniards.

We have already seen why most of this bullion finished up in Antwerp. As bills of exchange or as specie, it then circulated into other economies, facilitating further production and trade. All of it, in the final instance, was advanced against the credit of Spanish bullion.

In order for money to create wealth it had to be 'set to work'. Christian apologists of moneylending cited the parable of the talents, (*St Matthew* 25, verses 14–30). Injunctions against usury were replaced by laws regulating credit. By the eighteenth century, moneylending was being seen as one of the most admirable routes to a fortune.

own servants, and ... them his goods. And unto one he gave five talents, 15 to another two, and to another one; to every man according to his several ability; 16 and straightway took his journey. Then he that had received the five talents went and traded with the same, and made them other 17 five talents. And likewise he that had received two, he also gained other two. But 18 he that had received one went and digged in the earth, and hid his lord's money. After 19 a long time the lord of those servants cometh, and reckoneth with them. And so he 20 that had received five talents came and brought other five talents, saying, Lord, thou deliveredst unto me five talents: be-

Take, for example, printing – a key industry in the development of a sophisticated mercantile empire which needed maps, trade and financial manuals, news sheets and so on. Between £500 and £1,000 was necessary to set up a printshop in London in 1700, but the return on that investment might be considerable. Thomas Guy, the bookseller and founder of Guy's Hospital, amassed a fortune of half a million pounds, because, in Daniel Defoe's words,

> he was a thriving, frugal man, who God was pleased exceedingly to bless in whatever he set his hand to, so that, the natural improvements of this money, by common interest, after it was first grown to a considerable bulk, greatly increased the sum. (Defoe, *A Tour through the Whole Island of Great Britain*, 1724)

That is a politic way of saying that Thomas Guy made his fortune in many ways including lending money at the official rate of interest fixed at five per cent. Even more impressive, having started on credit and having prospered, he advanced credit to others against the collateral

of his own business; that is to say, he advanced credit on credit, not on specie. What a simple way of making money make money! Guy was also an astute gambler in South Sea Company stock, buying £45,000 worth of shares at £100 a share which he managed to offload at between £300 and £600 a share before the market collapse in 1720. All that was needed was money or credit to start with, because the opportunities in an age when traders lived on credit were enormous.

Even more capital (or credit) was necessary for other industrial ventures in the eighteenth century. Between £5,000 and £25,000 would establish a brewery; Whitbread's spent £20,000 on their first brewery in 1740. When Thrale's Brewery was auctioned in 1781, Dr Johnson was not exaggerating when he stated, 'we are not here to sell a parcel of boilers and vats, but the potentiality of growing rich beyond the dreams of avarice' (Boswell, IV, pp. 86–7).

Nevertheless, the amount of credit ultimately depended on bullion or other commodities of some description. The development of the sugar trade in the seventeenth century, and the conquest of India in the eighteenth, did much to provide more 'fat' for the body politic. The plunder of Bengal by Clive and other nabobs meant that £38 million was transferred from India to England between 1757 and 1780; Clive's share of this was about £1.2 million. This money was transferred legally through the English East India Company or illegally through French and Dutch bankers, who took a large cut as commission agents and discounters of bills. Once back in England, it circulated and stimulated further trade and manufacture through the massive creation of credit which it facilitated.

This shift – from advancing credit on bullion to advancing credit on credit – is one of the fundamentals of financial development. It explains why capital/lending ratios were progressively lowered from 1:1, under a 'bullionist' system of credit, to 50:1 in modern banking practice, where much of the collateral is itself credit from other financial institutions. This phenomenon later became known as 'the multiplier effect', which simply means that economic activity stimulates further activity, and so on. This is one of the basic principles which underpins Keynesian economics, which advocated the role of central government in stimulating economic activity when private enterprise is either stagnating or declining. However, widespread general confidence is necessary to support such ratios; it would only need a major banking collapse to demonstrate just how insubstantial is the whole banking edifice.

Not everyone benefits from the increasing availability of credit. In a dynamic economy, credit increases the money supply faster than the amount of goods on the market, thus creating price increases for scarce commodities and general inflation. When this phenomenon occurred in late seventeenth-century London, for example, workers in the city were often not paid at all or paid in bills which were discounted at a lower rate, or else paid in truck which bound them to the manufacturer's stores. Strikes were commonplace from the shipyards to St Paul's Cathedral, where everyone from the architect to the masons was owed money by the government. Petitioners suing for wages lined the halls of government offices and aristocratic debtors, and many were forced to settle for derisory sums. Astute jobbers, men like Thomas Guy, made fortunes buying up navy tickets from indigent sailors at a 50 per cent discount in the taverns of Rotherhithe. Small debtors too, could expect little mercy from their creditors:

'Such a spirit of cruelty reigns here in England among the men of trade, that is not to be met with in any other society of men, nor in any other kingdom of the world.' (Anon, *An Essay on Credit and the Bankrupt Act,* 1707, quoted in Marx, *Capital,* vol. 1, p. 135)

Furthermore, poverty was essential if money was to prosper, as Mandeville ironically observed in 1706:

In a free nation where slaves are not allowed of, the surest wealth consists in a multitude of laborious poor . . . To make the society happy and people easy under the meanest circumstances, it is necessary that great numbers of them should be ignorant

as well as poor . . . We have hardly poor enough to do what is necessary to make us subsist . . . Men who are to remain and end their days in a laborious, tiresome and painful station of life, the sooner they are put upon it, the more patiently they'll submit to it for ever after. (Bernard Mandeville, *The Fable of the Bees,* 1706, pp. 294–5)

This growing proletariat also saw nothing of what Jonathan Swift called 'the wealth of the nation, that used to be reckoned by the value of land, [but which now] is computed by the rise and fall of stocks' (*Works,* vol. III, p. 6). These were stocks in trading enterprises and increasingly in industry – a clear indication that the motor of the economy had shifted from agriculture. Furthermore, class divisions in seventeenth-century England were even more pronounced in the countryside than the cities. But in both town and country, the misery was largely a consequence of inflation, as Charles Mathon de La Cour, a radical French deputy, pointed out in 1788:

'Gold and silver, which are ceaselessly drawn from the bowels of the earth, are spread every year throughout Europe and increase the amount of coin there, but nations do not thereby really become more wealthy: the price of foodstuffs and other things necessary to life increases by turn, one has to pay more and more gold and silver to buy a loaf of bread, a house or a suit of clothes, but wages do not rise to the same extent. Just when the poor man needs more money to live, this very need makes wages fall or serves as a pretext to hold them at the old rate, and thus it is that the gold mines have provided weapons for the egotism of the rich, enabling them more and more to oppress the industrious classes.' (quoted in Braudel, vol. II, p. 428)

The difference between rich and poor in Europe was further exaggerated in the difference between core economies and their dependent colonies abroad. The official coinage of the colonies was coin of the 'mother' country, though for reasons already given, the progressive lowering of commodity prices and increase in the price of manufactures, meant that little official money circulated in the colonies and inflation was constant.

At independence, almost all colonies floated their own currencies on loans from the mother country banks. Now producer countries not only have their own domestic inflation, but are also subject to the constant devaluation of their currencies against core currencies. An extreme example of this is the case of Brazil, where, it has been estimated, the rate of inflation between 1900 and 1983 was more than 73 million per cent! Overall, inflation is yet another cause of the increasing immiseration of the mass of the population of the Third World.

BETTING, GAMBLING AND FORWARD TRADING

The sixteenth-century Antwerp bourse was also a money market in another sense. Following predictions by renowned astrologers, whom we can assume were open to bribery, the players on the exchange ran bets and lotteries. Initially, these were often bets on when a ship would return. Merchants quickly realized that they could 'hedge' their risks by betting on the bourse. If a ship went down or was sacked by Dunkirk pirates, they collected on the bet on the bourse. If the ship returned, they could sell the cargo.

So betting was a way of covering risks. Marine insurers also used the bourse, since they knew the ships better than the average gambler. As information was valuable it too became a commodity which was bought and sold. Players on the Antwerp bourse also betted on future prices such as the prices of Amsterdam corn, or English wool six months hence. In essence, they were gambling on the prices of 'forward' commodities.

All these operations became more sophisticated in seventeenth-century Amsterdam. The betting on future prices of corn was transformed into dealing in 'commodities to arrive'. This meant that merchants gambled on the future price of corn in the cornbin of Europe; if they thought that the estimated price was too low, they signed contracts agreeing to sell corn at a future date, though they did not yet own it. When the date for delivery came, they bought it on the spot market and sold it at the contract price. In other words they 'went long'

on corn, they sold it before they had bought it (which, confusingly, is also known as 'selling short').

Amsterdam also developed what was known as 'trading in air' – for how could one sell what one didn't own, indeed something that might not even exist? Yet, 'puts and calls' (options to buy and sell commodities of every description, at a stipulated price, with payment at specified times) were well developed in Amsterdam. With an 'options' contract the buyer could either accept the commodity when it arrived or else pay an agreed sum 'if the party doth repent of the bargain'.

By the 1620s, speculation with paper assets of all kinds was already being commented on by visitors to the city. The tulip mania of 1636–7 was perhaps the peak of this tendency, when Amsterdam collectors were paying thousands of florins and guilders for a single bulb and were gambling in 'paper tulips' (i.e. contracts which promised future delivery of exotic bulbs). The bubble burst in 1637 when the Dutch government passed a law which required contracts to be met with physical delivery and hundreds of speculators went bankrupt.

As far as English merchants were concerned, the bill of exchange on Antwerp was the paper money of international trade until the 1560s, and wool merchants increasingly provided banking facilities for fellow merchants. In London, as in Antwerp and Amsterdam the financial nexus was the Royal Exchange, built in imitation of the Antwerp bourse by a wealthy merchant, Sir Thomas Gresham and opened in 1567. During the Cromwellian period its fortunes took off. Since all colonial commodities had to be re-exported through the mother country, London increasingly became an international market for Virginia tobacco, Caribbean sugar, Newfoundland cod, Indian cottons and China tea, as well as providing a market for slaves and ships. Commodities were bought and sold in the exchange, both wholesale and retail. Joseph Addison, in 1711 described the merchants of his day, 'negotiating, like princes, for greater sums of money than were formerly to be met within the royal treasury' (*Spectator*, 69, vol. 1, p. 212).

In 1695, the exchange first saw the buying and selling of Bank of England stock and shares in the East India

Company, soon to be followed by speculation in exchequer bills, navy bills and shares in dozens of other companies. The facility with which commodities could be translated into paper money, and vice versa, was one of the key features of the London and Amsterdam exchanges. An Italian merchant, Torcia, in 1782 described Change Alley in London as 'a more precious mine than any which Spain possesses in Potosi or Mexico'.

By the 1690s, most of the wholesale London auctions were being held 'by inch of candle' in the coffee houses nearby. There was as yet no official stock exchange, though Jonathan's coffee house was already beginning to fulfil that function – daily commodity prices and exchange rates were posted on the walls, bankers, merchants and businessmen, exchange currency dealers, bankers' agents and brokers all congregated there, though access to the inner sanctum was closed to outsid-

ers, who had to rely on brokers for information about prices. Already there was a clear distinction between brokers and the speculators who risked their money following the brokers' self-interested (and often misleading) advice.

As in Amsterdam, some of the operations were nothing more than gambling, when speculators bought and sold shares which they would never own, simply speculating on future prices of stock. Some of the operations were downright fraudulent, when outsiders were fed inaccurate information and bought stock through the brokers on the strength of it. In such a context it was difficult to distinguish genuine commodity dealing from gambling mania – stocks, shares, mortgages and bills were even placed on gambling tables in lieu of specie.

And what, after all, was insurance but speculating on statistical odds? The science of statistics was more or less invented by Sir William Petty in the Restoration period.

Edmund Halley, the astronomer, also demonstrated how mathematical principles could be applied to the calculation of life expectancy. Both innovations led to a much more widespread use of life insurance – though even this was threatened by gamblers, who bet on the lives of prominent people and then insured their lives to cover their bets, until the activity was stopped in the Gambling Act of 1774.

But even insurance could be transformed to guaranteed advantage. A merchant could advance a sum of money to a trading enterprise for, let us say, a two-year run to Africa and the Caribbean. He then insured that sum plus expected profits or interest. If the ship sank, he recovered his money plus expected profit minus premium, and if it came home safe, he merely lost the premium but still made the profit on the voyage.

I bet you five guineas Halley drops dead before his Comet comes back!

OLD-FASHIONED LIFE INSURANCE

Speculation in stocks and shares, however, often destabilized the whole operation, as the South Sea Bubble in London and the Mississippi Bubble in Paris showed in 1720, when gullible punters bought shares in companies which could never conceivably pay a divi-

dend because they were not involved in trading operations or the production of sellable commodities. Somewhere in the chain of credit and speculation there has to be a commodity.

Many outsiders get their fingers burned on such occasions, and thus most speculative manias are followed by severe withdrawal symptoms. Even so, almost every generation sees some bubble or other floated to gull the punters with the shortest memories. Another bout of gambling mania in the 1840s saw manic speculation on the London stock exchange in canal bonds and foreign securities, with spin-offs into other commodities, until the mania got out of control. By 1847, speculation in railway shares had reached insane heights. Then the frenzy shifted to gambling in corn, as speculators anticipated high prices for corn because of the potato blight in Ireland. They went long on corn and sent the price rocketing. This merely compounded the misery of the Irish, of whom a million died, because their potato crop was ruined and they could not afford corn at the speculators' price.

It is useful to divide speculators into two groups: 'bulls' who go long on a market in expectation that prices will rise and whose interest is to make that market rise (a rising market is called a 'bull market'); and 'bears' who go short on a market, in expectation that the price will fall (a falling market is called a 'bear market').

The speculator's skill is knowing when to get in to or out of a market. In this, various factors have to be taken into account. On the one hand, there are the fundamental market conditions, the conditions of supply and demand. The conditions of supply are determined by factors like weather, political stability, new capital investment in a productive industry and so on. Demand is determined by factors such as consumer taste or a new industrial use for a metal. On the other hand, there is statistical ('chart') analysis, which is information concerning the cyclical behaviour of a particular market, because markets go up and down. Both 'fundamentals' and 'charts' generate their own information industries, and speculators who follow one or the other are called 'fundamentalists' or 'chartists'. Traders say that fundamentals give them the

139

direction ('bull' or 'bear') while the charts give them the timing.

Charts tend to make successful predictions because speculators make decisions according to their expectation of what other speculators will do, thus turning expectation into reality. For example, if everyone believes that the copper market is going to peak (at say $890 a tonne), they will all begin to sell simultaneously, and the market will indeed fall. Such a point is known as a 'trigger point', which is crucial in a highly geared market, such as a futures market, in which even a small drop in the value of the commodity will entail a 'margin' call.

The information available to speculators is also contingent upon their status within a market. Speculators or merchants who trade on the market floor, and who can generally take advantage of inside information, are known as 'insiders'. Those linked to the market by a phone to their broker, and who only have available the standard market information, are known as 'outsiders'. Outsiders are intrinsically at a disadvantage. They come into the market late, tend to buy at the top and sell at the bottom, before retreating having lost almost all their risk capital:

'Common sense teaches that booksellers should not speculate in hops, or bankers in turpentine, that railways should not be promoted by maiden ladies, or canals by beneficed clergymen.' (Walter Bagehot, 1852, quoted in Kindleberger, p. 273)

Despite such advice, gullible outsiders continued, and continue, to get caught by the speculative activities of insiders.

BANKING, TRADE AND EMPIRE

Bankers particularly prospered when their client governments went to war because all the wages and supplies ran through their fingers and into their ledgers. Even if their clients lost, the bankers got royal land and jewellery. If they won, they got new trading empires: Minas Gerais, Hong Kong, Calcutta, Ceylon, wherever.

Bankers liked to extend their tentacles even beyond such fat colonial pastures. By 1800 there were four banking capitals in the world – London, Amsterdam, Hamburg and Paris –all with distinct empires and monetary traditions. They were, however, all locked together in various ways, sometimes by family like the Hopes and Rothschilds, but as often as commission agents for each other. It was an alliance of Paris and London bankers who managed to get jewellery and gold out of France during the Revolution, even if they failed to save the aristocratic necks the jewellery had once decorated.

Bankers became more sophisticated in their techniques as their clients battled around the globe. Even when their clients were at war, they were forced to co-operate with each other, if only to solve their clients' financial problems. Ouvrard, the great financier and munitions entrepreneur, arranged to discount Spanish bills for the French government in 1803, when France and England were at war. He approached Hope & Co, the Amsterdam and London bankers. Together they arranged a deal whereby the British would allow the shipping of Spanish silver needed by Britain for the China trade and by Napoleon for his army in Spain. Some of the silver was sold in America against exports and some was bought with London bonds which were shipped to Amsterdam and converted into francs. The francs were then forwarded to Napoleon who used them to fund his campaign against the British in Spain. Thus the transfer of money was effected from one ally (Spain) to another (France) with the assistance of the enemy (Britain).

Throughout the Napoleonic Wars, bankers continued to operate in this way. Payment for American commodities, particularly Spanish silver, was through bills on London, Hamburg and Paris bankers. At times, the silver to pay Napoleon's armies was actually carried by British warships.

On one occasion, Rothschild, acting for the British government, bought bills of exchange on a network of bankers in Paris. The bankers were mostly Jewish, with branches in Spain and Portugal, and Rothschild bought their bills with gold (this shipment was permitted by Napoleon because he thought it would weaken Britain).

These bills were then forwarded to Wellington, who used them to buy supplies in Spain and to fund his Peninsular campaign against Napoleon. Later, when Wellington needed francs, Rothschild obtained them on the Amsterdam market, because francs had flooded into Holland in increasing quantities since the French Revolution.

Rothschild's banking operations were not his only profitable wartime venture. Having a speedy and efficient communications network, he was able to receive news of Wellington's victory at Waterloo in 1815, before other London financiers. He immediately invested heavily on the stock exchange. When the news became public and confidence in the British economy was restored, he made a killing on the stock market too. Recounting the stories of his financial operations years later, he recalled 'finance during wartime was the best business I ever did'.

The sale of Louisiana, the greatest land sale in history, was even more spectacular. As always, Napoleon was desperate for cash, since France lacked a central bank and during wartime, specie was gained more by conquest and the imposition of indemnities on conquered territories than by raising loans from reluctant bankers. But in 1803, the US government agreed to buy Louisiana from France for $15 million. Louisiana at that time was a vast territory stretching from New Orleans in the south to Nebraska in the north covering more than 800,000 square miles, an area twice as large as the US itself. But even at the knockdown price of $18.75 per square mile, this sum could not be raised by the American government and Napoleon needed bullion. Once again, the problem was solved by an alliance of bankers in different capitals. The Baring Brothers raised half of the sum on the London markets with a £6 million loan which sold at a premium. The Hope bank did the same in Amsterdam, and the transaction was completed by the regular shipment of bullion from these capitals to Napoleon at regular intervals over two years. Once again, money without frontiers.

Throughout the eighteenth century, the executive committee of British capitalism was the Whig elite, representing trade and empire. The Tories, representing the squirearchy and the country interest, remained more or less in permanent opposition. The operation was funded, as we have seen, by taxes on various commodities which paid the interest on government borrowing. The Whig oligarchy filled all the leading government posts. New money, like that of the nabobs, could always buy parliamentary seats, though the price rose from £10,000 in the seventeenth century to many times that before the reform of the franchise in 1832.

Coal mining, the iron industry and textile manufacture – the key sectors of the early Industrial Revolution – were generally financed not by banks but by landowners and individual entrepreneurs out of the profits of their operations. Nevertheless, the Industrial Revolution also stimulated the Financial Revolution of the nineteenth century. The growth of a middle class, benefitting from this accumulation of wealth, also provided a store of wealth – if it could be tapped. Several mid-nineteenth-century developments facilitated the channelling of savings from a multitude of small savers into the financial system. Such developments included the founding of provincial banks, building societies, mutual provident societies, and so on.

Legislation had been introduced after the South Sea Bubble, which had prevented incorporation of joint-stock companies without an Act of Parliament. All other companies were restricted to six partners who were liable to lose everything if the company collapsed. Although designed to control speculation it was a measure which clearly held back both country banking and investment in industry during the early Industrial Revolution. From a dozen country banks in 1750, there were over 500 in 1800. But they were local operations and many collapsed in the aftermath of the canal mania in the 1790s, others when a Lancashire calico printer failed for £1.5 million.

Merchant banking also followed and created commodity chains. Brown's bank, for example, of Baltimore and Liverpool, shifted finished linen and cotton manufactures to the US and imported raw cotton to Lancashire. But these banks did not, in general, tap middle class savings, which were either hoarded or spent

COMMODITIES

on luxuries. Legislation in 1826 and 1833 created a system of country banks, all with main offices in London – which gave them the privilege of issuing paper money – which speeded up both local exchange and the sifting of the surplus into the banking system generally.

The tapping of local hoarding and the turning into profitable loans paralleled earlier commodity dealing, though this time, the raw material was money not sugar, and the supplier was the English middle class, not plantations in the West Indies. Vertical integration followed, in banking as in tea and sugar capitalism. Since all discounting finished up in London, the money market became London. From the London clearing houses it went into stocks and shares and circled the globe in search of profit. In the US, on the other hand, there were hundreds of banks, many of them localized and dependent on the fortunes of the local commodity. However, the collapse of domestic corn and oil prices in the 1980s has led to a similar pattern of integration within the US banking system as well.

Great Hall, Bank of England, c. 1800

It is also worth pointing out in this context, that in many modern economies, like that of Britain, a proportion of most people's salaries goes into pension schemes and much of the rest of their savings goes into property via building societies. Pension funds and building societies have thereby become major mechanisms for the channelling of small savings into London's financial markets. Savings which finish up driving labour in the gold mines of South Africa, and buying paintings by Renoir at Sothebys – a shift which ironically parallels earlier money flows from the aristocracy to the financial system.

FROM COMMODITY MARKETS TO MONEY MARKETS

In the days when the East India Company had a monopoly on tea imports to Britain, shares in the company were synonymous with a stake in the tea market. But as the trading monopolies were either dissolved or undercut by the developing free trade interest in the eighteenth and nineteenth centuries, specialized markets developed on specific sites, each with their own institutional practices and traditions – the stock exchange, Lloyd's insurance market, the Baltic exchange (for shipping), the commodity markets around Mincing Lane, and so on. As ever, the relationship between money markets and physical commodity markets was closely linked. Banks advanced money to merchants to finance trade, and merchants had to contend with the problem of the different currencies they needed in order to purchase their raw materials. Today, currency fluctuation continues to be a factor which commodity merchants have to take into account but their main problem has always been the value of the stocks that they hold.

Forward buying of foodstuffs and other commodities had been a common practice since the fourteenth century, but a contract, in those days, was made between a merchant and a producer whom he knew. By the eighteenth century this process had been transformed into forward buying on a global scale, as well as being systematized and institutionalized around specific commodities of agreed weights and quality. In 1823, Parliament merely recognized what was a long established practice:

'Not only that the merchants of Great Britain are constantly in the habit of making advances on merchandise consigned to them for sale, to the extent of two-thirds or three-quarters of the value, but that they are also in the habit of obtaining advances themselves from bankers, corn factors, brokers and others, upon the goods so consigned to them, as well as upon their own merchandise . . . and it is carried on to such an extent that it may be considered essential to the carrying on of trade.' (Parliamentary Committee 1823, quoted in Rees, p. 29)

Forward markets could only succeed where the merchants had some control over the merchandise. The merchants advanced money or credit so that goods could be collected; it was they who insured the cargo and so on.

A similar problem emerged for corn growers in the American mid-west in the nineteenth century. They harvested corn and delivered it to the elevator owners in the autumn. The latter, however, could not get the corn to the grain silos in Chicago until the spring because of the winter freeze; they therefore lacked cash to pay farmers for their corn. By the 1850s, the 'river merchants', as the elevator owners were called, were travelling to Chicago and selling 'forward' to the Chicago mill owners, which provided them with cash to pay the farmers. The mill owners in their turn sold 'forward' to clients in New York and elsewhere. The problem for all of them was how to set the future price.

It was here that Chicago speculators, with risk capital, stepped in. If they thought that the future price offered was too low they bought forward, hoping to make a killing when corn reached the market in the spring. If it seemed too high, they sold corn (which they didn't yet possess) for future delivery, hoping that they could buy corn in the spring at a lower price. Such speculators were

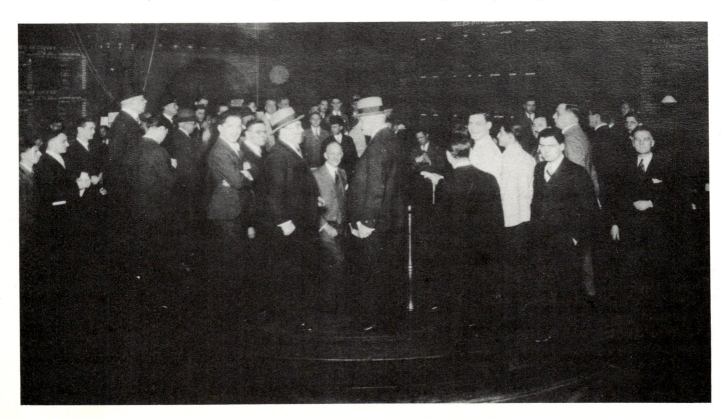

Futures market in coffee and sugar, New York, 1916

simply taking on the risk from the merchants and millers and, in the process, hoping to make a profit.

But one problem remained. The grain had not yet been sampled – indeed, it might not even have been grown when the contract was drawn up – there were often disagreements about the bargain when the grain was finally delivered. Since gunshot used to echo around the exchange in lieu of specie, it was rapidly systematized into a standard contract for the delivery of a standard quantity of corn, of standard quality, at a stated date and place. It was thus possible and easy to trade these standard contracts throughout the winter months – and the forward market in actual produce became a commodity futures market.

Although forward markets in physical commodities and commodity futures markets became essentially different operations, there are still crucial links between them. First, it is fundamental to the operations of both that when a contract 'matures', however many times it has changed hands in between, the physical commodity must be delivered, with agreed price variations for delivery of different grades of produce at different locations. Without that condition, futures markets become pure speculation with no relationship whatsoever to the material world. Equally important, is the relationship which merchants establish in the use that they make of a futures market to 'hedge' their risks in their physical commodity trading. The essence of a hedging operation is that a merchant who is holding stocks needs to protect himself against price variations, and hence changes in the value of his stock. This he can do by buying futures to the value of the stocks he holds. The reason why the merchant uses the futures market rather than hedging forward is that he does not have to put up the full value of the contract, only a 'margin' – which may be as low as ten per cent of the full value of the contract – in other words, the market is highly geared. The advantage of this margin system, is that by putting up only a percentage of the contract value he can speculate in the full value, which is many times his initial stake – in a stock market, on the other hand, the full value of the contract has to be staked. In the end, the rationale for the existence of futures

markets is that they provide a forum for merchants and speculators to meet, enabling the speculator to gamble and the merchant to limit his risks.

The Chicago Board of Trade, which established the first grain futures market in 1865, not only developed contracts for future delivery of corn of a specified quality, at a specified date, at an agreed price and at a specified place, but it also made one further crucial innovation. At the Board of Trade, 'ring traders' (whether speculators or merchants) did not have to buy or sell particular contracts but could sell a contract to one ring member and buy from another; the market itself would cancel the two operations. What this meant was that any member could trade with any other member. For the first time, contracts were not made between two named individuals; they could be bought and sold like any other commodity. Thus contracts themselves became commodities.

Finally, trading profits are made by buying cheap and selling at a profit. However, since crops tend to mature in the same month and ships tend to take time to reach the markets, most commodities were subject to massive price fluctuations. It is no coincidence that in the nineteenth century large amounts of capital were spent on developing faster and faster sailing ships (culminating in the tea clippers), and later, in developing fast steamships which could transport a greater weight of cargo, thus lowering the unit cost of the commodity. The opening of the Suez Canal in 1869 and the Panama Canal in 1914, of course, also shortened journey times.

Perhaps the most significant development of all, in its impact on commodity markets, was the laying of underwater telecommunications cables. The first permanent cable link between Europe and the US was in use by 1866, and other transcontinental cables were soon laid. Such links made instantaneous communication between producer countries and markets not only possible, but also a condition of the market. For the first time, there was a massive disparity between the arrival of news and the arrival of commodities. The combination of telecommunications with the underlying risk which every merchant had to take led to the formal separation of forward markets in physical commodities and commodities futures markets in specific places.

Futures markets were established in New York in grain, coffee and sugar in 1882. Liverpool traded grain futures the next year. London imitated Liverpool in 1887 and began trading coffee and sugar futures the next year. Today there are futures markets in pork bellies, orange juice, shell eggs, Idaho potatoes, rubber, coffee – almost every commodity which has a fluctuating price.

COMMODITY MARKETS TODAY

Today, coffee is bought and sold in a market which in many ways is similar to its seventeenth-century prototype. Then, there were merchants, brokers, roasters, and probably a few speculators, drinking coffee, tasting coffee and bidding for it by 'inch of candle' in Garraways. Later, when speculation in commodities became attractive to outsiders, those already in the game, the brokers, locked the doors of the coffee houses and formed 'rings'. When the brokers moved out of Garraways they built themselves a larger market building, and agreed that all trading should take place at specific hours and under agreed conditions.

The gambling operations inherited from Antwerp continued alongside coffee marketing, and occasionally they would intersect when coffee prices began to move up and down enough to attract speculators; this was not uncommon, given the unreliability of shipping and the increasing caffeine addiction of European consumers.

The London brokers also took on that other function of Antwerp moneylenders like Fugger; they drew outsiders' funds into the game. It was also a formal market where the insiders competed for commodities under an agreed set of rules, at a fixed place, usually called the 'floor' but often the 'pit'. (It is worth noting how much of the vocabulary of money capitalism derives from gambling and blood sports.)

Many of these roles and operations still exist in the modern coffee market, though it is now a global and not simply a metropolitan market. London is linked to New York, Paris and São Paulo, where the main coffee markets are, and to merchants and brokers throughout the world. There are, however, many more types of

coffee on the wholesale market today, whether forward or 'spot' (coffee available for immediate delivery). Some of it, like the *robustas*, will be of more interest to the big roasters, the manufacturers of instant coffee; other finer *arabicas* will be bid for by the more specialist coffee men.

They all know what kind of taste they are looking for; their problem is to find enough of it in bulk at the right price. The roasters almost always start with samples and the coffee merchant's job is to find it for them and sell it to them. He ensures that the coffee is shipped and delivered on time and that it is of the right quality. The merchant also has to ensure that it is accompanied by the correct paperwork, which, in the case of coffee, includes the documentation for export and import under the market controls imposed by the International Coffee Organization (see below under Commodity Agreements).

To be able to buy large amounts of coffee on the forward market, a trader needs to have credit of some sort; indeed a large amount of the world's credit is tied up in financing trade. Bankers who advance this credit to merchants usually demand, as a condition of the loan, that the merchant hedges the value of his coffee on a

Futures market, New York, 1980s

coffee futures market, whether in London or New York. The banks want to ensure that the coffee against which they have made the loan is not going to lose its value. Trading on the 'floor' of the futures market is restricted to members of the Market Association, who not only act as principals on their own account, but also as middlemen, who buy and sell for others and who ultimately must accept responsibility for their clients' debts if they default. The biggest traders will almost certainly also be brokers, but they are as likely to buy through other brokers, so that they can conceal their actions from other trade houses.

Despite the domination of most commodity markets by the big operators, they nevertheless continue to provide a medium for speculation which is particularly attractive to those who have the liquidity to withstand big losses and who are attracted by the potential windfall profits which a highly geared market provides. In the late 1970s, such markets were particularly attractive because the rate of interest was below the rate of inflation. Therefore, speculative money was not interested in fixed-interest investments, as a contemporary commodity broker comments:

> It's a very clean-cut business – one telephone call and you're in a market and another one and you're out. So they're an exceptional way of using up your risk capital. Commodity markets are attractive in that there are situations in the world of raw materials and commodities whereby the supply/demand balance shifts. There might be a drought which would affect grain prices in the States, or there might be a coup in Peru which would affect copper production, and one can really benefit in a very clean-cut way from a price movement in the underlying raw material . . . The underlying commodity often gets forgotten about in the price movements. A lot of money comes from European markets (which is obviously not liable to UK tax), or is money that's off-shore and likes to remain off-shore. (John Burridge, Interview from the *Commodities* series, 1984)

In such markets, therefore, speculators have no interest in the underlying physical commodity material. For them, a commodity futures market is merely another paper money market. Should prices cease to fluctuate speculators will put their money elsewhere.

FROM STERLING TO THE DOLLAR

Mine eyes have seen the glory of the coming of the Americans – substantial dollar bringing virgins . . .
e.e. cummings, 'Memorabilia'

During the nineteenth century, the British financial and industrial revolutions were matched, and in some ways surpassed, by similar developments in Germany, France, the US, Japan and Russia. They all developed central banking systems, joint-stock legislation, provincial banking networks and invested in new technology. The Bank of England had become the central bank for the whole sterling trading area, not just the British economy, while other central banks took on similar roles.

As trade between the different trading empires increased, the responsibility fell on central banks to maintain the parity of their currencies against gold and against each other. This accompanied the competition for colonies and new trading areas not under direct colonial control, like Latin America. This competition was itself a major cause of the First World War. The main belligerents financed their war economies by a mixture of taxation and government borrowing. While the British opted for a 50:50 mix, the Germans and the French financed their war effort by 85 per cent borrowing, in the expectation that the losers would be compelled to make reparation for the war debt of the victors.

The result was financial mayhem. Germany was never able to meet the reparation payments exacted by the Treaty of Versailles (1919), but the payments which it did make contributed to the massive inflation of the Weimar period (1918–33). Neither the dollar, the franc nor sterling (which had the added responsibility of being used as a reserve currency by other powers) succeeded in stabilizing their parity with gold again after the war. In the case of sterling this parity had been more or less maintained since the early eighteenth century. In the inter-war period, however, sterling was undermined by the growing power of the dollar, the massive European indebtedness to the US, the capital flows necessitated under the reparation agreements, and national competitiveness between the US, French and British governments. Rather than striving for international cooperation, each government saw its currency as a virility symbol of the national economy.

The Stock Market Crash of 1929, and the consequent fall in commodity prices, led to a general loss of confidence in the banking system. The bankruptcy of the Creditanstalt bank in Austria (leaving only $14 million debts) triggered off a chain of bankruptcies throughout Europe, which central bank cooperation was unable to prevent. In 1931 Britain came off the Gold Standard; from then on the big question became not, 'what is the exchange rate of the pound?', but 'what is that of the dollar?'

During the 1930s, there were many attempts to reactivate and regulate the stagnating world economy through international financial institutions. These included international commodity agreements, and suggestions for the creation of an international central bank to act as a lender of last resort. None of these suggestions, however, were implemented. Most governments retreated behind tariff walls and attempted to revive their national economies by printing money and reducing unemployment through public sector investment and rearmament. Hitler built the autobahns, Mussolini the autostrade, Roosevelt's 'New Deal' in the US saw massive government spending on welfare and public works, and Keynes's theories were put into practice in Britain by government spending on housing and education. In the end, however, it was war spending which revived the economies and mopped up the reserve army of unemployed.

In 1945 it seemed that the financial lessons of the 1930s had been learned. The allied war effort was funded by the 'Lend-Lease Agreement', under which the US provided arms and supplies to the Allies, agreeing to settle accounts after the war. The recipients collaborated with

'PHEW! THAT'S A NASTY LEAK. THANK GOODNESS IT'S NOT AT OUR END OF THE BOAT' (1932)

the US in constructing a multilateral world trading system different from the bilateralism which had prevailed before the war. This guaranteed the US entry into traditionally protected European trading areas. Since the US was the only major industrial nation not to be crippled by war, 'Lend-Lease' underpinned the emergence of the dollar as the dominant force in post-war reconstruction. The Bretton Woods conference of 1944 led to the creation of the International Monetary Fund and the World Bank – the remit of both was to assist the Third World.

European reconstruction was funded by US bankers through the Marshall Plan of 1947, on the condition of political loyalty to the US. This lent money to Europe at fixed rates of interest, principally in the form of trade credits, which not only financed European recovery but also further stimulated US industrial production. The Marshall Plan was essentially the application of Keynes's theory on an international scale. With the consequent growth of the world economy and the dissolution of bilateral trade agreements, a new tariff agreement was established under the General Agreement on Tariffs and Trade (GATT) of 1948. Through such institutions the Western economies strove towards world domination under a banner of free trade which disguised the reality of protectionism and the Third World's comparative disadvantage.

COMMODITY AGREEMENTS

Following the Second World War, attempts were made to regulate international trade in many basic commodities. These were influenced by pre-war measures, and by US-imposed wartime quotas intended to encourage Latin American economies to align themselves with the Allied war-effort rather than the Axis powers (Germany, Italy, Japan).

Commodity agreements were sponsored under the direct aegis of the United Nations (coffee) or under the aegis of the UN Conference of Trade and Development (rubber, wheat, cocoa, sugar, tin, and others). Commodity agreements aimed to regulate the price paid to producers. This was achieved in two ways – by the creation of a 'buffer stock' or by a quota system.

For many years the Tin Agreement (1954) was perceived as the model of all commodity agreements. It operated through a buffer stock mechanism. The manager of the agreement was financed by member governments (both producer and consumer countries) to purchase excess tin on the international market if prices fell below an agreed trigger price; thus the manager would create a 'buffer stock', from which he would make sales when the price rose above an agreed upper limit.

However, the US, despite being the major user of tin, now refuses to support the agreement for ideological reasons. Bolivia, the third largest producer, also dropped out because it lacked the financial resources, though it also benefited from the higher prices the agreement brought. Despite the fact that the agreement covered only 65 per cent of the world tin market, it operated successfully to control prices for thirty years.

The effect of the Tin Agreement was to keep the price within an internationally negotiated price band. However, technological developments in the motor industry, and packaging innovations in the 1960s and 1970s, reduced the international demand for tin. Producers were unwilling to allow the price band to fall since their economies depended on their tin exports.

Consequently, by 1985, the tin buffer stock manager was defending a price of about £8,000 a tonne, when the estimated 'free market' price was around £4,000. The buffer stock got bigger and bigger as the manager spent more and more money buying surplus tin from producers who were able to stay in production because of the high price. Since the manager was the biggest buyer on the international tin market and was apparently financed by governments, he was advanced substantial credit by metal merchants, particularly on the London Metals Exchange. In 1985, the London Metals Exchange suspended trading in order to buy time for the member governments to negotiate additional finance, which, however, was not forthcoming when member governments refused to recognize their debts. When the buffer stock manager finally ran out of credit and could not meet his obligations, both the tin market and the Tin Agreement collapsed.

The collapse of the tin price bankrupted many brokers on the exchange and undermined its credibility as the price setter of the international metals market. It also precipitated economic, political and social upheaval in tin exporting countries like Malaya and Bolivia who were crucially dependent on tin revenues.

THE COFFEE AGREEMENT

The International Coffee Agreement, on the other hand, operates with an export quota system, under which the burden of warehousing surplus production falls on the producer country and not on a buffer stock manager. Each exporting country is allocated a quarterly quota which it undertakes to export. If the international coffee price rises above an agreed range, each country's quota is increased; if it falls below the agreed range the quota is reduced. The task of administering the system falls on the International Coffee Organization. The task of overseeing the quotas falls on the Customs and Excise authorities in importing countries, who collect the shipping and export documentation and deliver it to the ICO to ensure that quotas are adhered to.

Unlike the buffer stock system, the mechanism is bureaucratic and still subject to misuse. Producer countries, for example, sometimes undership their quotas to increase prices. Speculators sometimes stockpile coffee in tax free ports when prices are low; when prices rise and quotas are suspended, they import it and sell it at the higher price.

Nevertheless, over 90 per cent of the world's coffee is covered by the Agreement. The benefit to producer countries is that their coffee income is stabilized even though the price of coffee has not risen as much as the price of industrial imports. However, they are burdened with the enormous cost of purchasing and warehousing surplus coffee production. For example, the National Coffee Federation in Colombia, like Marketing Boards in other countries, is essentially a government within a government, with immense financial and industrial responsibilities. The Colombian Federation is responsible for the income of 300,000 coffee producers, it warehouses up to 13 million sacks of coffee (the current value of which is around $3 billion). It has its own instant coffee plant, fleet and bank, and is responsible for the construction of roads and the electrification of the coffee growing areas in Colombia.

For consumer countries the benefits of the Coffee Agreement are political rather than financial. There would be a direct economic benefit if coffee prices were prevented from going through the roof – which they did in 1975, after the Brazilian frost – yet 'the real reasons why they are in the ICO is for reasons for foreign policy' (Octavio Rainho Neves, Director of the Brazilian Coffee Institute, 1982, interview from the *Commodities* series).

After the Cuban Revolution and the Cuban Missile Crisis, the US government attempted to link Latin American development even further to US needs. Because of the importance of coffee in many Latin American economies, the first International Coffee Agreement of 1962 was supported by the US.

Almost all the other commodity agreements have collapsed, in part because the commodities can be grown in consumer countries, or replicated by other commodities produced there. Rubber can be replaced by oil-derived substitutes, sugar and wheat are grown in temperate climates, and others collapsed because consumer countries lacked the will to make them work.

Despite the current antipathy of Reagan and Thatcher to commodity agreements because of their dislike of

COMMODITIES

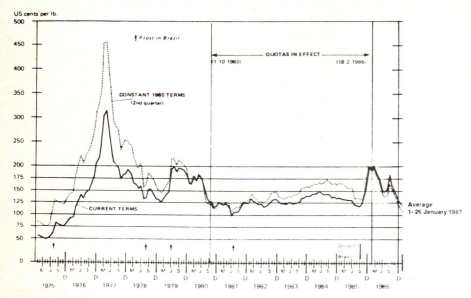

US cents per lb.

Frost in Brazil

QUOTAS IN EFFECT
(1.10.1980)   (18.2.1986)

CONSTANT 1980 TERMS
(2nd quarter)

CURRENT TERMS

Average
1- 26 January 1987

1975 1976 1977 1978 1979 1980 1981 1982 1983 1984 1985 1986

Coffee prices have been more stable while quotas were in force

commodity mountains financed out of the profits of trade – unlike the wheat, sugar, beef and milk mountains which are the results of policies introduced to placate the domestic agricultural vote – the Coffee Agreement is one of the few to have survived. As coffee is the second most valuable traded commodity after oil, and important to an increasingly unstable Latin America, the political will to make it work exists:

> We see the importance of the revenue of developing countries in terms of political stability and planning, because most of these countries have very large foreign debts, and they need to service them. So it's in our interest to keep the purchasing power of developing countries intact because we are also selling to them. So our interests are interlinked, we have mutual interests and this flow of money must be kept intact. (Abraham van Overbeeke, Netherlands Undersecretary for Trade, Interview from the *Commodities* series, 1984)

However, even the Coffee Agreement may not survive. In 1986, when the price of coffee remained above $1.40 a pound for more than a month, quotas were automatically suspended. When the price subsequently fell again,

consumer country hawks (the US, Britain and the Netherlands) used their powers of veto over the reintroduction of quotas as a platform to renegotiate aspects of the Agreement. They objected to the alleged undershipment of coffee by some producer countries, and to the selling of cheap coffee on the 'parallel' market, non-ICO member countries like South Africa, Hong Kong and Israel; and they demanded the reallocation of export quotas to match increased consumer demand for higher grade mild *arabicas*. But under the leadership of Brazil, the country most threatened by this latter demand, the producers refused to budge. In March 1987, coinciding with Brazil's moratorium on debt repayment, the Agreement collapsed. The coffee price plunged to below one dollar a pound, no doubt to the satisfaction of the hawks, and to the pleasure of the coffee multinationals who need not pass on the reduction in price to the individual consumer.

If the Coffee Agreement remains dead there will be no significant commodity agreement left in operation. It will be the final nail in the coffin of the integrated commodities programme of the United Nations Conference on Trade and Development – a programme which had attempted to establish a common fund which would finance commodity agreements in 18 commodities, but which never worked because the Western powers refused to co-operate. The resulting loss to producer countries is, of course, immense, the resulting benefit to consumer countries in terms of low commodity prices, hardly needs to be stressed.

MONEY NOW

Since the Second World War, there has been a huge growth in the scale and complexity of the world's financial system. The period also saw a shift from highly regulated war economies throughout the world, to (in theory) an increasingly global 'free market' economy.

Given the pre-eminence of the US economy in the post-war period, it was the dollar, convertible to gold at $35 an ounce, which became the core currency for international settlements. This meant that while the settlement of balance of payments within trading blocks could be effected in the currency of that block (for example, the

150

use of sterling within the Commonwealth) settlements between trading blocks and national economies were effected either in dollars or gold.

The world's liquidity was therefore based on the accumulation of gold by the US government which backed the printing of dollars by the US Treasury. This meant that it was the US economy which regulated world development. This responsibility was assumed, if not actually seized, by the US after Bretton Woods, through interventions like the Marshall Plan, and through institutions like the IMF and World Bank.

As the post-war world reindustrialized, the financial system had a more stable base, but it also required modification and development. In the Cold War era there was a perceived need for the construction of a European trading block to counter the US and the Soviet world, for why should all country to country transactions be effected in dollars? Increasingly, there was pressure on the recovering European powers to replace the system of bilateral capital transfers, effected in dollars, with a system which was multilateral and more flexible.

Following the creation of the EEC, a new method of currency convertability was introduced in 1958. This permitted francs to be exchanged directly for marks and so on, and thus, at a time when central banks were still responsible for the parity of their currencies, there was an established and quoted rate which did not have to be first translated into dollars. Even so, the dollar retained its status as the core currency of value.

British policy makers, at that time, still saw Britain's destiny in terms of its Commonwealth, with Britain retaining control of financial structures through control of sterling. But, with Britain's poor post-war performance, there was a growing pressure on sterling to be devalued, in order to improve Britain's industrial competitiveness. It was now perceived that Britain's place in the international economy could not be ensured merely by stimulating the national economy through Keynesian measures. Devaluation in 1949 was followed by another in 1967. Both devaluations were seen as symbolic of the collapse of Britain's economic primacy and virility.

There was, however, a developing threat to western financial stability caused by the US's developing balance of payments deficit from the 1960s onwards. By the early 1970s, there was a massive accumulation of dollars in the reserves of Europe's central banks. It was argued that the dollar was overvalued in relation to European currencies, for if the dollar was lower, US exports would be more competitive and the US trade deficit would be reduced. However, this would be breaking the sacred cow of dollar parity with gold. The only alternative would have been a massive exodus of gold from the US. So in a simultaneous move in 1971 the core European currencies were, by international agreement, revalued in relation to the dollar and the dollar was devalued against gold to $38 an ounce.

However, the devaluation was not sufficient since the other core powers were not content to sacrifice their own competitiveness. By 1971, the pressure was such, reinforced by speculation, that the dollar had to come off the gold standard. Thenceforth, gold became just another commodity, albeit with special status, (current value around $400 an ounce). All currencies were allowed to float against each other and currencies came to be traded like any other commodity.

It was argued that market forces should be allowed to determine exchange rates and thus the relative competitiveness of national economies, because it was no longer possible for any single national, or indeed international institution, to regulate the international economy. But such a free market was inevitably prone to the cyclical exaggerations caused by speculation in currencies. Therefore the international role of central banks is now limited to intervening to even out excessive fluctuations in exchange rates.

The absence of exchange rate policies, meant that governments had to rely on interest rate manipulation and control of the money supply to influence the national economy and the exchange rate. If national interest rates are high, speculative capital flows into a country and raises the exchange rate; although the exchange rate is still seen as a virility symbol, the industrial competitiveness of a country is reduced and it makes it more difficult to finance investment. It also reduces the money supply,

'Try to think of something that doesn't require dollars'

COMMODITIES

since high interest rates make overdrafts and lending more expensive. If interest rates are low, competitiveness is increased, the exchange rate goes down, money is cheaper, demand for money increases faster than the supply of goods and inflation results. As the core economies of the US, Europe and Japan shifted to a more integrated trading system, national economies became more difficult to control.

It is significant that the 1970s became a period of considerable inflation in the western world, when the rate of inflation rose higher than interest rates. This meant that in real terms there was a negative interest rate. This encouraged borrowing both nationally and internationally. Internationally the flow of funds to the fast growing economies in the developing world led to the debt crisis of the 1980s, while nationally this borrowing fuelled further inflation. The only measure left to the Western powers to regain control of the global economy, and in particular to put an end to the high growth rates of developing industrial competitors of the south, was to pull in the reins by raising interest rates, reducing the money supply and putting up protectionist barriers.

Exchange rate parities had to be abandoned as a key component of both international and national economic management, giving way to 'monetarist' policies in the mid-1970s. Central banks printed less money, governments cut public spending, the money supply was reduced and capital investment was increasingly subjected to market forces. The theory was that the resulting growth in competition would weed out inefficient industries and make capital and labour available for new industrial initiatives. But, in reality, labour forces cannot be re-educated, retrained and relocated without massive social and political upheavals. The result, therefore, has been bankruptcy of industries throughout areas of Europe and the US, and the increasing shift of industrial power from the Atlantic to the Pacific basin, and from the declining north of the US to the developing industrial economies of the south. The one area in which the northern economies continue to dominate is in the financial services sector, because the immobility of labour contrasts with the startling fluidity of capital.

CURRENCY FUTURES

Throughout the 1970s, and in particular after 1973, there was a boom in the financial services industry, for now, every market was connected to every other market and there was no point of stability which was defended by any international institution. The value of shares affected interest rates, interest rates affected commodity prices, commodity prices affected exchange rates, exchange rates affected the policies of governments, these affected the value of gilts, which were themselves affected by what the governor of the Bank of England said over dinner, or what the IMF was doing to Brazil.

Information about the state of the markets and any factors which might affect the markets became so valuable that information itself became a key commodity (the information industry has become one of the leading sectors in the international economy of the 1980s). Smart money now shifts around from market to market and plays one off against another (arbitrage) often within seconds.

It is in this context that in 1972 the Chicago Mercantile Exchange launched the International Monetary Market in which the principles of the futures trading of physical commodities were applied to currencies, the stock exchange index, interest rates and other financial indicators, thus marking the latest move of money to its status as commodity.

Financial futures became a virtual necessity within a free market economy for those with capital. Capital has to be held in some material form; if that material form is inherently unstable and subject to speculative manipulation, then capitalists, if they do not wish to speculate, need to hedge their financial risks. For example, an industrialist who is making a forward contract for the construction of (say) a dam in Kuwait, for which he will need dollars a year hence, would not be able to cost the project if he did not know what the cost of dollars will be in a year's time. Instead of buying the dollars forward, which would tie up his capital, he can lock in a price on the currency futures market by buying a futures contract to the value of the dollars he will need. On the futures market this merely involves the outlay of a small percentage of the full value of the contract.

Likewise, capitalists can hedge the value of currencies they actually hold; they can hedge the value of their stock exchange investments, or any other financial instrument they hold for which there is a futures market. As with physical commodities, hedging only works where there is speculative capital which will take on the hedger's risks, and which makes a profit out of the successful trading of the markets. It is worth pointing out again that there is a fundamental difference of interest between the speculator and the hedger, for while the hedger's aim is to stabilize his production costs and the value of his assets (and thus he does not mind how the futures market moves), the speculator's aim is to exploit market movements. The delicacy of the distinction between speculative (risk) and productive capital, is that if productive capital is not hedged a risk is being taken – not to hedge is to speculate.

For speculators, financial futures markets provide yet another medium for gambling with their risk capital. The gearing on these markets is even higher than it is on traditional commodity markets, that is to say, the percentage of the face value of the contract which has to be put up, is very low. For example, for £1,000 down he can speculate on the shift in value of £1 million worth of dollars or marks. In 1984, 180 million futures contracts were traded world wide, of which about half were in the financial sector. The astronomical growth in twelve years from zero to some 100 million traded contracts, with a face value of around a million dollars each is still increasing exponentially. The latest growth area is in options contracts, which are future options to buy a futures contract – a further shift of money into the realm of pure abstraction!

The variations in the values of national currencies against each other led central bankers to devise new financial tokens, like the European Currency Unit (ECU), which is a basket of European currencies. This was intended to act as a stable measure of value, being abstracted from and balancing out the shifting values of the currencies in the basket. But money can never be that abstract, for it can never forsake its historical origins. It is

always also a currency – and now of course, there is a futures market in ECUs!

Given the increasing mobility of capital, and the reliance of the City of London, in particular, and the British economy in general, on the financial services industry, the British government has embarked on a harmonization of British financial practices with those of the rest of the world. This deregulation ('the big bang') is creating a revolution in the structure of the City. The self-regulating practices built up since the seventeenth century are being disbanded, directly opening up the markets to foreign capital and companies. The result will be the gradual elimination of the traditional smaller City partnerships and enterprises as they get taken over and absorbed by the financial services transnationals. In the same way that industry is now controlled by corporations such as ICI and Unilever, the financial sector will be controlled by Nat West, Amex and Citicorp.

The rationalization of the world financial system under the control of a few huge financial bureaucracies will eliminate competition, and this might impose some order on the markets. But it is doubtful whether it will do so in the interests of the majority of the world's population.

So, while the commercial markets are spinning into a dizzy flow of electronic digits, made possible by the high-tech revolution, the core powers are faced with the task of preventing the world's financial system spinning out of control. For this they have to rely on constant international negotiation and on institutions like the IMF and the Bank of International Settlements, whose task it is to ensure that capital is redistributed to parts of the globe from which commercial capital has flown in its pursuit of higher profits elsewhere. But it still remains to be seen whether institutions like the IMF have the skill, and whether the core powers have the political will, to prevent the whole edifice collapsing.

Commodity Capitalism Today six

*Our target market is the 18–30 year-old male reader.
The prime interest of such people is sport, music,
clothes, cars and women. We shall provide an ample
sufficiency of those commodities in addition to top
quality news reporting.*
David Sullivan, prospective publisher of the new
Sunday Sport, May 1986

Almost everything in the present world system is potentially a commodity. Women, and images of them, are treated as commodities. Drugs, information, televisions, videos, high technology are all commodities with a market price. Goods from all over the world, dressed up and promoted by advertisers, continue to flood onto Western markets; the same goods are on sale throughout the world – wherever there is money to pay for them. The world's labour force is now organized worldwide and almost everyone, in varying degrees, has been sucked into the vortex. In this final chapter, therefore, we look at some of the forces which have created such patterns of global integration and inequality.

COLONIALISM AND CAPITALISM

*Whatever happens we have got
The Maxim gun and they have not.*
Hilaire Belloc

The nineteenth century saw a massive extension of European colonialism, particularly in Africa; by 1914 only two African countries, Liberia and Ethiopia, were not controlled by some European power. India, Burma and Sri Lanka were now European plantations; south east Asia was divided up between the British, French, Dutch and the US. The richest segments of the Chinese Empire were largely in the hands of the Japanese, British and French, though Germany and Russia also grabbed some

of it. Although the independence of Latin America had been 'guaranteed' by the Monroe Declaration of 1823, it was effectively an Anglo-American economic colony, with Haiti, Cuba, Costa Rica and Panama already established as US satellites.

The motive behind US and European policy was to secure raw materials for industry and food for the rapidly growing urban workforce. The development of new technology required new raw materials; tin, copper and rubber for electricity; rubber, petroleum and many metals for the car industry; aluminium for aeroplanes and so on. The industry behind this global land grab and the greatest consumer of its resources was, of course, the arms industry.

The wholesale destruction of resources in the First World War increased the demand for raw materials and thereby the demand for labour in the producing countries. More and more miners were sent down the gold mines of the Rand and the copper mines of the Congo. Everywhere, labour was forced onto plantations to grow whatever the gullet of capitalism demanded.

This global carve-up destroyed local economic systems everywhere. People who had enjoyed the use of the land for centuries were forced off it, if that land was in any way exploitable by Western interests. Colonial governments set up departments which sold concessions to favoured white colonists such as Lord Delmare, who got a thousand acres of prime Kenyan farmland at a penny an acre. And everywhere, the indigenous population was evicted onto marginal land, which eroded

Anti-government graffiti, Jamaica, 1986

provide labour to work in the mines and on the plantations for wages fixed by the foreign companies with the connivance of colonial government officials. This system was established in German Tanganyika, French West Africa, the five Portuguese colonies and in most of the territories under British control.

Often, where land was not directly expropriated, land taxes were introduced, allegedly to pay the costs of colonial government, and peasants were compelled to grow cash crops in lieu of money taxes. The Europeans also took land they did not cultivate in order to force native labour into the mines and onto the plantations, where they were paid as much for a week's work as European labour was paid in an hour. For example, in Enugu, Nigerian coalminers in the 1930s were paid one shilling a day (5p), when European miners were earning five shillings an hour. In Northern Rhodesia, mine labourers were earning seven shillings a month, agricultural workers 15 shillings a month, and so on. The European powers saw non-European peoples as commodities which could be transported around the world like slaves. Indians were shipped to Africa and the Caribbean to work on plantations; Chinese and Lascar sailors were recruited for European navies, and regiments were raised in India and Africa for the defence of white imperialism at home and in Europe.

The consequent expansion of production based on cheap supplies of raw materials meant that, under pressure from organized trade unions, capital was able to pay higher wages to the working class at home. Within Europe, after the 1880s, there was therefore a retailing revolution, as companies expanded to supply the hitherto neglected working-class market, particularly in groceries like tea, sugar and soap. The more successful companies bought out their competitors and expanded both at home and overseas. The biggest companies were obviously in a position to undercut the rest because of economies of scale – the larger the operation, the smaller the individual unit cost. Lipton cut a shilling off a pound of tea, Lever cut fourpence off a pound of soap, and so on.

By a process of mergers many commodities like tobacco, soap and tea were soon dominated by a handful

quickly, causing floods, drought and finally famines – a process which gave rise to the convenient myth that the natives had always been poor farmers.

The scale of these expropriations was colossal. Between 1934 and 1940, one and a half million acres of the best food-growing land in Egypt was taken by foreign companies to grow export crops like cotton, while the Egyptian populace starved. Lever Brothers negotiated a single concession of a million acres in the Congo to grow palm oil for their soap and margarine factories. US corporations took over the sugar plantations of Cuba and established banana dictatorships throughout Latin America. Almost everywhere in the Third World, the story was the same.

Land, however, could only be sold if native claimants were evicted, but the eviction of native populations itself created a labour shortage. This problem was solved, particularly in Africa but elsewhere as well, by the 'forced labour system'. Villages were compelled to

of companies – a process which has continued. By the 1980s, five companies controlled more than half the grocery retailers in Britain, and single companies like Unilever and General Foods have turnovers greater than the gross national product of the 20 poorest countries in Africa.

RISE OF THE TRANSNATIONALS

The roots of transnational corporations can be traced back to the big trading operations of earlier centuries which had depended on the subjugation of indigenous peoples by the imperial powers. We have already examined many examples of this: the East India Company with its opium plantations in Bengal, tea warehouses in Canton, and a fleet which carried the wealth of Asia back to London, enjoyed effective monopoly trading rights in three continents by the 1830s. Lipton's – with its plantations, factories and grocery outlets – had achieved, by 1900, complete vertical integration of the tea production and marketing process from Sri Lanka to Europe.

In the 1860s, however, a new kind of trading company emerged. Manufacturers like the US Singer Sewing Machine Company established factories abroad using local labour and management to supply local markets with patented goods. Profits were repatriated and transport costs were minimized. The new technology of the period – steamships, railways and the telegraph – meant that central control of the operation could be maintained, even at a distance of thousands of miles.

The advantage of this corporate strategy became clear in the period of protectionism which followed. By 1900, the industrialized European countries had begun to erect tariff barriers to protect their own industries from foreign competition. The tariffs raised the prices of imported goods and manufactures above those of locally produced goods, encouraging the development of industry and agriculture. Between 1871 and 1914, Germany industrialized at a massive pace behind protectionist tariffs; its coal output increased from 38 million to 279 million tons, iron production increased tenfold, and its steel, electrical and chemical industries became the

'Shipping in the Hooghly', Calcutta docks, 1890s

157

most advanced in the world. Russia and France followed suit in the 1890s, developing their own heavy industries behind tariff barriers.

Protectionism hit foreign companies badly, since it either wiped out their export markets entirely or forced them to compete with locally produced goods. For these reasons, many of the biggest companies established plants within the 'protected' country itself; Dutch companies established margarine factories in Germany, German and Swiss companies built textile factories in France, the Germans built chemical factories in Russia, and so on. If profit repatriation proved difficult, the profits were reinvested in the new 'host' country, often leading to rapid expansion and local takeovers.

By 1914, other US firms like Ford Motors and Standard Oil had moved into Europe; European companies like Lever Brothers, Courtaulds and Royal Dutch Shell were established in North America. Today, perhaps 70 per cent of the biggest transnationals are US based; yet until the mid-1950s, European companies had more investments in the US than the US had in Europe.

The transnationals also expanded where they could, buying up competitors in order to lower their costs, and then, from a position of strength, setting the market price. Many also attempted to corner the market by forming cartels, in order to hold the prices of raw materials down and the prices of manufactured goods high. This happened with chemicals, explosives, oil and aluminium.

By the Second World War, seven oil companies, 'the Seven Sisters', controlled the world oil market; only two, Shell and BP, were not US based. Together this oil-marketing cartel controlled the price of oil worldwide until the mid-1970s. By the 1980s, Ford had plants in 25 countries and ranked among the ten biggest corporations in the world. Standard Motors (later General Motors) followed; like Ford, it bought up smaller competitors as they went bankrupt as a result of price undercutting by the biggest transnationals.

In general, each of the early transnationals concentrated on a single commodity: Coca Cola, motor cars, rubber, oil, whatever. But after the Second World War

they began to diversify and since the mid-1970s they have rapidly accelerated this process. Many of the biggest companies have now merged with other companies or have been taken over by them; food manufacturers have been absorbed by property companies, hotels by airline companies, property companies by newspapers and so on. Many of these mergers are effected by holding companies or finance houses which operate as front men for anonymous backers, so the ultimate source of control is unknown. Often too, the motive behind a takeover is 'asset stripping' – the sale of less profitable sectors and then the revival of what remains before it, too, is sold to another company.

Most transnationals, for administrative purposes, are based in one country, but many, for financial reasons, are registered in countries which offer corporate tax benefits, (like Britain, Luxembourg and Lichtenstein) or in tax havens (like Andorra, Monaco, Bermuda and the Cayman Islands). Many, also take advantage of 'free production zones', where local labour produces manufactures for export and where transnationals enjoy major tax and customs benefits.

Structurally, transnationals differ. Some adopt a policy of 'vertical integration' attempting to control the whole operation from the extraction of the raw material, through processing and transport, to marketing the product. The big oil companies are good examples of this. Others adopt a policy of 'horizontal integration', buying up competitors until they dominate the market and are in a position to fix prices for that product. Unilever and General Foods demonstrate both tendencies very well. They not only operate worldwide as buyers and producers of raw materials, but have diversified into innumerable manufactured commodities. Although less visible than better known companies with brand-name products, they are now two of the biggest companies in the world. Significantly, Unilever attempted a takeover of General Foods in 1984.

UNILEVER

The history of Unilever is instructive. It was the product of an amalgamation in 1931 of two companies – Lever Brothers of Britain and Margarine Unie of Holland. Lever Brothers was itself founded by William Lever, who started off as a Bolton grocer in 1867. In 30 years his company and his product, Sunlight Soap, dominated the British soap market. Lever employed American advertising techniques, spending a fortune on promoting his product. Despite low profit margins, his high turnover enabled him to put his rivals out of business.

Next, in order to protect his supplies of raw materials, Lever bought up vast land concessions in Africa. When the First World War broke out he moved into margarine, hitherto a German monopoly, though customers said that his margarine tasted like soap, and the troops refused to eat it. Soon, through one of his subsidiaries, the United Africa Company, he had control of the Nigerian market in groundnuts, cotton, cocoa, hides and skins. Free from competitors, his company could set the price it paid for raw materials; for example, palm oil fell from 14/- (70p) a gallon to 1/2d (6p) between 1922 and 1929.

After the merger with Margarine Unie, the operation diversified even further. Both soap and margarine are compound products, made from different fats and oils, and both were 'inventions' which necessitated scientific research and controlled manufacture. Increasingly, this was the direction which Unilever took – inventing new commodities – because there is much more profit in, say, a hundredweight of fish fingers than in a hundredweight of cod. Food processing became more cost effective, with waste products being sold as animal feed and fertilizer by Unilever subsidiaries, while the nutritional value of the foodstuffs they produced declined.

In the 1930s, Unilever courted Hitler, and established

cheese, hair dye and ice-cream factories and fish processing plants in Germany. Since foreign companies in Nazi Germany were not permitted to repatriate their profits, they were spent on the construction of a fishing fleet in Hamburg; when war broke out, the fleet sailed out of Germany and became part of Macfisheries, another Unilever subsidiary.

In 1943, Unilever bought Birdseye and Bachelor's Canning; in 1944, Pepsodent and Lipton's. Acquisition of John West and Walls followed. With the advent of fridges and washing machines, Unilever capitalized with specialized soap powders and convenience foods, aimed at a working population where women were increasingly drawn into full-time employment. Unilever bought Vesta and Fray Bentos; Oxo was gobbled up in 1984. Once Brooke Bond was acquired, Unilever had control of 60 per cent of the world tea market. Now Unilever is the largest food corporation in the world, with a turnover of £13 billion a year. It has ocean-going

159

freighters, factory ships, trawler fleets, oil and timber mills, slaughter houses, sausage factories, advertising agencies, chemical plants, perfumeries, even vinyl floor covering companies; it also has overall control of 500 other companies.

TRANSNATIONALS AND UNDERDEVELOPMENT

Today, 200 transnationals control one third of the world's Gross Domestic Product. Certain commodities like oil, bananas, tea, bauxite, copper, iron ore, nickel, lead, zinc and tin are completely in their hands. In both the Third World and Europe, tariff policy, economic development, trade treaties and political and economic unions have been influenced by the transnationals' need to make profits. Their power as buyers also made it difficult for local industries to develop in response to local needs, which, in part, explains why transnationals expanded so rapidly in the Third World countries as the suppliers of processed foodstuffs.

This domination continued even after colonies achieved independence in the post-war period. The withdrawing colonial powers often succeeded in establishing puppet governments which could be relied on to maintain trading and commercial links. And even where land was nationalized, this didn't much matter, since the greatest profits, as we have seen again and again, are not made by the producers of raw materials. Those producers still had to sell to the transnationals, at prices fixed by the latter so the ex-colonial powers still controlled the processing and marketing of the commodities.

In many instances, the new governments collaborated completely with their old masters. In Sri Lanka, for example, the government sold plantations cheap to foreign tobacco companies, thus forcing the peasants off the land to work in the factories, hotels and brothels of the cities. The rhetoric of 'the free world' is often revealing. When uranium was discovered in the Congo, a US adviser on aid, Clarence B. Randall commented:

'What a break it was for us that the mother country was on our side! And who can possibly forsee today which of the vast unexplored areas of the world may likewise possess some unique deposit of a rare raw material which in the fullness of time our industry or our defense programme may most urgently need.' (Clarence B. Randall, quoted in Hayter, p. 68)

Later, when a socialist government led by Patrice Lumumba became imminent in the Belgian Congo, the CIA staged a coup to protect US economic interests.

The discovery of raw materials has never significantly improved the standard of living in those producer countries. Semi-processing which, the UN estimated in 1975, might have earned Third World countries an additional $27 billion per year was not permitted by the transnationals. Throughout the twentieth century, the price of raw materials has fallen relative to the price of manufactured goods, forcing producing countries to produce more and more cash crops and minerals which they are able to exchange for fewer and fewer imports.

Furthermore, the power of the transnationals prevents indigenous manufacture from developing. Foreign companies raise on average 80 per cent of the capital they need in local money markets in developing countries. So, even though capital is available, local investors prefer to lend it to the big foreign companies rather than local enterprises, thus further increasing the drain of capital from the Third World.

Few of the biggest companies pay tax. Because they control the whole operation, their accounts can attribute their profits entirely to subsidiaries based in tax havens. Real rates of profits, if measured in world market terms, are often several times the declared rates, ranging from 50 per cent to 400 per cent a year in certain reported cases. In the final instance of course, since they are so secretive about their operations, none of these figures are at all exact. Only someone with access to the central computing system of the biggest companies could hope to unravel the complexity and scale of the operations, as this quote reveals:

A Swiss holding company with a majority share of a West German manufacturing company turned out to be controlled from New York by agents, who in turn, were acting for companies in Saudi Arabia and Brazil, which were part subsidiaries of intermediaries registered in the Cayman Islands, the largest owners of which were insurance companies and pension funds in Sweden and Britain. (Harris, p. 123)

OIL AND CAPITALISM

Our dependence on foreign oil is a clear and present danger to our national security.
US President Jimmy Carter

Oil, the most valuable commodity in world trade, has immense strategic and political importance for several reasons. It is not simply the major energy source of all industrial societies but an essential component of the plastics and chemical industries as well. Three countries –

the US, the USSR and Saudi Arabia – produce over half the world's oil and still have enormous reserves. However, since the two 'superpowers' consume all the oil they produce for their own industry, the Middle East remains by far the greatest supplier of oil on the world market.

Until 1939, most of the oil-producing countries were under foreign control. The Seven Sisters of the international oil cartel (Shell, Exxon, BP, Texaco, Mobil, Gulf and Socal) took advantage of this. For the payment of small initial concessions, they took what they wanted and made enormous profits. Kuwait, Oman and Iraq were British 'protectorates'; Persia (now Iran) was partitioned between Russia and Britain; the Red Sea coast of Saudi Arabia was under Ottoman (Turkish) control; and Saudi Arabia only became an independent kingdom in 1932. However, the surge of independence movements after 1947 changed the picture. Kuwait became independent in 1961; Aden was evacuated by the British in 1967 to become capital of the Republic of South Yemen; Oman, Bahrain, Qatar and the United Arab Emirates followed in 1971. But all these ex-colonial states were essentially Third World economies, since none had hitherto profited from the processing and marketing of oil; they lacked development advice and the technical and financial skills because the oil companies had no incentive to help them acquire these.

The Seven Sisters had almost total control of the 'free world' oil market until the early 1970s. They controlled the operation both 'downstream' (the refineries) and 'upstream' (the wells). Since they ran the whole operation, they felt no need to negotiate other terms with the producers. As a consequence, the price of crude oil dropped steadily in the post-war period, from $2.30 a barrel in 1948 to $1.30 in 1960.

It was against this line-up that OPEC was formed. By 1960 the oil-producing countries realized that they could increase their revenue from their oil exports only if they formed a producer cartel and if all the members of the cartel acted in unison to hold prices up by restricting production. Initially it comprised Venezuela, Saudi Arabia and five other smaller producers. For the first ten

(left) **OPEC's first meeting, 1960**

161

years of its existence it was totally ineffective. The Seven Sisters refused to recognize OPEC, let alone negotiate with it. Their policy of 'divide and rule' easily played off one producer against another. However, after the cutting of the oil pipeline between Iran and Syria during the Yom Kippur War (1973), the West suddenly became aware of the ease with which producer countries might cut off supplies; prices doubled to $2.70. In the same year OPEC instituted a boycott against the West for its support of Israel in the war; the price rose further to $7 a barrel, to $11 the next year, and again to $15 in 1977. After the fall of the Shah of Iran, the West panicked in response to the threatened shortage; speculation pushed the price up to a peak of $40 a barrel in 1980.

Initially, however, the Seven Sisters benefitted from the OPEC price increase because it increased the Seven Sisters' profits and made it economically more viable to extract oil from less accessible places. But the frenetic exploration which resulted contributed to the glut and subsequent fall in oil price in 1985/6, when oil dropped again to $10 a barrel. Meanwhile some countries, like Algeria and Libya, nationalized the oil fields and took over the running of the business.

In the 1970s, however, the Middle Eastern countries lacked the financial and governmental institutions to take advantage of these massive oil revenues. They were obliged to depend on the Western banking system to handle the revenues, and on Western construction companies to develop their oil fields, roads, ports, airports and so on. They imported food rather than developing their own agriculture. They also spent a massive amount of the surplus on arms, mostly bought from the West, but also from the Soviet bloc. Western producers of luxury goods also benefitted from the influx of petrodollars.

But the high price of oil encouraged oil-importing countries everywhere to find alternative energy sources – coal, natural gas, nuclear power, and, in the case of Brazil, fuel alcohol from sugar. Energy-saving programmes and the decline of industry in developing countries, which could not afford oil at OPEC's prices, both lessened the demand for oil at OPEC's prices. Non-

OPEC producers like Britain and Norway benefitted from the high OPEC price, while undercutting it and maximizing production to take advantage of the boom. All these factors contributed to the halving of the demand for oil on the free market between 1980 and 1985.

The consequent oil glut sent prices falling again, to $27 a barrel in 1985, and then to $10 in 1986, a price at which it was no longer economic for many producers to keep wells open. The price drop caused immense problems for developing countries like Mexico and Nigeria for whom oil was the major source of foreign earnings, and for new producers like Britain and Norway as their tax revenues from oil fell and their oil industries floundered.

The full effect of the collapse of oil prices has still not been registered. The Middle East, despite its vast petrodollar reserves abroad, has failed to buttress itself against dependency. In order to stave off budgetary deficits and internal crises, it will have to repatriate its holdings in Western banks. This in turn will effect stock market and property prices everywhere – for what went up with the petrodollar will have to go down with the glut.

But even this scenario is tentative. The 1986 Chernobyl nuclear plant disaster will affect power policies as countries reconsider their nuclear programmes. The prices of oil and coal are likely to increase, which may make abandoned pits and oil wells financially viable again. And funding of research and development of solar, wind and wave power, and geothermal energy, hitherto all rejected as being too expensive, could radically alter the energy map of the world.

THIRD WORLD DEBT

After 1973, the Western banking system was awash with petrodollars from the Middle East. Domestic investment in 'developed' economies was sluggish due to rising unemployment and industrial decline. Governments and banks chose not to reverse this decline through investing in new industries with low immediate returns; they chose, instead, to make short-term profitable loans to Third World governments. These loans also seemed to be profitable, because, for Third World countries the rate of interest was lower than the rate of inflation – in effect, Third World countries were being paid to take the money off the bankers' hands. But 'developing' countries, having embarked on a process of modernization and industrialization, then found that the prices of their raw materials were falling and the costs of oil and machinery were rising. In order to stave off collapse, they took up further loans, courted by Western bankers. As Armen Kouyoumidjian, a Mexican banker, recalls:

> There was a lot of glamour associated with it. The jetsetting banking crowd arrived in private planes, had meetings with Finance Ministers, were entertained at the highest level, and then came back saying 'this country is very good because the golf course is excellent, and the Central Bank serves a first class lunch'. Some of the basic principles of banking, such as credit analysis, caution and moderation, were thrown out of the window, and some banks didn't even bother to consult economists. And international lending for a while was a very profitable activity. (Interview from the series, 20 June 1985)

The first loans were fixed interest at six per cent, but gradually they were replaced by variable-interest loans, which in five years hit a peak of 17 per cent on a much larger debt. As the oil price went up, so borrowing too

increased; but as the crisis in industrialized countries worsened, commodity prices tumbled as manufacturers closed down. Developing countries were forced to export more raw materials for lower returns, as well as borrowing more money, at higher rates of interest, in order to import essential goods, oil and food. The debt became a vicious circle.

It might be assumed that such massive loans would have increased the productive capacity of developing countries, but this was rarely the case. Western banks seem not to have cared or monitored how it was spent. In Gabon, for instance, $1.2 billion went on a triumphal highway linking the airport and the President's Palace, prestige government buildings for a non-existent bureaucracy, hotels for a non-existent tourist industry, a fleet of jets which is now mothballed and a railway system which does not work. In Honduras, it was spent on a new jail. Some of it was appropriated by local dictators who squandered it on jewellery and real estate in Europe and the US. Some was spent on arms, finding its way back to the biggest arms manufacturers – the US, the USSR, Britain, France and Italy. And some of it, syphoned off by corrupt politicians and financial speculators, finished up in Swiss banks. Whatever the case, most of the money found its way back to the West.

Hitherto, the basic assumption which underlay foreign lending was that the outflow of money to debtor countries would always be greater than the sums necessary to service the loans, until, at some future date, the borrower was strong enough to repay the debt out of increased export earnings. Until that time came, unmanageable debts would be 'rolled over' with new loans at higher rates of interest.

In the early 1980s, Western bankers and economists in developing countries woke up to the problem. A third of the petrodollar lending had been funneled through the 'money centre' banks, mostly based in New York, a third through Lloyds and the Midland and other European banks, and a third through Japanese banks. They were most exposed in Latin America. If Mexico, Brazil, Venezuela and Argentina defaulted, this would wipe out their entire capital reserves. Although the African debt was smaller, it was being repaid from a lower standard of living, causing widespread malnutrition and famine. Many banks were overextended, having lent even more capital than they had in reserve; the Midland (205 per cent), Lloyd's (165 per cent), and US money centre banks (127 per cent), were the most vulnerable.

The accounting was also extraordinary. Words like billion (in US terminology, one thousand million) entered everyday language. The total Third World debt was around $850 billion, though estimates varied. Much of this debt was not in the borrower country at all, but merely 'paper money' – that is, money in the form of promissory notes and agreements to reschedule, which were accumulating hypothetical interest. The net outflow of money from debtor nations was colossal. In certain cases, one third of their exports went towards servicing the debt, yet it was getting bigger and bigger.

WORLD BANK

YOUR LOSS IS OUR PROFIT

AUSTERITY IMPOSED

Finally, in the late 1970s, the troubleshooters of capitalist banking, the International Monetary Fund (IMF), the World Bank, and the US Agency for International Development (AID) bank, intervened. The IMF insisted on austerity measures in developing countries as a precondition for rescheduling their debts. Wages and luxury imports were to be cut, the currency devalued to make exports cheaper and essential imports more expensive in order to balance their budgets. Thus the brief 'petrodollar boom' of the 1970s was followed by swift economic and industrial collapse; local industries were deprived of essential raw materials and components;

strikes, riots and widespread unemployment ensued.

Even before the debt crisis, the US had freely intervened to head off opposition to its favoured model of dependent 'development'. For example, after Jacabo Arbenz was elected President of Guatemala in 1950, with 63 per cent of the vote on a platform of extensive land reform, his government redistributed 162,000 hectares of uncultivated land to 100,000 peasant families. Despite paying compensation to the US United Fruit Company, Arbenz was ousted (and later murdered) by a handful of disgruntled mercenaries, financed by the CIA in June

The Brazilian tinderbox

Ten thousand enraged rural workers recently set fire to crops, destroyed public buildings and fought pitched battles with riot police in the town of Guariba, in São Paulo's rich farming belt. A year ago mass rioting and looting by unemployed industrial workers broke out in the state capital.

Incidents such as these, together with bloody anti-IMF riots in the Dominican Republic, have forced bankers to consider the social effects of the economic readjustment policies being imposed on Latin American debtor countries.

The revolt in Guariba ended after an ... higher piecework ...

1954. The puppet government of Castillo Armas returned the land to the previous title holders, peasant and labour unions were crushed and at least 100,000 opponents of the regime were murdered. A 1981 Amnesty International report on Guatemala concluded 'torture and death are part of a deliberate long term programme in Guatemala.' (Jonas et al., p. 235). Moreover, when Chile elected a left-wing government in 1970, Henry Kissinger, Nixon's Secretary of State commented, 'I don't know why we should stand by and watch a country go Communist due to the irresponsibility of its own people' (quoted in Hayter, p. 116). In Chile's case, aid was reduced from $130 million to zero and World Bank loans were frozen. But after the 1973 CIA-organized coup which brought Pinochet to power, money from US banks flooded back in. The same thing happened in Colombia in the mid-1970s, when the government attempted to nationalize a forest concession belonging to a US company. Once again, a withdrawal of aid was threatened.

By the early 1980s, such overt coercion could not so easily force compliance, as the Third World's ability to repay the debt was ever receding. Initially, the petrodollars had caused inflation since they were used to stimulate a consumer boom (Coke, Pepsi, TVs, radios, and so on). It was hoped that the boom would stimulate production, as people moved into the factories to assemble components, cheap textiles, toys and consumer goods for export. Others would move onto the plantations ('the green revolution') and grow crops for northern markets. By 1980, the soaring price of oil and the collapse of Western markets had revealed the emptiness of this cheap industrial dream; many factories were closed and the prices paid for export crops had dropped by about a third.

In Brazil by 1982, over ten million people were earning less than half the official minimum wage and malnutrition had spread to a third of the population. The next year, spontaneous riots and looting broke out; 225 supermarkets and shops were broken into. Scavengers rooted and fought among the garbage tips; people were driven to extraordinary feats of improvisation in order to stay sheltered and alive. For the cuts demanded by the IMF were cuts in real incomes which were already critically low.

Between 1979 and 1981, interest rates in debtor countries rose faster than inflation; the (theoretical) outflow rose from $15 billion to $44 billion. Much of it was paper money rolling over the debt. Over the same period, oil prices also rose, creating a further paper money burden. In certain countries too, inflation had spun right out of control. In Brazil, annual inflation had reached 400 per cent by the end of 1985, which led the military to hand

Road-block constructed by protesters after news of oil price rises, Jamaica, 1985

the responsibility of the debt over to a civilian government. In the year before it fell, the military government had been issuing a mass of short-term bonds, index linked to inflation, in which the (paper money) rate of interest worked out at 30 per cent. Thus in less than a year, Brazil theoretically spent $4.3 billion paying interest on a money loan which its people never actually saw!

All the countries were forced to float their currencies against the dollar in order to raise the loans in the first place. Inflation attracted speculators who made fortunes in a bull market which pushed the peso, cruziero and other currencies higher and higher. This rise in real exchange rates between 1980 and 1983 (Argentina 60 per cent, Mexico 41 per cent, Brazil 34 per cent) made imports even cheaper and exports more expensive. It also made foreign assets cheaper (palaces abroad, real estate, Swiss bonds). Over the same period, it is estimated that

165

$28 billion was transferred out of Mexico, $21 billion out of Venezuela, and $11.5 billion was smuggled out of Argentina. In the Philippines, Fernand Marcos's loot alone is reckoned at $5 billion. 'Baby Doc' Duvalier in Haiti and Samoza in Nicaragua also escaped with vast fortunes, and others like Suharto in Indonesia have millions of dollars in Swiss banks.

DEFAULT

By 1986, most debtor nations had called a halt. When Poland defaulted first in 1981, the IMF was forced to negotiate rollover terms with a Soviet puppet, General Jaruzelski. He proved as adept as any Third Word dictator in smashing the unions and imposing austerity measures, so the Polish crisis was temporarily averted. But the Western ban on eastern European food exports following Chernobyl, makes another Polish default almost inevitable.

In 1982, Mexico defaulted. In the jittery language of international banking, it 'temporarily suspended interest repayments on its debt'. Like Nigeria, it had been hit first by falling commodity prices, and then by falling oil prices. The $49 billion debt was rolled over on IMF terms within a few months. But then earthquake damage in 1985 added $3 billion dollars to its (by now) $70 billion debt, on which it was expected to pay $8 billion a year in interest. By 1986, it had shot up to $92 billion following a 30 per cent devaluation of the peso and a 25 per cent fall in oil revenues. Mexico, though, is unlikely to default formally. Half its oil goes to the US; if oil exports were blocked in retaliation, Mexico would be in dire financial trouble.

In 1984, Bolivia suspended payments on its debt of $3.6 billion because it could no longer pay for essential imports and inflation was out of control, running at something between 9,000 and 34,000 per cent a year. The population was near starvation. The debt in terms of IMF loans was relatively small, so it was quietly shelved, to be put on the negotiating table again if the Bolivian economy recovered.

More worrying for Western bankers was Peru's line after the election of a civilian president, Alan García. In 1985, García announced that his government, already $425 million in arrears, would pay only ten per cent of its export earnings ($310 million) to service its $13.6 billion debt. As he argued, 'The destiny of the poor and condemned comes first. If I were to impose the sort of austerity the IMF wants, I would be facing 40,000 Maoist guerillas, not 4,000'. When the US cut off aid to Peru, García retaliated, saying that the ten per cent would be paid only to those Western banks which continued to offer credit to Peru.

After the fall of the military in Brazil, Sarney's civilian government followed Peru's lead. In 1985, it refused to reschedule on IMF terms, instead introducing a package which promoted growth and reduced social inequality. At the same time, foreign bankers were told that they would not be compensated for the loss of $415 million incurred in 1984 when three Brazilian banks collapsed. The bankers panicked, since one third of Brazil's debts were similar loans, unsecured by the government. But the governor of the central bank was adamant, stating that

> this is a democracy. We cannot take taxpayers' money to cover risk operations. Bankers had other lending alternatives at the time, but they preferred non-guaranteed, bank-to-bank loans. (The *Guardian*, 30 December 1985)

And he added, essentially in line with Peru's argument, 'if money comes in, then money will be allowed to go out'. Nigeria followed suit in January 1986, deciding to repay a maximum of 30 per cent of foreign earnings – which, after the collapse of the oil market, is 30 per cent of very little. In the aftermath of the Johnson Matthey Bank scandal, and in the light of the notorious corruption of the contractors and politicians of the ousted military government, the new government asked, 'since many of the debts are dubious, why should Nigeria pay?'

Meanwhile, at a conference held in July 1985 for delegates from debtor nations, Fidel Castro, the Cuban President, produced four arguments in favour of default:

1. Latin America has a moral duty to cancel the debt because it has been exploited by the West for centuries.
2. The West would only use the money to buy arms.
3. Non-payment would actually help the West, because the increased purchasing power of debtor countries would boost production and reduce unemployment in the West's industrial sector.
4. Because the West keeps commodity prices low and interest rates high, the debt can never be repaid anyway, so it is better to default now rather than later.

(Castro failed to mention that Cuba is in debt to the USSR for $32 billion, as well as receiving a $3 billion a year subsidy.)

The world debt crisis is not over, despite the pretended optimism of the world banking system. The whole structure of debt is too fragile to withstand prolonged, unilateral default by one of the major debtor nations: once one country defaults, there is every reason for others to follow. If Western bankers attempt to freeze the debtor countries' assets abroad – which legally in the West would be very difficult, if not impossible – then the debtor countries could easily retaliate and nationalize foreign assets at home. The only real weapon open to Western banks is to withhold trade credit; since the West is a net importer of Third World manufactures and raw materials, such a response would be economically suicidal.

Privately, many bankers now acknowledge that Latin America's total debt to the West of around $360 billion is both unpayable and uncollectable. There is nothing novel about this apart from the scale of the debt. Philip II of Spain defaulted on his Antwerp bankers three times in the 1550s; Brazil defaulted on several occasions in the nineteenth century and the 1930s. Already, Swiss banks have refused to roll over many bad debts, instead writing them off. Many smaller US banks have sold the almost worthless debts at big discounts to bigger banks who attempt to maintain an appearance of normality. But now it seems likely, even in that bastion of free enterprise, that the US government will eventually be forced to step in to save its banking system from total collapse.

TURNING THE TABLES?
Unlike other debtor nations, Brazil used much of its borrowed money to develop its own advanced indus-

167

tries. Potentially, it is one of the richest countries in the world, with its vast undeveloped territories and abundant untapped resources; and with a population only three times that of Britain, it produces most of what it needs. On the other hand, access to those resources has always been restricted to a small elite of planters, financiers and industrialists who still hold down a vast, impoverished labour force. In less than ten years, Brazil has become one of the major industrial economies in the world. It is now the fifth largest aeroplane manufacturer; its essential transport system is now almost self-sufficient in fuel alcohol from sugar – which when oil prices were higher than $35 a barrel was an economic substitute; it manufactures its own computers; it builds highways, dams and irrigation systems in Africa and the Middle East. It has a net balance of trade surplus of $12 billion. For these reasons, it has little interest in servicing its debt on IMF terms: even so, all the surplus is swallowed up in debt repayments.

But significantly, when Brazil attempted to turn the tables on its old masters by trying to export steel to the US, it was blocked by tariffs protecting the US steel cartel. The same happened in the case of aluminium to Jamaica under Michael Manley, before he was toppled under pressure from the CIA and the transnationals. In the 1970s, Manley's government sponsored the development of a local aluminium industry, processing its bauxite deposits – but exports of aluminium were again embargoed by Western cartels.

It would therefore seem that there is little that Third World countries can do to protect themselves against falling prices of raw materials, none of which are effectively protected by commodity agreements. If they attempt to nationalize their resources, as Chile did with its nitrate deposits, the CIA moves in and destablizes the government; and if they attempt to industrialize, they cannot sell to the West.

The most obvious alternative is the promotion of 'south-south' trade, which is trade in raw, processed or manufactured commodities between Third World countries. For example, Brazil, Uruguay and Argentina have recently established a common market; Colombia,

Bolivia, Equador and Peru have formed 'the Andean pact', and so on. There have also been proposals for the establishment of a 'South Bank' – a central bank, established not in Paris, but in Tahiti or wherever. However, it could only operate with a new monetary unit and this itself would eventually have to be valued against the dollar – thus the old problem of dollarization remains.

'BARTER DEALING'

Another healthy shift – and one, naturally, which Western economists dislike – is the development of 'counter trade', or barter deals. For Third World countries, such deals have the advantage that they cut out the Western banks and the capitalist middlemen, and enable countries to trade directly, exchanging oil for coffee, radios for rubber, and so on. Today, perhaps a third of all world trade takes this form, and some of the deals are both inventive and revealing. A Chinese-Brazilian consortium is currently constructing a $1.4 billion hydro-electric scheme in Iraq, to be paid for in oil. And even Thatcher's government in Britain, which was resolutely opposed to counter trade, announced in 1986 that it was prepared to promote barter deals with Nigeria. With trade between the countries at a standstill, there was no alternative.

OPEN DOOR TO CHINA

We are going to break the rigid model of our national economy and import knowledge, experience and management methods from capitalist countries. By 1987, we will implement a full set of reforms.
Chinese Vice-Premier Tian Jiyun, 1986

In such a situation, it is not difficult to understand why Western capitalists were so keen to get into China with its abundant raw materials, cheap labour, and a potential market of one billion people – more than the combined populations of the USSR, the USA and the EEC. Mao's death in 1976 was followed by the 'open door' policy of Deng Xiaoping – a reversal in almost every way of Maoist dogma: an end to class struggle was announced; the Chinese were encouraged to become rich again; China was to be decollectivized and decentralized; bonus systems were introduced for high productivity; and Western companies were invited in to help China spend its $14 billion reserves.

Links between Western and Chinese companies were formally organized as 'joint ventures' in which Western companies provided finance and technical support, and the Chinese provided cheap labour to produce goods for export and the growing Chinese consumer market. Foreign companies thus made a double profit – interest on the loan to establish the factory and then profit from marketing the product. The alleged advantage to the Chinese was that in the process they would be trained in the necessary technical skills. To some extent this has happened, but the eventual replacement of skilled foreign workers by Chinese will take a very long time.

In the process, China has increasingly spent its dollar reserves which dropped from $17 billion in 1984 to $11 billion in 1985, and then to a staggering $18 billion deficit in 1985/86 – the money having being spent on iron, steel, machinery and consumer goods. In the wake of Western capital goods, there came cheap consumer goods – T-shirts, second-hand TV sets, transistor radios, drugs, anything for which there was a demand.

Peasants were also permitted to sell their surplus on local markets once they had fulfilled their quota requirements. Much of this surplus went into the cities with their expanding markets. Peasants who had once been fêted for their commitment to collective programmes were forgotten, while others earning 60 times the average wage were elevated to prestigious organizations like the People's Congress.

The pattern of urban life has also been transformed. A vast variety of black market goods flooded in; rickshaws, once condemned as degrading, reappeared on the streets; private restaurants, shops and barbers now flourish; private theatre groups, advertising companies and shipping companies are permitted, along with private medicine and dentistry.

Unemployment, once unknown in China, now runs at 12 per cent in certain cities. Hustlers, black marketeers, speculators and profiteers all flourish. Corruption goes right to the top. For example, in 1984, leading officials in Hainan Province were convicted of appropriating $1.5 billion of state funds, which they converted into US dollars on the black market. These dollars were then

(left) **Margaret and Denis Thatcher, Shanghai, 1982**

169

Toshiba billboard in China, 1986

spent, mostly in Japan, on 89,000 motor vehicles, 2.9 million TV sets and 252,000 video recorders, which were smuggled into China and sold at 300 per cent mark-ups on the Chinese black market.

Such reports suggest that the Chinese government will reimpose a clamp down on expenditure of its dollar reserves. However, the 1985 freeze on foreign-exchange purchases – imposed by the government to cope with its trade deficit – merely fuelled inflation and further stimulated the black economy. At the moment it is still tolerated. Were it to be completely suppressed, the economy would collapse and inflation would increase even more.

China is clearly moving away from socialism towards membership of the capitalist sector. Interesting evidence of this was the announcement, in May 1986, that China's Great Wall Industry Corporation, which produces the Long March III rocket, had agreed with Texas Telesat to

launch satellites, following the collapse of the US Space Shuttle programme after the Challenger disaster. The Chinese offer won because its price – due to low labour costs – was 15 per cent lower than that of Western competitors.

HIGH TECH, HIGH COSTS

In the West, the post-war development of the world arms industry, space programmes and nuclear power gave birth to a new stage of production – high technology. High tech involves the linking up of computers and communications networks in order to speed up and control design, communications, manufacturing and commerce. In the process, high tech has transformed economic systems, the sexual division of labour, the politics of the workplace, the nature of work and leisure, as well as relations between the developed and the Third World countries. High tech is also a commodity in its own right; through its power to define and process knowledge, it makes knowledge itself into a commodity, renamed 'Information'.

While automation contributes to massive job losses in heavy industry, increasingly, the remaining jobs are disciplined by high technology systems. In Britain more people (most of them low-paid young women) now work in front of VDUs than are employed in the steel, shipbuilding, coal and car industries combined. In the US, high tech has created a massive shift in investment from the declining East Coast to California; in the process, it has overtaken the declining US motor industry with an estimated turnover of $110 billion (about 3.5 per cent of the Gross National Product). While traditional industries decline, high tech is predicted to contribute 15 per cent to the GNP of most Western economies in ten years time.

The high tech industry at the most basic level involves the transformation of sand into silicon chips and fibre optics and the assembling of semi-conductor circuits. At the capital intensive end, in Silicon Valley and Silicon Fen, photographic chemistry transforms sand into electronic circuitry. Once the circuits have been designed and the production line built the labour-intensive work is done by young women, mostly in south east Asia; their health in general and their eyesight in particular, is ruined through this work. The main beneficiaries of their work are Japanese and the Western transnationals. The US and Japan each control a third of the high tech market, with the rest divided between Europe and the USSR.

Some advocates of high tech foresee a more democratic, prosperous world, where all have access to the benefits which this technology brings. The sceptics reasonably point to the fact that capitalism, high tech or otherwise, has never hitherto invested in a project for any reason other than the making of money. Neither is high tech likely to diminish disparities between the 'developed' and the 'developing' worlds, much less to bring benefits to people in the Third World. Advantage is determined by global power and technological know-how, not by access to labour and raw materials; a supply of cheap labour is no advantage for a Third World country trying to industrialize along high tech pathways. High tech is also the most innovative of all industries; obsolescence is now a matter of years rather than decades, as it was in the case of the railways and the motorcar. All these are factors which accentuate the advantage of those countries (presently the US and Japan) which are already producing 'fifth generation' computers, associated with 'artificial intelligence', and which are trying to prevent countries like Brazil developing their domestic computer industries.

JAPAN

The emergence of Japan as a world power has been so rapid that few people foresaw the effect its primacy would have on patterns of world trade and development. But Japan has continued to grow and innovate faster than any other world power. It has had such large trade surpluses that the maintenance of advantageous trade between itself and its competitors has even become threatened.

Japan, like West Germany, gained from the 'permanent arms economy' of the US and its NATO satellites in the post-war period. Forbidden to rearm, they spent more on research and non-military production – a crucial

factor underlying their much vaunted 'economic miracles'. In the 1950s, Japanese industrialists, protected by tariffs and with a massive, cheap, skilled labour force on tap, concentrated on rebuilding Japan's industrial base and producing cars, cameras and ships. By the mid-1970s, Japan had become the world's third industrial nation, and was already a leading producer of cheap televisions and computers. By 1980, it had overtaken the US as a motor manufacturer (11 million vehicles, 44 per cent more), as well as building half the world's ships. In 1985, all the big US motor companies were losing money: Chrysler, $1.7 billion; Ford, $1.5 billion; General Motor, $763 million. Yet Toyota had overtaken General Motors as the largest single motor company in the world, and had a profit of $1.2 billion. In 1986, the US government announced a budget deficit of $180 billion. Today, the revaluing of the yen against the dollar is making it increasingly difficult for the Japanese to export goods to the US, hitherto its major foreign market. Japanese goods are now too expensive; if they are cheap, they are kept out by protectionist legislation. On occasion, Japanese goods have even been boycotted. Thus, Japan is being forced to open up new trading networks which are not limited by the weakness of the dollar. Not simply the terms of trade, but also the balance of power had shifted across the Pacific.

One reason for this is the Japanese skill in the creation of 'flexible manufacturing systems', combining robots, lasers and computers. These allow short-run, high quality production of all manner of goods, while eliminating many of the dull, dirty, dangerous tasks. But in the development of this technology in the 1970s, hundreds of thousands of women in Pacific basin countries (like Taiwan, South Korea, Hong Kong, Singapore and Indonesia) had to assemble the circuitry, often going blind after ten years.

Japan is now the world leader in many aspects of high tech. By 1982, it had 14,000 robots in operation, compared to 4,000 in the US and 600 in Europe. Japan's are mostly in car assembly, electronics, plastics and textiles. Japan began investing abroad in the early 1960s, in low-cost neighbouring economies like Taiwan, Hong Kong and South Korea, where it exported the plant and capital to produce cheap consumer goods like textiles, cameras, motor bikes and cars for Western markets.

In the 1970s, Japan began to export plant and capital further afield, taking advantage of lower energy, raw material and labour costs abroad. By 1985, it had steel plants in Malaysia and Brazil, aluminium plants in Indonesia and the Amazonas, and petrochemical plants in Iran. Japan also invested in declining industrial economies like Britain, setting up high tech assembly factories producing cars, TVs and other consumer goods. The north east of England and Wales are now becoming Japanese economic colonies. Japan is also investing heavily in the US, where, because of the fall of the dollar

Our Look East Policy is directed not so much at investment from Japan but acquiring the kind of policies, systems, and work ethics that the Japanese have.

Looking East means we are also looking towards what we consider — and what the whole world considers — as the best technology. If we are going to learn we should learn from people who are the best in the field.

Dr. Mahathir Mohamad, Prime Minister of Malaysia, 1982.

against the yen, US labour is cheaper than labour in Japan.

The rapid rise of Japan, today controlling ten per cent of the world's GNP, has focussed attention on research and development in high tech. Its rise has encouraged the belief that only investment in high tech can help the world out of its present crisis. Some of its successes are indeed remarkable. Microcomputer control systems get hens to lay more eggs; pigs fatten faster and produce bigger litters; plants mature faster with greater yields; processing everywhere is more efficient with less wastage; new medicines and vaccines against killer viruses like hepatitis B are developed; a super bullet train with speeds of 500 kilometres per hour is in production; solar power systems for south east Asia are in operation; and so on. Japanese corporations have taken the lead in calls to transform the world, using high technology. The Mitsubishi Research Institute is currently campaigning for the rich countries to devote $13 billion a year – the amount they spend in one and a half weeks on arms – on a series of grandiose high tech designed and assisted projects. These include an artificial lake in the heart of Africa, bringing irrigation, vegetation and rain to the parched desert; a channel from the Mediterranean to the Qattara Depression in Egypt, creating another artificial lake; a dam across the Bering Straits to moderate the climate of the North Pacific; a tunnel under the Himalayas to tap the waters of the Ganges and the Brahmaputra for hydro-electric power; a second channel south of the Panama Canal; and a tunnel linking Gibraltar and Africa. In all, the estimated cost of these projects totals $500 billion. That such schemes are possible is beyond doubt. That they would play havoc with the environment and undermine many people's livelihoods is also certain.

THE PACIFIC RIM
The weakness of the dollar and the strength of the yen has already seriously begun to undermine Japan's markets in the US. In response, Japanese transnationals have moved into declining economies, like Britain and the US, and expanding economies in the Third World, like China and

Brazil. By making comfortable profits in both, through the introduction of highly efficient manufacturing systems, Japan has further strengthened its ability to withstand downturns in the world economy. And being free of the US umbrella, it has developed trading links with countries in every continent, through barter deals, technical agreements and capital loans, indifferent to the ideologies of its trading partners.

This shift to the Pacific Rim has radically altered patterns of growth and decline both in Europe and the US. By 1984, US trade with the Pacific Rim countries was worth more than its trade with Europe. In the ten years following the first oil shock in 1973, 14 million jobs were created in the US, especially in California, while Japan created three million new jobs and Europe lost two million. The Pacific area has a GNP of $200 billion and is growing at ten per cent a year, while Europe's average growth rate is four per cent, and Britain's is even lower. Already Japan's products have taken large chunks out of Europe's traditional markets – cars, motorbikes, textiles, footware – as well as supplying most of the mass-produced, low cost, high tech products like videos, cameras, computers and so on.

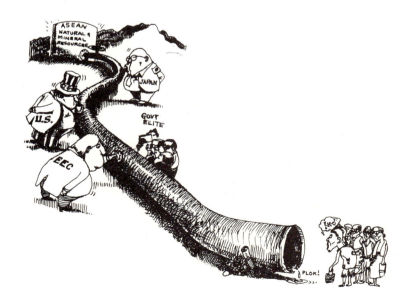

COMMODITIES

The rapid expansion of Japan, with a population of 120 million on an island little bigger than Britain, has meant that it has become increasingly dependent on food imports. So Japan, imitating the tactics of earlier European colonialism, has transformed its neighbours into Japanese orchards and plantations, investing not only in south east Asia, but in Brazil and Argentina to secure its grain and beef supplies. This international division of labour guarantees Japan's continued dominance. Starved of aid and crippled by debt, Third World countries have welcomed Japanese encroachments into traditional Western areas of influence, but the net result is the same – the colonies still supply cheap raw materials and cheap labour for foreign industry. The masters have changed, but the yoke is the same. Elsewhere, Japan has provided 'aid' to countries like Turkey and Pakistan, encouraged by the US, which, in the continuing debt crisis, cannot raise much capital for investment in developing countries. As is everywhere the case, aid is geared to the givers' needs, not the needs of the recipient countries. Following the examples of Europe and the US, Japan now uses the host country as an offshore production facility for its own capital.

'The winds of change' of south east Asia and elsewhere, now blown by the Japanese as well as Western capitalists and the ideologues of the Pentagon, mean more of the same – more environmental and health damage, lower wages, fewer political rights, and final loss of control.

SURVIVING IMMISERATION

In 1985, the net transfer of resources from the Third to the developed world was $22 billion. The truth is that the poorest parts of the world are still subsidizing the richest.
Roy Hattersley, The *Guardian*, 10 June 1986

Today, five hundred million people live in a state of permanent malnutrition, and as many starve every year as died in the Second World War. But they do not starve because the world is overpopulated, or because there is not enough food. Far from it. One of the 'problems' of

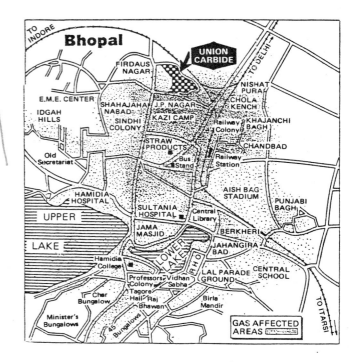

the world is the overproduction of foodstuffs; wine and milk lakes, butter, cheese, and beef mountains in Europe; a world 'glut' of sugar; and grain rotting in the silos of Europe and North America. Each year, the Common Market spends more ($18 billion) storing and disposing of its surpluses than it provides in famine relief. There is no shortage of food. Why then are people starving? 'Because the limits of production are determined, not by the number of hungry bellies but by the number of purses able to buy and to pay.' (Marx and Engels, p. 199) Bourgeois society does not and cannot wish to produce any more. The hungry bellies, the labour which cannot be profitably employed and therefore cannot buy, is left to die.

The arms bill is another contributory factor as the world spends half a million dollars per minute on arms. The Western powers are careful to ensure that they are mostly used, not at home, but abroad, leading to even greater misery in countries overrun by the armies and competing dictators who nominally represent 'the free world'. And nearly every economy is geared to maintaining this militarization of the planet. Over sixty million people worldwide serve in uniform, or provide civilian support for their armies. There are only half as many teachers and one twentieth as many doctors. Furthermore, many skilled workers leave the Third World, where they are urgently needed to work in the industries and social services of Western countries.

It cannot even be argued that disasters and famines are 'acts of God'. In every instance, if not preventable, they could have been ameliorated by rational human intervention. In the 1974 Rangpur famine, for instance, when 150,000 people starved, they died because they were compelled to sell their crops for future delivery while the crops were still in the ground; they then sold their draught animals and land, and finally their clothes and their bedding, in order to buy rice at the speculators' prices. When they ran out of money they died, though there was still plenty of rice in the warehouses. Meanwhile, Europe was feeding its wheat surplus to cattle, which then finished up on a refrigerated beef mountain, before it was dumped on the market as petfood.

Marx and Engels saw the solution in 'the crisis of capitalism', when the proletariat would seize power from a collapsing bourgeois class. But capitalism has a remarkable ability to deflect class struggle. Even the traditional militant trade unionism has declined with the factory systems which gave rise to it. By threatening to move plants abroad where labour is cheap and compliant, transnationals have weakened traditional unionism even further. In the US, trade unions have collaborated with management in cutting wages and jobs but even that hasn't prevented the flight of capital either from the unionized North to the anti-union South, or from the US to the Third World.

In Japan and its factories abroad, company unions have no bite, being run by the companies and not by the union members; there are no secret ballots and no criticism of union policy is allowed. In the Third World the problem is even worse, reminiscent of the early years of unionism in Britain, with very few workers being members of unions and a mass army of unemployed people, desp-

'For the fatherland to the slaughter': the German arms industry as depicted by George Grosz, 1924

erate for work. The lack of union rights in particular attracts foreign companies, as this glowing report on investment opportunities in Indonesia by World Bank advisers makes clear:

Indonesia has the largest remaining pool of inexpensive and relatively literate labour in East Asia. Even before the recent devaluation, wages for unskilled labour were the lowest in the world; lower than in Singapore, Hong Kong, South Korea and Taiwan. Labour is not unionised. (*Far Eastern Economic Review*, 23 May 1980)

COMMODITIES

But even wages at this level can still be cut:

> Singapore Prime Minister, Lee Kwan Yew, today warned Singapore's 75,000 unemployed that they must expect wage cuts in their next job, and reported an average 35 per cent reduction in new wage rates. (The *Guardian*, 1 May 1986)

When Prime Minister Thatcher toured south east Asia she revealed that she had forgotten where she was, while making a speech, because to her, one cheap labour paradise is much like another.

In these countries, many of the workforce are women, hired in their teens and fired at thirty. In Hong Kong, 60 per cent of adults work a seven day week; 34,000 children work, half of them a ten-hour day; in South Korea the seven-day, 84-hour week is normal, and it sometimes lasts for two or three days on end. The workers are supplied with pep pills to keep them awake. Predictably, South Korea has the highest industrial accident rate in the world. And throughout south east Asia, wage rates for identical jobs are twelve times lower than those in the US, though the productivity of the workers is actually higher.

The alternatives are few. In some Third World countries, local capitalists have developed enterprises for local markets. But if they want to expand and need cash, they are forced to gear production to export markets; thus they lose the profit from the goods, which are marketed by the transnationals abroad. More profitable, perhaps, is production for the huge counterfeiting industry which has grown up all over the developing world, where factories produce everything from brandname videos, TVs, cassettes and watches to military components for NATO, and even, it was discovered, the US Space Shuttle. This counterfeiting accounts for something between three and nine per cent of world trade. Taiwan is the largest source of fakes, followed by the UK and then Indonesia.

Illegal drugs too, although equally difficult to quantify, are crucial to many Third World economies for a number of reasons. First, the prices of illegal drugs tend to rise and tend not to be subject to the price cycles which characterize most other commodities. Second, it is a trade which remains unaffected by protectionist and tariff legislation – in this sense its illegality acts in the interests of Third World countries. The illegality of the trade also allows refining to take place in the producer countries. In the case of opium to heroin this rarely occurs; most refining is carried out in Europe. In the case of cocaine, much of the processing is carried out, if not in Bolivia, then in Colombia. Thus, a greater share of the final market price is taken by the producer country, even if the bulk of the profits are still made by traders in consumer countries. Third, the world drug currency is US dollars; a major advantage of the dollar is that it does not depreciate in value, whereas currencies like the Bolivian peso are subject to astronomical inflation. Furthermore, the operations which have been set up to launder 'narcodollars' allow massive amounts of cash to flow in and out of Third World countries. In the case of countries like Bolivia and Peru, crippled by debt and faced by the collapse of key commodity prices like tin, narcodollars

Lot Six –
South America!

are essential to the running of government. To a significant extent the domestic inflation of these countries is caused by the government's printing of pesos with which to buy illegal dollars. Narcodollars, of course, are also used to finance other forms of contraband trade from industrial components and arms to clothing and luxuries, through free-trade zones like Panama and Paraguay. Some of it, inevitably, filters into the poorest sections of the economy, encouraging peasants, no longer able to make a living from crops like coffee and tobacco, to switch to more profitable crops like marijuana and coca. Ironically, however, and perhaps predictably, the organization of the drugs industry is increasingly being taken over by big business operations. For example, verbal forward contracts are now widely used in Colombia in the production of cocaine. Peasants are paid cash in advance to supply coca leaves at an agreed price at some future date – though that price is almost invariably lower than the market price. In Jamaica, bulk buying of marijuana allows the big exporters to dictate prices and to use the profits to buy protection from the government. The large-scale warehousing of stocks also helps buttress the entrepreneurs against price fluctuations in Western markets, though, as always, such organizational shifts take an increasing amount of the profit away from the actual growers.

As alternative cash crops, illegal drugs are now as important as legal crops in many countries. Marijuana is the major cash crop in at least ten US states; the value of the 1984 domestic US crop was estimated at $16.6 billion, second only to maize ($20.4 billion). Perhaps 50 per cent of Bolivia's and Colombia's foreign earnings derive from the cocaine trade. Colombia also supplies about 30 per cent of the US marijuana market, followed by Jamaica, where marijuana earns drug traffickers around $1 billion a year, twice what the island earns from all legitimate exports. In the Lebanon, the $1 billion earned from cannabis production goes largely on buying arms. Burma, producing perhaps a quarter of the world's raw opium, earns only $90 million a year for it (though its street value is at least a hundred times that). While at the consumer end, according to the US National Institute of Drug Abuse, 'the growing use of dope on the job is costing the US economy $70 billion a year' (The *Observer*, 11 May 1986).

THE FUTURE OF COMMODITY CAPITALISM

Today, almost 500 years after Columbus 'discovered' America in his delirious quest for gold, the world remains very much the victim of that dream. Vast tracts of land, once fertile, have been rendered sterile; forests have been cut down; and rivers flood and then dry up as the vegetation disappears. People once free are now enslaved, once fed are now hungry. The forces which sent Columbus on his voyage still control the territories which he and those who emulated him stole. But the balance of global power has now shifted. Control passed from Spain and Portugal to Genoa and then Antwerp. Amsterdam followed to be overtaken by London. The balance then shifted to New York and the US between the first and Second World War, before shifting again to Japan and the Pacific Rim. And as each new power emerged, it first collaborated with and then colonized the economy it displaced.

The shift of Western banks and transnationals to the Pacific Rim is a further reminder of the impotence of nation states to control the movement and operations of capital. Even some Western governments are now reduced to bargaining with the transnationals for investment by promising them better terms. The ruling class, increasingly an international class, remains in power because it controls the increasingly sophisticated means of production. It owns and designs the communication networks, the robots, the flexible manufacturing systems. A commodity broker in London who plugs into satellite information systems knows more about crops, soil, minerals and other resources in the Third World than the governments of those countries.

At the same time, financiers argue that the fundamental problems of the world economy can be solved by further increasing the mobility of capital and the flexibility of labour. Of course, from the point of view of capital, labour has already become internationalized. Yet politically, the working class is fragmented, both within

177

the workplace and within the nation state. In order to ensure economic survival, workers are compelled to work harder for lower rates of pay, in the interests of the firm and even the nation. Some countries demand protectionist measures but this merely places the burden on other workers abroad. In the case of commodity capitalism, there seems to be no end to its logic – a logic which conflates people's survival with that of 'the economy'. For this reason, potential alliances between 'rival' workers are undermined by the competition for work and jobs. There has been little organized resistance which might challenge the right of capital to decide what is produced and how it is produced.

From the point of view of commodity prices, there are two distinct interest groups – consumers and producers. Western consumers, who benefit from the cheap commodity prices provided by Third World countries, are unlikely to welcome a system which demands that they pay at least a third as much again for their commodities, in real terms, to the producers of the myriad tropical and subtropical commodities which they consume. But unless commodity prices are increased by at least a half and possibly more, the massive capital flows from producer to consumer countries will intensify the widespread immiseration of Third World economies.

In another sense, however, workers in both Third World and industrial societies have a potential common interest. They can continue to submit to the imperatives of agrarian and industrial capitalism which demand that they reproduce capital by selling their labour as a commodity on terms dictated by capital's ever-pressing need to make profits. Or they can refuse to do so, instead reappropriating their labour and the world's resources to serve human needs.

Bibliography

All titles are published in London unless otherwise stated.

Addison, Joseph and **Steele**, Richard (1711–14) 'The Exchange', in Smith, G., ed. *The Spectator*, 4 vols. Everyman, 1945.

Aubrey, John (1667–92) *Brief Lives*, Dick, O.L., ed. Harmondsworth: Penguin, 1961.

Barraclough, G., ed. (1984) *The Times Atlas of World History*. Times Books.

Biddulph, William (1600) 'Travels in the Levant', in Purchas (1625), vol. 8.

Boswell, James (1791) *Life of Johnson*, Hill, G.B., ed. Oxford: Oxford University Press, 1934–64.

Braudel, F. (1981, 1982, 1984) *Civilization and Capitalism*, vol. 1, *The Structures of Everyday Life*; vol. 2, *The Wheels of Commerce*; vol. 3, *The Perspective of the World*. Collins.

Calder, A. (1981) *Revolutionary Empire*. Cape.

Collis, M. (1959) *Marco Polo*. Faber & Faber.

Conner, P. (1986) *The China Trade 1600–1860*. Brighton: The Royal Pavilion, Art Gallery & Museums.

Craton, M., **Walvin**, J. and **Wright** D.W., eds (1976) *Slavery, Abolition and Emancipation*. Longman.

Cribb, J. (1986) *Money: From Cowrie Shells to Credit Cards*. British Museum Publications.

Davatz, T. (1951) *Memorias*. São Paulo: Livraria Martins.

Dean, W. (1976) *Rio Claro, A Brazilian Plantation System*. Stanford, CA: Stanford University Press.

Defoe, Daniel (1724–6) *A Tour Through the Whole Island of Great Britain*, Rogers, P., ed. Harmondsworth: Penguin, 1971.

Dufty, W. (1975) *Sugar Blues*. New York: Warner Books.

Equiano, O. (1789) *The Interesting Narrative of the Life of Olaudah Equiano or Gustavus Vassa the African*, Edwards, P., ed. Heinemann, 1967.

Evelyn, John (1620–1706) *The Diary*, de Beer, E.S., ed. Oxford: Oxford University Press, 1959.

Exquemelin, A. (1678) *The Buccaneers of America*, Brown, A., trans. Harmondsworth: Penguin, 1969.

Ford, F. (1970) *Europe 1780–1830*. Longman.

Furber, H. (1976) *Rival Empires of Trade*. Minneapolis, MN: University of Minnesota Press.

Gatt-fly (1984) *Sugar Workers Round the World*. Canada: Gatt-fly.

Goodman, G.J.W. ('Adam Smith') (1982) *Paper Money*. Macdonald.

Gordon-Ashworth, F. (1984) *International Commodity Control*. Croom Helm.

Guha, A. (1977) *Planter-Raj to Swaraj*. New Delhi: Indian Council of Historical Research.

Harris, N. (1983) *Of Bread and Guns*. Harmondsworth: Penguin.

Hay, D. (1966) *Europe in the Fourteenth and Fifteenth Centuries*. Longman.

Hayter, T. (1981) *The Creation of World Poverty*. Pluto.

Henman, A., **Lewis**, R. and **Malyon**, T. (1985) *Big Deal: The Politics of the Illicit Drug Business*. Pluto.

Hill, C. (1980) *The Century of Revolution*. Nelson.

Hobbes, Thomas (1651) *Leviathan*, Macpherson, C., ed. Harmondsworth: Penguin, 1968.

Hobhouse, H. (1985) *Seeds of Change*. Sidgwick & Jackson.

Hobsbawm, E.J. (1962) *The Age of Revolution*. Mentor Books.

Inglis, B. (1976) *The Opium War*. Hodder & Stoughton.

Jacob, H.E. (1935) *The Saga of Coffee*. Allen & Unwin.

Jonas, S.L., **McCaughan**, E. and **Martinez**, E.S., eds (1974) *Guatemala, Tyranny on Trial*. San Francisco: Synthesis Publications.

Kidron, M. and **Segal**, R. (1981) *The State of the World Atlas*. Pan Books.

Kindleberger, C. (1984) *A Financial History of Western Europe*. Allen & Unwin.

Koenigsberger, H.G. and **Mosse**, G.L. (1968) *Europe in the Sixteenth Century*. Longman.

BIBLIOGRAPHY

Kurian, R. (1982) *Women Workers in the Sri Lanka Plantation Sector*. Geneva: International Labour Office.

Leary, V.A. (1983) *Ethnic Conflict and Violence in Sri Lanka*. Geneva: International Committee of Jurists.

Lever, H. and Huhne, C. (1985) *Debt and Danger*. Harmondsworth: Penguin.

Ligon, Richard (1673) *A True and Exact History of the Island Barbadoes*.

Lyttleton, Edward (1689) *The Groans of the Plantations*.

Mandeville, Bernard (1706) The Fable of the Bees.

Marx, Karl (1844) *Economic and Philosophic Manuscripts*, Struik, D.J., ed. Lawrence & Wishart, 1970.

—— (1852) 'The Eighteenth Brumaire', in Fernbach, D., ed. *Surveys from Exile*. Allen Lane, 1973, pp. 143–249.

—— (1857–8) *Grundrisse*, Nicolaus, M., ed. Allen Lane, 1973.

—— (1887) *Capital*, 3 vols. Lawrence & Wishart, 1970.

Marx, K. and **Engels**, F. (1842–83) *Selected Correspondence*. Lawrence & Wishart, 1956.

Mintz, S.W. (1985) *Sweetness and Power*. New York: Viking.

Morse, H.B. (1926–9) *The Chronicles of the East India Company*. Oxford: Oxford University Press.

Mortimer, T. (1769) *Every Man His Own Broker*.

Mukherjee, R. (1974) *The Rise and Fall of the East India Company*. New York: Monthly Review Press.

Mun, Thomas (1621) 'A discourse of trade from England unto the East Indies', in Purchas (1625), vol. 8.

—— (1664) *England's Treasure by Foreign Trade*. Oxford: Blackwell, 1928.

Ovington, J. (1699) 'An essay on the nature and qualities of tea'.

Padfield, P. (1979) *Tide of Empires 1481–1654*. Routledge & Kegan Paul.

Palacios, M. (1980) *Coffee in Colombia 1850–1970*. Cambridge: Cambridge University Press.

Pelaez, C.M., ed. (1973) *Essays on Coffee and Economic Development*. Rio de Janeiro: Instituto Brazileiro do Cafe.

Pepys, Samuel (1660–9) *Diary*, Wheatley, H.B., ed. Bell & Sons, 1893–9.

Perlman, F. (1972) *The Reproduction of Daily Life*. Detroit, M: Black & Red Books.

—— (1985) *The Continuing Appeal of Nationalism*. Detroit, M: Black & Red Books.

Petty, William (1691) *Political Anatomy of Ireland*.

Pirenne, H. (1936) *Economic and Social History of Medieval Europe*. Routledge & Kegan Paul.

Purchas, Samuel (1625) *Purchas his Pilgrims*, 20 vols. Hakluyt Society, 1905–10.

Ralegh, Sir Walter (1610) 'A discourse of the invention of ships', in Oldys W. and Burch, T., eds *Works*, vol. 8. Oxford: Oxford University Press, 1829.

Rees, G.L. (1978) *The History of the London Commodity Markets*. Commodity Analysis.

Richards, R.D. (1965) *The Early History of Banking in England*. Frank Cass.

Rodney, W. (1972) *How Europe Underdeveloped Africa*. Bogle-L'Ouverture Publications.

Rumsey, Walter (1657) *Diverse New Experiments of Tobacco and Coffee*.

Sandys, George (1615) 'Relation of a journey', in Purchas (1625), vol. 8.

Selbourne, D. (1983) 'International conference on the problems of plantation workers of Sri Lanka', *Bulletin* 4. Sri Lanka Research and Information Group.

Sieghart, P., ed. (1982) *Microchips with Everything: Consequences of Information Technology*. Comedia/ICA.

Silva, S.B.D. de (1982) *The Political Economy of Underdevelopment*. Routledge & Kegan Paul.

Swift, Jonathan (1696–1739) *Works*, Davis, H., ed. Oxford: Blackwell, 1948–68.

Tanner, J. (1982) *The Tea Trade*. World Development Movement.

Thomas, Sir Dalby (1690) *An Historical Account of the Rise and Growth of the West India Colonies*.

Tugendhat, C. (1971) *The Multinationals*. Eyre & Spottiswoode.

Tussac, F.R. de (1808) *Flora des Antilles*. Paris.

Ukers, W.H. (1922) *All About Coffee*. New York: Tea and Coffee Trade Journal Co.

—— (1935) *All About Tea*. New York: Tea and Coffee Trade Journal Co.

Waley, A. (1958) *The Opium War through Chinese Eyes*. Allen & Unwin.

Wallerstein, I. (1983) *Historical Capitalism*. Verso.

Walpole, Horace (1737–1797) *Letters*, Toynbee, P., ed. Oxford: Clarendon Press, 1903–5.

Williams, E. (1942) *The Negro in the Caribbean*. Washington, DC: The Association of Negro Folk Education.

Winstanley, G. (1649) 'A declaration from the poor oppressed people of England', in Hill, C., ed. *The Law of Freedom and Other Writings*. Harmondsworth: Penguin, 1973.

180

Further Reading

All titles are published in London unless otherwise stated.

GENERAL BACKGROUND

Fernand Braudel, *Civilization and Capitalism*, vol. 1, *The Structures of Everyday Life*; vol. 2, *The Wheels of Commerce;* vol. 3, *The Perspective of the World*. Collins, 1981, 1982, 1984. Three books which explore on a global canvas the minute and fascinating details of economic life over two thousand years of history; well illustrated.

Immanuel Wallerstein, *The Modern World System*, 2 vols. New York: Academy Press, 1974, 1980. A more theoretical account of the historical development of the modern capitalist system.

Geoffrey Barraclough (ed.), *The Times Atlas of World History*. Times Books, 1984. Indispensable background text with excellent maps and data.

Eduardo Galeano, *Open Veins of Latin America*. New York: Monthly Review Press, 1973. A classic book describing the pillage of a continent over five centuries.

Teresa Hayter, *The Creation of World Poverty*. Pluto Press, 1981. A short history of how producer countries became dependent on Western markets, which provides a scathing indictment of the notion that charity will solve the problem of Third World poverty.

Henry Hobhouse, *Seeds of Change*. Sidgwick & Jackson, 1985. A readable account of the crucial importance of five key plants – quinine, sugar, tea, cotton and potatoes – in the development of world history.

EUROPE TAKES CONTROL

Walter Rodney, *How Europe Underdeveloped Africa*. Bogle-L'Ouverture Publications, 1972. An essential text by the Caribbean Marxist assassinated in 1980.

Christopher Hill, *The Century of Revolution*. Nelson, 1980. A classic analysis of the economic and political changes in seventeenth-century England which underpinned Britain's emerging role as a mercantilist and imperialist power.

Angus Calder, *Revolutionary Empire*. Cape, 1981. An extensive account of the evolution of the British Empire, with material on slavery, the Caribbean and India.

Ralph Davis, *The Rise of the Atlantic Economies*. Ithaca, New York: Cornell University Press, 1973. A basic, descriptive history of the early growth of Italy, Portugal, Spain, Antwerp, Amsterdam and London as the controlling powers of world trade.

Holden Furber, *Rival Empires of Trade*. Minneapolis, MN: University of Minnesota Press, 1976. A detailed account of the early conflicts between the Portuguese, Dutch, French and English for control of the India trade.

SUGAR

Sidney W. Mintz, *Sweetness and Power*. New York: Viking, 1985. A history of the West's craving for sugar, and how the Caribbean was exploited to satisfy it.

M. Craton, J. Walvin and D. W. Wright (eds), *Slavery, Abolition and Emancipation*. Longman, 1976. An anthology of the arguments that raged over slavery in the eighteenth and nineteenth centuries.

Olaudah Equiano (1789), *The Interesting Narrative of the Life of Olaudah Equiano or Gustavus Vassa the African*, ed. P. Edwards. Heinemann, 1967. A classic account of slavery by one of the key figures in the abolition movement who was himself enslaved in Africa at the age of eleven.

William Dufty, *Sugar Blues*. New York: Warner Books, 1975. A powerful indictment of the evils of sugar.

World Development Movement, *Sugar: Crisis in the Third World*. World Development Movement, 1980. A scathing analysis of the causes of the current crisis in the sugar industries of Third World countries, in particular Jamaica and the Philippines.

FURTHER READING

TEA

Ramkrishna Mukherjee, *The Rise and Fall of the East India Company*. New York: Monthly Review Press, 1974. The most readable and perceptive account of the iniquities of the English East India Company.
William H. Ukers, *All About Tea*. New York: Tea and Coffee Trade Journal Co., 1935. A romantic but encyclopaedic history of tea (for the connoisseur).
Amalendu Guha, *Planter-Raj to Swaraj*. New Delhi: Indian Council of Historical Research, 1977. A detailed analysis of the complex interrelationship between tea and politics in Assam.
John Tanner, *The Tea Trade*. World Development Movement, 1982. A short description of the misery of contemporary conditions on the tea plantations.
Rachel Kurian, *Women Workers in the Sri Lanka Plantation Sector*. Geneva: International Labour Office, 1982. The official report of a detailed and extensive research project on the condition of female tea workers in contemporary Sri Lanka.
'Sri Lanka', *Race and Class* **Special Issue.** Race and Class Publications, 1984. Well-researched analysis of the legacy of migrant labour.

OPIUM

Michael Greenberg, *British Trade and the Opening of China 1800–1847*. Cambridge: Cambridge University Press, 1951. A lucid, classic analysis of the economic and political reasons for the British incursion into China.
Brian Inglis, *The Opium War*. Hodder & Stoughton, 1976. A readable and reliable history.
Arthur Waley, *The Opium War through Chinese Eyes*. Allen & Unwin, 1958. A remarkable account, based on primary source material, of the crisis in Chinese society when confronted by British trading demands and gunboat diplomacy.

COFFEE

Warren Dean, *Rio Claro, A Brazilian Plantation System*. Stanford, CA: Stanford University Press, 1976. A fascinating history of the development of Brazilian coffee-plantation agriculture in the nineteenth century.
Marco Palacios, *Coffee in Colombia 1850–1970*. Cambridge: Cambridge University Press, 1980. An academic, classic account of how a whole economy comes to depend on a single commodity.
William H. Ukers, *All About Coffee*. New York: Tea and Coffee Trade Journal Co., 1922. Like his book on tea, an encyclopaedic and romantic text for coffee buffs.
Campaign Co-op, *The World in your Coffee Cup*. Campaign Co-op, 1980. A direct and straightforward analysis of the world coffee trade as it affects the consumer.

MONEY

John Cribb, *Money: From Cowrie Shells to Credit Cards*. British Museum Publications, 1986. A useful pictorial history of money and money tokens over three thousand years of world history.
Charles Kindleberger, *A Financial History of Western Europe*. Allen & Unwin, 1984. The best single-volume history of the European monetary system.
G.J.W. Goodman ('Adam Smith'), *Paper Money*. Macdonald, 1982. A humorous, extremely well-informed account of the operations of the world's financial system.
Fiona Gordon-Ashworth, *International Commodity Control*. Croom Helm, 1984. A dry but thorough analysis of how international commodity agreements have, or have not, worked.
Harold Lever and Christopher Huhne, *Debt and Danger*. Harmondsworth: Penguin, 1985. A short, basic current affairs analysis of the events of the 1980s world debt crisis.
Cheryl Payer, *The Debt Trap: The IMF and the Third World*. New York: Monthly Review Press, 1974. A seminal text on the role played by financial institutions like the IMF in exerting control over Third World economies.

COMMODITY CAPITALISM NOW

Michael Kidron and Ronald Segal, *The State of the World Atlas*. Pan Books, 1981. A basic survey of contemporary developments in all the key commodities, with brilliant and imaginative visuals.
Nigel Harris, *Of Bread and Guns*. Harmondsworth: Penguin, 1983. Both an academic and a political analysis of the iniquitous inequalities of the world trade system.
Barbara Dinham and Colin Hines, *Agribusiness in Africa*. Earth Resources, 1983. A basic account of the transformation of Africa into a commodity producer for Western markets.
Roger Burbach and Patricia Flynn, *Agribusiness in the Americas*. New York: Monthly Review Press, 1980. Ditto for the Americas.
Anthony Henman, Roger Lewis and Tim Malyon, *Big Deal: The Politics of the Illicit Drug Business*. Pluto, 1985. The most up-to-date analysis of the increasing importance of illicit drug production in the world economy.
Latin American Bureau, *The Poverty Brokers*. Latin American Bureau. 1983. A survey of the IMF's stringent policies in Latin America.
Peter Evans, *Dependent Development: The Alliance of Multinational, State and Local Capital in Brazil*. Princeton, NJ: Princeton

University Press, 1979. Traces Brazil's development during the 1960s and 1970s into a highly capitalized satellite of Western transnationals.

Transnationals Information Exchange, *Brazil, The New Militancy: Trades Unions and Transnational Corporations*. Transnationals Information Exchange, 1986. An account of contemporary developments in debt and politics since the demise of the Generals.

Acknowledgements

Author's Acknowledgements

This book is indebted to many people who have been generous in supplying original research material, criticism and advice. In particular I would like to thank Allister Goulding for help with the chapter on tea, Chaim Litewski and Anthony Henman for material on coffee and Latin America, and Anne Simpson of the Trans-nationals Information Centre, London. I am also indebted to Les Levidow and Charlotte Greig of Free Association Books for devoting a great deal of time to discussing, editing and improving the book. Finally, I have to acknowledge an enormous debt to Sue Clayton and Jonathan Curling, who read the manuscript through at every stage and made numerous valuable comments; the chapter on money, in particular, is as much Jonathan's as mine.

Illustrations

Anglo-Chinese Educational Institute, 169;
Anon., El Ancora Editores, Bogota, 121;
Arrow Books [*Hell is a City*], 117;
BBC Radio Times Hulton Library, 16, 88, 104;
T. Beswick, Newcastle, 87 left;
Bristol City Art Gallery, 43;
British Library, 25 lower, 28 right, 31 lower, 32, 58, 77, 83 left;
René Caillié, *Travels* (1830), 26;
Cambridge University Press, 30;
Terry Cannon, 170;
Colombian Coffee Delegation, 118
Belinda Coote/Oxfam, 46, 67, 165;
Cork Public Library, 20;
Counter-Information Services, 97 left, 178;
Jonathan Curling © Firefret Ltd/Channel 4 TV, 71, 100, 123 left (from *Alternativa*);
Eilles Kaffee, Munich, 107;
Phil Evans, 6, 22, 44, 70, 72, 94, 98, 116, 123 right, 124, 127, 141, 154, 159, 168, 171 (collage), 176;
Far Eastern Economic Review, 172, 174;
Marc Ferrez, 112, 115;
R. Fortune, 75;
Germanisches Nationalmuseum, Nuremberg, 40;

Gluck Press, 101, 102;
Allister Goulding, 93, 97;
George Grosz,13, 175;
Guardian (Oct. 1986), 177;
Guildhall Library, City of London, 140, 142;
Illustrated London News (1896), 91;
International Coffee Organization, 150;
Knockabout Comics, 148;
Lloyd's of London, 106;
Longman [Craton *et al.*, *Slavery, Abolition and Emancipation*], 60;
Lopex Public Relations, 64, 74 top;
Louvre, 15;
David Low, 147;
Mansell Collection, 11, 12, 24, 29, 54, 103, 128, 133 left;
Mary Evans Picture Library, 85, 105;
Massachusetts Horticultural Society, 74 bottom
Mayhew's London, 8;
Musée de Cluny, Paris, 35;
Museo Nacional do Brasil, 48, 108, 113;
National Coffee Growers Federation of Colombia, 119;
National Maritime Museum, London, 37, 38, 78;
Nationalmuseum, Stockholm, 39;
New Testament, 135;

ACKNOWLEDGEMENTS

New York Coffee, Sugar and Cocoa Exchange, 143, 145;
OPEC, 171;
Robert Opie, 100;
Ordonnances de la jurisdiction de la prevote des Marchands de Paris
(1528), 31 upper;
The Picture Magazine (1893), 9, 10;
Felipe Guaman Poma de Ayala, *Neuva coronica y buen gobierno*
(1615), 25 left;
Punch, by permission of, 19, 151;
The Queen's Empire (1901), 65, 81, 87, 157;
Rijksmuseum, Amsterdam, 41;
Royal Commonwealth Institute, 89;

Royal Pavillion, Art Gallery & Museums, Brighton, 28 left;
South (July 1985), 68, (Aug. 1984), 164 right;
Laurie Sparham/Network, 21;
Jo Spence/Photography Workshop, 92;
United Society for Propagation of the Gospel, Jamaica, 50;
Wayne Tippetts, 156;
Unknown, 33, 52, 110, 114, 133 right, 164 left, 173;
Wedgewood Museum, 61;
West Indies Committee, 55;
Richard Wilson, 162, 166;
Witt Library, Courtauld Institute of Art, 82, 83 right;

Commodities: The TV Series

Six films which explore the development of the modern world economy, focussing on the key commodities of sugar, tea, coffee and money.

FILM ONE: *White Gold – Black Market* looks at the early capitalist sugar industry in Amsterdam and Brazil, and at the opium and tea trades in London and the Far East in the early nineteenth century.

FILM TWO: *Leaving Home for Sugar* examines the development of the sugar industry in Zimbabwe in relation to its history in the Caribbean.

FILM THREE: *Tea Fortunes* explores the development of the tea trade in China, Assam, Sri Lanka and East Africa, and its continuing domination by London companies.

FILM FOUR: *Coffee is the Gold of the Future* tells the history of the peasant production of coffee in Colombia.

FILM FIVE: *Free Markets for Free Men* explores the relationships between the City of London and producer countries, examining the nature of futures markets and the history of Third World debt.

FILM SIX: *Grow or Die* looks at the growth of one transnational corporation – Unilever – and speculates on the future of the world financial system in an era of debt and commodity mountains.

Index

INDEX

This first edition of
Commodities: How the World was Taken to Market
was finished in September 1987.

It was phototypeset in $10^1/2/12^1/2$ CRTronic Bembo
and printed on a Miller TP 41, on blade-coated cartridge 135 g/m^2

The book was commissioned by Robert M. Young, edited by Les
Levidow, copy-edited by Charlotte Greig, designed by Sonia
Alexis and produced by David Williams and Selina O'Grady for
Free Association Books.